Deviance

Deviance

Theories on Behaviors That Defy Social Norms

**Duane L. Dobbert
and Thomas X. Mackey, Editors**

 PRAEGER™

An Imprint of ABC-CLIO, LLC
Santa Barbara, California • Denver, Colorado

Library of Congress Cataloging-in-Publication Data

Deviance (Praeger)
    Deviance : theories on behaviors that defy social norms / Duane L. Dobbert and Thomas X. Mackey, editors.
        pages cm
    Includes bibliographical references and index.
    ISBN 978-1-4408-3323-6 (print : alk. paper) — ISBN 978-1-4408-3324-3 (e-book)   1. Deviant behavior.   2. Social norms.   I. Dobbert, Duane L.   II. Mackey, Thomas X.   III. Title.
    HM811.D532 2015
    302.5'42—dc23   2015007657

ISBN: 978-1-4408-3323-6
EISBN: 978-1-4408-3324-3

19 18 17 16 15   1 2 3 4 5

This book is also available on the World Wide Web as an eBook.
Visit www.abc-clio.com for details.

Praeger
An Imprint of ABC-CLIO, LLC

ABC-CLIO, LLC
130 Cremona Drive, P.O. Box 1911
Santa Barbara, California 93116-1911

This book is printed on acid-free paper ∞

Manufactured in the United States of America

Contents

Preface

Duane L. Dobbert

This book is a unique demonstration of the blending of Scholar/Practitioner and Socratic pedagogic theoretical perspectives. The editors of this book are Scholar/Practitioners with a combined excess of 75 years as practitioners in the criminal justice system in the United States. They are also accomplished researchers and publicists in the public sector and academe.

They are both committed to the Socratic method of teaching, particularly with university graduate students. Unless a course is especially esoteric, there is no "Sage on Stage." Rather, the Socratic method is a dialogue between students and faculty rather than a faculty monologue by acknowledging that each participant, faculty and students, brings unique and authentic perspectives to the content knowledge. Dogmatism is frowned upon; however, healthy debate, supported by credible research documentation, is encouraged. The Socratic method provides for a plethora of wide-ranging perspectives and opinions in an environment free from fear of criticism.

Each individual's perspective on a social problem is influenced not only by discipline or course of study but also by their unique frame of reference. Commonly, the new student to the Socratic method is not cognizant of their individual frame of reference and how it precipitates skew on their view of the world. The frame of reference is dynamic, ever changing as one encounters the world in which one exists. The views of the wealthy are significantly different from the views of the poor. Ethnicity, religion, education, parental indoctrination, and peer association influence the individual's frame of reference. These experiences determine tolerance and acceptance of persons different from oneself. These referential parameters are also developed by legitimate institutions: parents, schools, and government.

A Scholar/Practitioner curriculum at the upper-undergraduate and graduate-student level is applied. Acquired content knowledge in and of itself is insufficient for application in the solving of social problems. The skill sets of intelligence analysis, critical thinking, and communication are of equal importance. Comparative analysis of classical and contemporary theoretical perspectives with contemporary research is mandatory in assessing the efficacy of theoretical perspectives. Theory in the absence of practice is merely that—theory.

The Scholar Professor lecture format often restricts freedom of thought, opinion, and expression. It precipitates dogmatism and cloning of the skewed perspectives of the graduate faculty member. Challenging the professor is often intimidating and humiliating. Intelligent debate is discouraged as disrespectful. Consequently, the scholar's theoretical perspectives become "fact" in the eyes of the student. This is a tragic error in applied disciplines and sentences society to the historically failed solutions to social problems. History repeats itself again and again.

Effective graduate education demands student analysis of seminal work, not the interpretation of classical theory by a textbook author. Critical authentic thinking begins by examining the original work of the theorists. Utilizing the research question, "The Proliferation of Violent Street Gangs," examination of the seminal work of Durkheim, Merton, and Thrasher is required. Anomie, anomie and social structure, and play group confrontation are foundation principles that offer insight into the research question.

Generally speaking, textbook authors are university professors with specific academic knowledge and skill sets. While there is value in reading the interpretation of theory and research by the textbook author, it is naturally skewed by the author's frame of reference. Graduate student examination of the original work is also skewed by their personal frame of reference, and this is the same of each student in the class. There is a natural difference of opinion for each student. The Socratic method entertains vigorous informed critical thinking, challenges the frame of reference–precipitated skew, and scholarly debate.

Many university faculty are not practitioners in their discipline. Research and publishing are significantly relevant; however, some disciplines also require a practitioner's perspective in problem solving. Hours, days, weeks, and months spent inside a maximum-security penitentiary is valued knowledge pertaining to prison reform. It is inconceivable that an academician can offer valid applicable theoretical perspectives in the absence of that practitioner's experience. Knowledge honed through practical application is requisite to the criminal justice, public safety, homeland security, forensic behavioral analysis, and intelligence analysis disciplines.

This book is the product of the editors' frustration. Books authored by Scholar/Practitioners that examine the sociological and psychological variables that precipitate deviance are nonexistent. There are a plethora of books authored by academicians with no experience as practitioners. If one truly wishes to examine the variables associated with the proliferation of violent street gangs, one does not need to have previous membership with a street gang but a professional responsibility involving gang activity. This experience adds credibility to the research conclusions.

This book examines the seminal work of 20 classical and contemporary theorists from psychology, sociology/criminology, political science, and philosophy. It differs from other books as the content knowledge of each theorist has been examined, analyzed, and debated by 35 graduate students with the goal of reducing skew. It also examines the contextual frame of reference that influences the theorist's perspective.

Have you wondered how Sigmund Freud and B. F. Skinner developed such significantly different views on the human personality?

This book does not propose to accurately answer these questions but rather to present an opportunity for the audience to determine their own inquiries for future research. The ultimate goal is to challenge current perspectives on deviance. Do these perspectives that drive the implementation of deviance prevention and elimination programs have efficacy in accomplishing their objectives? Is there value in the integration of different perspectives in synthesizing new multidisciplinary perspectives that accurately understand the variables that precipitate deviance?

Acknowledgments

To Joyce Elaine Dobbert, my wife, my life, and my partner in everything important.

To Liam and Sheila Mackey. Your strength has made this book possible.

To Vanessa Cournoyer and Andi Benscoter for their excellence in technology and manuscript preparation.

To Christina Molinari, Sarah Norman, and Jessica Vena. Thank you for your relentless commitment to this book.

1

Introduction

Thomas X. Mackey

Deviance is relative. At the level of individual recognition, as well as at the level of societal parameters, the concept of deviance is fluid in nature and consistently evolving, albeit most often slowly. Deviant behavior is a reality that has been documented since the dawn of recorded time. The term "deviance," by its very nature, identifies divergence from the norm. Over time, society has come to understand the term "deviant" as a negative separation from the cultural norm. In fact, deviations may occur on either side of the culturally acceptable middle ground, the societal "norm." Behaviors may be perceived as positive deviance, negative deviance, or deviance absent any particular connotation.

For example, if an individual takes their entire savings and utilizes the money to begin a Ponzi scheme, designed to steal money from innocent victims, they would likely be perceived as engaging in "negative" deviant behavior. If an individual takes their entire savings and utilizes the money to buy food to feed the homeless, at the risk of their own financial security, they would be seen as engaging in "positive" deviant behavior. Yet an individual who utilizes their entire savings to buy dry goods by the case and stores them in the basement would also be engaging in deviant behavior, a behavior that departs from the cultural norm. Yet this survivalist hoarder deviant behavior lacks any particular connotation, negative or positive. It is just "different" from behavioral cultural norm expectations and therefore, by its very nature, deviant. Three distinct behaviors have transpired; one positive, one negative, and one just different. Yet all three are deviant in their own way. While all three examples would qualify as deviant, society tends to reserve the term "deviant" for individuals engaged in negative behaviors that travel outside the realm of social acceptability. We as a society generally categorize deviant individuals to be those who are engaging in negative behaviors.

This text looks at some of the foremost recognized authorities in the area of deviant and criminal behavior. It analyzes the theorists and their theories from a fresh perspective. The chapters look at the theorists themselves and then build the foundation of the individual's maturity before the presentation of their theory. This initial information on the biographical and developmental background of the theorist is designed to shed light on the perspective of the scholar, leaving out the explanation of their theory. This background elucidation establishes insight into the people themselves and allows the reader an opportunity to view their theory after development of a fundamental understanding of the theorist.

These theories, like their authors, vary greatly. The text shows individuals who were raised and educated in many different environments and developed many varied theories. As the book shows, not all environmental and educational variables resulted in the logical correlating theory. In other words, not every theorist who grew up in a challenging urban environment developed a theory on deviance that identified urban social challenges as primary motivators for deviant activity. Likewise, individuals who were raised in wealthy families with top-notch education did not all compose theories that identified excessive greed as the primary motivator for crime. While the theorists' upbringings and their theories were not all consistent, some correlations between developmental exposures and subsequent theory may be observed throughout the text. Having identified deviance and the developmental aspects of the theorists, a look at the idea of "social norms" is in order. Each of us develops a perspective on what is right and proper. The growth of this perspective is usually attributed to interactional developmental components. Our families, our peers, and our educators all play a role in the molding of our particular viewpoint on what is right and what is wrong. The lens through which we develop this "normal to deviant" continuum is often called our personal perspective or personal paradigm. Each individual paradigm develops slowly and, most often, imperceptibly. However, in most personal experiences, there are certain significant singular events that cause a radical shift in a personal paradigm.

For example, an individual may live in a middle-class neighborhood with a small number of homeless population in the area. The person may live in the neighborhood for years and not think much of the homeless issue in their neighborhood. Yet, if the person is exiting a convenience store and is mugged by an individual who is unkempt, disheveled, and appears to have poor hygiene—characteristics that individual normally associates with a homeless person—the individual's perspective on the homeless in the area may change instantly. This singular incident may radically alter that individual's view of the homeless. In this case, a personal paradigm has been altered considerably by one event.

Rapid radical paradigm shifts are the exception rather than the rule. In most cases, our paradigms, or lenses, alter slowly over time. They move like the hour hands on a clock. We understand that they move, yet we never actually witness or perceive the movement. The minor events of our lives shape us daily, in a very subtle fashion. Routine observations, everyday interactions and conversations with peers and coworkers, media observations that bombard us every waking moment—these all affect our personal paradigm, our lens through which we view the world.

Additionally, it should be noted that the vast majority of us are not cognizant that our personal paradigms exist. Even though they influence daily decisions, we are not aware of the role our past experience plays in relation to present decision making. Most of us make decisions because we feel that the action is the right thing to do. Underlying motivation is rarely analyzed when we decide on any given course of action, particularly routine daily decisions. Yet past experience serves as the baseline for all decision making. We draw upon our past experiences in an effort to make the best possible decisions in our present situation. That repository of data, which becomes the lens through which we view our present circumstances in making choices, is our personal paradigm.

Personal paradigms become the foundational perspective by which personal lines of normal versus "deviant" behavior are established. It is vital to recognize that the line of acceptable versus deviant is different for every individual. Society's perspective on any given topic or decision will most often vary to differing degrees. If 1,000 individuals were interviewed and asked if they felt that homicide was a deviant behavior, it is likely that a vast majority would concur. On the other hand, if 1,000 individuals were interviewed and asked if they felt that personal marijuana usage inside the home was a deviant behavior, the results may be mixed. In a majority of states in this country, both incidents would be a violation of law. Yet, based upon personal paradigms and opinions, the level of consensus on behavioral acceptability may vary.

Taking the concept of personal paradigms and personal perceptions of the "norm" relative to deviant behavior, the variations are now apparent. How, then, are these personal perceptions of the norm ultimately translated into the larger perspective of the cultural norm? Most often personal paradigms, absent radical shifts, develop slowly over time. Likewise, societal norms develop slowly. In fact, it could be argued that societal norms develop even more slowly than personal norms. Moreover, these societal norms tend to lag behind personal norms in terms of societal acceptance. It should be pointed out that there are exceptions. September 11, 2001, was a single day in history where it may be argued that both personal and societal paradigms changed dramatically in the course of a day.

Societal norms tend to change as a majority of the public in any given culture begins to adopt a different perspective on a particular issue. Cultural acceptance of a previously deviant behavior normally follows acceptance or indifference established by a majority of the public. In addition to this personal acceptance or indifference, there is usually a vocal minority actively seeking change on the issue. Personal use of marijuana inside the home may serve as a recent example of a previously deviant behavior. In U.S. society today, marijuana use appears to be a behavior that is slowly transitioning into cultural acceptability. The vocal minority advocating marijuana use, along with the accepting and/or indifferent majority, fuels the slow-moving motivation toward acceptance within the realm of societal norms. This societal acceptance is usually followed by a legislative adaptation eradicating the criminality of the behavior.

Personal perspectives of normal versus deviant tend to develop slowly and imperceptibly. This personal set of norms, held by a majority of the population, establishes the foundation for societal norms. These societal norms are the impetus for the legislative action that establishes deviant behavior as criminal behavior. It should be noted that not all deviant behavior is criminal, yet an overwhelmingly large percentage of criminal behavior would be classified as deviant.

Having established the rudimentary foundation for personal and societal norms, the value of theory must be examined. What is the purpose of theory? We each have our own perspective of normal versus deviant. The influence of societal opinion establishes a portion of deviant behavior as criminal. We make conscious decisions as individuals, if healthy, to obey or not obey these laws. We choose to live within the societal realm either of "normal" or of "deviant." If we choose to be openly deviant in a noncriminal manner, we may face societal stigma. If we decide to be criminally deviant, we run the risk of facing the penal law consequences associated with our behavior.

The issues discussed thus far relate to behavior. Behavior is the consequence of motivation. Whether impulsive or carefully planned, motivation precipitates behavior. After you read this chapter, you can go apply for a job at a local restaurant or you can go rob a bank. Both are behaviors. Both are designed to result in the procurement of money. Yet they would be viewed as significantly different from the perspective of societal acceptability within the realm of cultural norms. Cultural norms will tell us how these behaviors will be perceived, but what can help explain why these behaviors will take place?

Theory

Theory can help us make sense of the underlying motivation of an individual who chooses to engage in deviant and even criminal behavior. Cultural norms help establish the parameters; theory helps to explain the deviation from those parameters. Consequently, theory is vital to the development of a societal understanding of deviant behavior.

The book starts with an analysis of behavioral theory as examined by a scholar who changed the face of behavioral analysis, Charles Darwin. Darwin's view went right to the heart of the development of man. Inherent in that concept of development was the theory that behavior is intertwined with biological development. Darwin's theories altered the view on issues far beyond the concept of deviant behavior. In subsequent chapters, the text looks at two more theorists whose work was centered outside the concept of deviance, yet deeply rooted in behavioral motivations: Karl Marx and Sigmund Freud. These groundbreaking scholars focused on other concepts, namely, political unrest and underlying psychological motivations for behavior. Yet both touched on the potential for human actions that might be classified as deviant in the eyes of the cultural modes of their time—and even today.

The next chapters begin to focus on classical deviant behavior motivations. Sociologist Emile Durkheim made clear the idea that behavioral theory cannot identify individuals but rather only groups. This one of his many contributions showed us the value of those groups as they relate to classification. Durkheim also identified the reality that in order to understand deviant we need to understand the norm. German psychoanalyst Karen Horney is the only female theorist discussed in the text. She has often been identified as the founder of feminist psychology. Her neo-Freudian perspective focused heavily on the concepts of culture and societal influences over fundamental biological motivation. This is a brief sampling of some of the many significant behavioral theorists examined. Some focus heavily on the concept of deviant behavior, while others only touch on deviance as a part of their larger theoretical perspective.

The book goes on to identify some of the most significant behavioral theorists of the last 200 years. While it will be nearly impossible to gather the significant contributions made by all deviant behavioral theorists in the last few centuries, the book attempts to enlighten the reader to some of the more significant classical thinkers in the field. The individuals chosen for analysis were selected not because of their similarities but rather due to their differences. In analyzing different and varied perspectives, the recognition of the myriad of possible explanations for deviant behavior becomes more apparent. It is clear that no one theory explains all deviant behavior and no deviant behavior is completely explained by just one theory.

The text concludes with two chapters that step outside the essential theme of the book. The first of these final two chapters discusses pedophilia. By presenting a chapter on a deviant behavior, rather than the theory of a deviant behavioral theorist, the reader has an opportunity to apply the perspectives of some of these theorists to actual deviant behavior. The reader can examine the paraphilia of pedophilia through the lens of a number of different theoretical perspectives. The final chapter discusses competency and culpability.

The purpose of this chapter is to show that classical deviant behavior theories are not always applicable to all deviant behavior. Mental age, and the ability to understand right from wrong and normal from deviant, is a variable that needs to be considered in certain instances.

In introducing the reader to numerous and divergent perspectives, the text attempts to broaden the recognition of varied possibilities to explain deviant behavior. Additionally, the biographical and developmental components of the lives of theorists are reviewed. Just as deviance is a relative concept, fluid and changing over the experiential evolution of time, so too is its counterpart, the norm. Both individually and societally, experiences influence individual and societal perspectives on deviance. Likewise, both individually and societally, the experience of the theorist influences, in some fashion, the theory. We are a conglomeration all of our prior thoughts and experiences. Our prior realities affect our perception of life. Our perception of life influences our theory. So, whether the focus is on deviance and its separation from the norm or on biographical data and its relationship to theory, the influence of experience is a consistent theme.

2

Charles Darwin

Joseph McCluskey and Lucy Papp

When examining theories of deviance, Charles Darwin is not considered a dominant figure. It is Darwin, and creative thinkers like him, who did not accept the popular beliefs/dogma of the time but instead questioned those beliefs, sometimes at great risk to personal and professional reputations. These bold advances paved the way for others to develop new and different ideas and theories.

Early Life and Education

Darwin was born in 1809 in Shrewsbury, England, into a fairly prominent family.[1] One grandfather was an industrialist, and the other, Erasmus Darwin (Erasmus), was a freethinking doctor, poet, and naturalist.[2] (A freethinker was one who did not feel constrained to follow or agree with the existing ideas of the time). Erasmus also had an interest in zoology and wrote *Zoonomia: or The Laws of Organic Life*, which Erasmus explained was his attempt to break "ANIMAL LIFE into classes, orders, genera, and species; and by comparing them with each other to unravel the theory of diseases."[3] Erasmus's connection with zoology may help explain, in some small part, Darwin's lifelong interest in nature.

Darwin was one of five children. His mother died when he was about eight. She did not seem to have a lasting impact on Darwin's life.[4] Darwin's father, Waring, was a physician who was overbearing and showed little affection for his children, instead opting to teach them about proper behavior, or what he deemed to be proper behavior.[5]

Darwin went to a day school in Shrewsbury for about a year when he was eight years old. He was told that he was much slower at learning than his younger sister. Darwin recalls that by this time his "taste for natural history, and more especially for collecting, was well developed."[6] In 1818, Darwin's father sent him to the traditional Anglican Shrewsbury boarding school where he stayed for approximately seven years. The school taught the classics, such as geography, language, and ancient history. Darwin did not enjoy the rote learning that was such an integral part of the school's classical training.[7] About his time at the Shrewsbury school, Darwin recalled "[t]he school as a means of education to me was simply a blank."[8] Darwin "was considered by all of [his] masters and [his] father as a very ordinary boy, rather below the common standard of intellect."[9] At the time, science was considered dehumanizing in English public schools. Darwin's headmaster criticized him for dabbling in chemistry.[10] It may have been this failure to live up to the expectations of his father and the educational environment that helped Darwin evolve into a collector of nature and become absorbed in the sciences.

While studying medicine, a profession he did not enjoy, Darwin met a freed South American slave at the Edinburgh Museum who taught him how to stuff birds and how to identify rock strata and colonial flora and fauna. His experiences at the museum were what Darwin felt was enlightening.[11] Darwin preferred to be outdoors collecting specimens, hunting, and riding instead of learning to be a doctor. Darwin also attended student societies where he listened to freethinkers speak, for example, critically about the generally accepted divine design of human facial anatomy and supportively about the relatively new idea that animals and humans shared all the human mental faculties. He also attended an "underground" society where students read papers on the natural sciences, and he joined the Wernian Society where published natural science papers were discussed.[12] Darwin's father disapproved of his son's seeming lack of interest in his studies and once told him "[y]ou care for nothing but shooting, dogs and rat catching, and you will be a disgrace to yourself and all of your family."[13] Again Darwin suffered the disapproval of his father.

During his stint at Edinburgh, Darwin met Robert Edmont Grant, who was a disciple of French biologist Jean-Baptiste Lamarch. It was Grant who first mentioned to Darwin Lamarch's beliefs concerning evolution. Lamarch's theory dealt with plants and animals attempting to adapt to the environment in a way that enhanced their abilities to prosper in the environment.[14] A notable example given by Lamarch was that of the adaption of the giraffe's longer neck to allow it to be able to feed on leaves higher up in trees.[15] Darwin later said, "I listened in silent astonishment, and as far as I can judge, without any effect on my mind."[16] Later in his life, referring to reading his grandfather's *Zoonomia* and to learning of Lamarch's views on evolution, Darwin said, "it is probable that the hearing rather early in life such views maintained and praised may have favored my upholding them under a different form in my 'Origin of Species.'"[17] Grant became Darwin's mentor and taught him about the growth and relationship of primitive marine invertebrates. Darwin believed that these primitive marine invertebrates held information relevant to the origin of more complex creatures learned from Grant and tackled the larger questions of life through a study of zoology. He made his own. Darwin, encouraged by his observations on the larval sea mat, announced his findings at different student societies.[18]

Waring Darwin learned that his son did not want to become a physician and, not wanting Charles to become "idle" by leaving school altogether, Waring had his son transfer to Cambridge to study for the clergy.[19] Darwin believed that the time he spent at Cambridge "was wasted as far as academical studies were concerned as completely as at Edinburgh."[20] While at Cambridge, Darwin continued to enjoy hunting and riding, and he also collected beetle specimens. Darwin embraced the study of religion and finally received his bachelor of arts degree in 1831.[21] At that time, Darwin "did not then in the least doubt the strict and literal truth in every word in the Bible."[22]

The *Beagle* Expedition and Darwin's Views on Creationism Begin to Change

One of the key turning points in Darwin's life was when John Stevens Henslow offered Darwin the opportunity to serve as a botanist on the HMS *Beagle* for an around-the-world voyage.[23] The ship was to map sea routes along South America. Darwin originally refused the opportunity because his father did not approve of the trip. His father eventually relented when Darwin satisfied his father's request that Darwin find one respected gentleman who could vouch for the importance of this type of study.[24] Darwin's cousin Josiah Wedgwood convinced Darwin's father that the expedition was significant, and Darwin signed on to the expedition.[25] In an ironic twist of scientific fate, Darwin was almost excluded from the voyage because the ship's captain believed in the then popular practice of physiognomy, which was the "scientific" study of assessing people's character by their facial appearance.[26] The captain wanted to exclude Darwin from the expedition because he thought Darwin's nose was the wrong shape.[27] The captain eventually relented, and Darwin was given permission to join the crew.

The outset of the five-year voyage was miserable for Darwin because he suffered from severe and constant seasickness, his quarters were cramped, and the crew (not including Darwin) was disciplined brutally. Despite the difficult start, Darwin said, "I have always felt that I owe to the voyage the first real training and education of my mind. . . ."[28]

Throughout the expedition, Darwin saw examples of phenomena that seemed to contradict the creationist providential design belief. For example, in San Salvador, Darwin made an observation that made him wonder whether plants and animals adapted and evolved. He observed a narrow band of seashells on a rock ledge; however, the ledge was much higher than the sea level. It seemed incongruent that the seashells would be so far above the sea. In Tierra del Fuego, Darwin came across some natives who behaved with animal-like qualities. This made him question how God could have created both humans who were so "low" as to behave like animals and so "high" as the humans he knew from Cambridge.[29] Darwin began to believe that humans' origins were deeply rooted in the animal kingdom.[30] This was inconsistent with the generally accepted creationist view that God designed and created all living things at a single time.[31] While exploring the Galapagos Archipelago, Darwin noted that certain species had different characteristics, depending on where they lived on the island.[32] He noted, for example, that the beaks of the finches had variations. His doubts about creationism were confirmed by the realization that species could evolve and that species were not fixed as stated in the Bible.[33] In describing the "gelling" of his ideas on evolution while on the expedition, Darwin explained:

> During the voyage of the *Beagle* I had been deeply impressed by discovering in the Pampean formation great fossil animals covered with armour like that on the existing armadillos; secondly, by the manner in which closely allied animals replace one another in proceeding southwards over the Continent; and thirdly, by the South American character of most of the productions of the Galapagos archipelago, and more especially by the manner in which they differ slightly on each island of the group; none of the islands appearing to be very ancient in a geological sense. It was evident that such facts as these, as well as many others, could only be explained on the supposition that species gradually become modified; and the subject haunted me.[34]

The ship returned to England in 1836. During the voyage, Darwin had collected 1,500 animal samples and 4,000 plant samples.[35] Darwin's place in the scientific community was secure.[36] Darwin married his cousin Emma Wedgwood and had 10 children, seven of whom survived into adulthood.[37]

Darwin said that his theory of evolution was "clearly conceived" in 1838.[38] However, he wanted to develop a comprehensive and complete explanation for evolution before he published his theory.[39] He collected any ideas expressed by others that seemed to contradict his theories so that he could address and refute them in his treatise. Darwin ultimately developed overwhelming evidence to support his theory of evolution. In 1842, he wrote a 35-page abstract of his theory, and by 1844, the document had grown to 230 pages.[40] Throughout the 20-year period during which Darwin refined his theory of evolution, Darwin discussed his ideas with others who had similar interests. Darwin did not believe that they understood the import of his theory.[41] Darwin's theory of evolution was first presented to the scientific community in 1858 and published as *On the Origin of Species* in 1859.[42] Thus, Darwin refined and perfected this theory for over 20 years before he was willing to make it public. Many found Darwin's theory revolutionary and believed it explained comprehensively the inconsistencies between what they had actually observed and the creationism teachings. For example, one noted botanist of the day, Joseph Dalton Hooker, said, "I must own that my faith is shaken to the foundation [and] that the sum of all the evidence I have encountered since I studied the subject is in favor of the origin of the species by variation."[43] In contrast, Louis Agassiz, a leading naturalist in the United States, declared, "Evolution in any form, whether it was Darwin's or any other, was sacrilegious."[44] Darwin believed the religious who clung to the biblical explanation of creation had attacked him "fiercely."[45] Darwin stood by his work, even though it was mocked and ridiculed and had become the central issue for creationists versus Darwinists. The fundamental concept of evolution developed by Darwin and others essentially turned the world of science upside down. The great debate that resulted was the Bible versus nature.

Impacts of Life on Theory

An extended discussion of Darwin's theories on evolution would not advance the premise of this chapter. It is sufficient to say that Darwin's 1859 publication of *On the Origin of Species*, his 1871 publication of *The Descent of Man, and Selection in Relation to Sex*, and the 1872 publication of *The Expression of the Emotions in Man and Animals* changed views on creation that had been held for thousands of years. In his later works, Darwin looks into human reactions such as crying or the furrowing of lips in children. Darwin examines the idea that humans and their bodies will react to emotion and other stimuli in similar ways. He describes that these behaviors become somewhat predictable within individuals. Darwin explains the evolution of these behavioral responses and the expression of emotion.

Modern deviance theories can be applied to Darwin and his life. For example, a cause of delinquent behavior is ascribed to the labeling (labeling theory) of an individual, such as "slow" or "intellectually inferior," as Darwin was labeled. One could point to the impact, or lack thereof, of his mother's death, which seemed to have little effect on Darwin, as a deviance from the norms of the day for children who suffer from attachment issues specifically with a maternal figure. Similar parallels can be drawn between Darwin, who faced parental and peer rejection, and modern research that has shown a significant impact of rejection on the delinquent behavior of children.

Although one can point to events in Darwin's life that could cause him to deviate from the norms of the day, this is not his true contribution to deviance theory. Rather, it is his refusal to simply accept the religious and "scientific" dogma of the day and instead pursue his steadfast search for explanations for things that were different. He was a keen observer who took copious notes. But he was more than just an observer; using his informal scientific training, he tried to make sense of the many anomalies he came across that seemed to contradict· the accepted biblical explanation for creation. Upon his return from the voyage, his significant collection of plant and animal life gave him immediate credibility, celebrity status, and a voice in the scientific community. Nevertheless, he spent the next 20-plus years developing what he considered to be a virtually ironclad explanation of evolution. This explanation is, in a sense, a continual explanation of nature's deviation from the status quo to adapt to conditions of the time, much like deviant behavior is a way to adapt to or cope with a hostile personal environment.

Darwin was not a maverick or contrarian; rather, he followed his passion to be a natural scientist and shifted the debate about creation from the Bible to nature.

Notes

1. Charles Darwin, *The Life and Letters of Charles Darwin, Including an Autobiographical Chapter*, ed. Francis Darwin (London: John Murray, 1887), 27.

2. Francis Darwin, ed., *Charles Darwin, His Life Told in an Autobiographical Chapter, and in a Selected Series of Published Letters* (London: John Murray, 1892), 5, https://play.google.com/books/reader?id=j9MEAAAAYAAJ&printsec=frontcover&output=reader&authuser=0&hl=en&pg=GBS.PR1; *Charles Darwin: Evolution's Voice*. United States: A & E Biography Series, 1998. DVD.

3. Erasmus Darwin, *Zoonomia: or The Laws of Organic Life, Vol. I*, produced by Greg Alethoup, Robert Shimmin, Keith Edkins, and the Online Distributed Proofreading Team (Project Gutenberg Ebook, 2005), Preface.

4. Darwin, *The Life and Letters*, 27.

5. *Charles Darwin: Evolution's Voice*.

6. Darwin, *The Life and Letters*, 27.

7. F. Darwin, *His Life, Told*, 7.

8. Darwin, *The Life and Letters*, 8.

9. Ibid., 32.

10. F. Darwin, *His Life, Told*, 7.

11. Ibid., 14.

12. Ibid., 37, 40.

13. Ibid., 37.

14. Charles Darwin and Edward O. Wilson, *From So Simple a Beginning: The Four Great Books of Charles Darwin* (New York: W.W. Norton & Co., 2006), 438.

15. Ibid.

16. F. Darwin, *His Life, Told*, 11.

17. Darwin, *The Life and Letters*, 38.

18. F. Darwin, *His Life, Told*, 39.

19. Ibid., 45.

20. Ibid., 46.

21. Ibid., 45.

22. Ibid.

23. Ibid., 54.

24. F. Darwin, *His Life, Told*, 25.

25. Darwin, *The Life and Letters*, 32.

26. Sharrona Pearl, *About Faces: Physiognomy in Nineteenth-Century Britain* (Cambridge, MA: Harvard University Press), 1.

27. F. Darwin, *His Life, Told*, 27; Darwin, *The Life and Letters*, 27.

28. Darwin, *The Life and Letters*, 62.

29. Darwin and Wilson, *From So Simple*, 199, 208.

30. Ibid.

31. Mark A. Noll, "Evangelicals, Creation, and Scripture: Legacies from a Long History," *Perspectives on Science and Christian Faith*, 63, no. 3 (September 2011): 149, http://web.a.ebscohost.com/ehost/pdfviewer/pdfviewer?vid=3&sid=3f284638-08aa-4244-9da0-8364441705a4%40sessionmgr4004&hid=4209 (accessed April 4, 2014).

32. Darwin and Wilson, *From So Simple*, 330.

33. Ibid., 331.

34. Darwin, *The Life and Letters*, 82.

35. *Encyclopedia Britannica Online*, s.v. "Charles Darwin" (accessed March 21, 2014).

36. E. J. Browne, *Charles Darwin: The Power of Place* (New York: Alfred A. Knopf, 2002), ch. 1.

37. Ibid.

38. Darwin, *The Life and Letters*, 88.

39. Ibid., 82.

40. Ibid., 84.

41. Ibid., 87.

42. Brown, *Charles Darwin: The Power*, ch 2, pt II.

43. Ibid.

44. Ibid.

45. F. Darwin, *His Life, Told*, 17.

Bibliography

Browne, E. J. *Charles Darwin: The Power of Place*. New York: Alfred A. Knopf, 2002.

Charles Darwin: Evolution's Voice. New York: A & E Biography Series, 1998. DVD.

Darwin, Charles. *The Expression of the Emotions in Man and Animals*. New York: D. Appleton & Co., 1872, edited by Francis Darwin. London: John Murray, 1888.

Darwin, Charles. *The Life and Letters of Charles Darwin, Including an Autobiographical Chapter,* ed. Frances Darwin. London: John Murray, 1887.

Darwin, Charles. *The Origin of Species & The Descent of Man*. New York: The Modern Library, 1977.

Darwin, Charles. *On Natural Selection*. New York: Penguin Books, 1859.

Darwin, Charles, and Edward O. Wilson. *From So Simple a Beginning: The Four Great Books of Charles Darwin*. New York: W. W. Norton & Co., 2006.

Darwin, Erasmus. *Zoonomia: or The Laws of Organic Life, Vol. I* (1976), produced by Greg Alethoup, Robert Shimmin, Keith Edkins, and the Online Distributed Proofreading

Team. Project Gutenberg Ebook, 2005. http://www.gutenberg.org/files/15707/15707 -h/15707-h.htm.

Darwin, Francis, ed. *Charles Darwin, His Life Told in an Autobiographical Chapter, and in a Selected Series of Published Letters.* London: John Murray, 1892. https://play.google .com/books/reader?id=j9MEAAAAYAAJ&printsec=frontcover&output=reader&aut huser=0&hl=en&pg=GBS.PR1.

Encyclopedia Britannica Online, s.v. "Charles Darwin." http://britannica.com/EBchecked/ topic/151902/Charles-Darwin (accessed March 21, 2014).

Johnson, James. "Survival of the Fitted: God's Providential Programming." 2010. http://www .icr.org/article/survival-fitted-Gods-providential-programming (accessed April 4, 2014).

Noll, Mark A. "Evangelicals, Creation, and Scripture: Legacies from a Long History." *Perspectives on Science and Christian Faith* 63, no. 3 (September 2011): 147–58. http:// web.a.ebscohost.com/ehost/pdfviewer/pdfviewer?vid=3&sid=3f284638-08aa-4244 -9da0-8364441705a4%40sessionmgr4004&hid=4209 (accessed April 4, 2014).

Pearl, Sharrona. *About Faces: Physiognomy in Nineteenth-Century Britain.* Cambridge, MA: Harvard University Press, 2010.

Ruse, Michael. "Charles Robert Darwin and Alfred Russel Wallace: Their Dispute over the Units of Selection." *Theory in Biosciences* 132, no. 4 (September 7, 2013): 215–24. doi:10.1007/s12064-013-0190-7.

3

Karl Marx

Inna Angelina Olson

Throughout history, from the Dark Ages to the modern era, one can apply a Marxist perspective and draw a fundamental correlation between poverty and violent behavior. Karl Marx was greatly influenced by the Hegelians' idealism and historical inevitability. Nonetheless, he counterargued that human behavior is dependent upon financial matters—economics at large. Karl Heinrich Marx, the renowned German sociologist, socialist, philosopher, and politician, attempted to closely examine the nature of individuals "conditioned" under a materialistic living environment. In other words, Marx believed that the level of productiveness and/or social behavior of any individual is more likely to be affected by one major factor, which plays not only as a final determinant but directly relates to deviance, the gap between social classes. Throughout his numerous works he stressed that social norms and behavior are vested solely in the material base and its financial aspects; they are detrimental in the future (behavioral) development of any individual.

Consequently, the class itself or the gap between the classes have become the foundation and cornerstone of the Marxist theory. His theory established the main principles for many modern theorists and criminologists that the (financial) environment is a significant variable in the decisions related to the commission of crime and deviant behavior, where the latter stands at opposite ends of a continuum—within its outliers. For instance, in the Communist Manifesto, Marx and his comrade Friedrich Engels were able to manipulate the masses by inspiring, calling out, and finally provoking the "proletariat" (i.e., commonly known and further referenced as the "bourgeoisie" class) to unite in revolution, strikes, and hostility against existing regimes. In its broader scope, seen as capitalism, is the concentration of all evil in the Marxists' eyes. Soon after its publication in 1848, numerous revolutions ensued across Europe, echoing the "ideas" or propaganda in the Marx and Engels work.

Some may argue that these two factors (i.e., economic conditions and the gap between classes) are integral variables of society and are interrelated entities.

It is believed by many that lower socioeconomic status (SES) may result in a strain between two classes—poor and rich, (defined by Marx: "bourgeoisie" as capitalist class and "proletariat" as working class). Marx saw an issue in the differences or discrepancies between the two SES of people—wealthy (including the middle) class and working (including the poor) class. In his work he argues that the higher the gap in SES, the bigger the problem may be in terms of social alienation, leading to unrest, revolutions, and aberrant behavior, including violence and other deviant acts.

The German socialist believed that "oppressed masses"—the proletariat—come from lower SES; they are the victims of capitalism. The latter class—the bourgeoisie—come from higher SES: entrepreneurs, property, small or large business owners, and alike, respectively. Consequently, Marx's main argument is extended to a sub-argument that the ownership class, or the bourgeoisie, therefore produces "egocentric, greedy, and predatory human beings."[1] These predators abuse the working class, or the proletariat. Thus, the Marxist position and explanation for unsuccessful economy—or even self-destruction—is capitalism.

Marx argues that capitalism is the central reason for violent behavior in society through unequal distribution of financial resources, a socioeconomic gap between poor and wealthy.[2] His own, and also modern, interpretation of this doctrine clearly demonstrates that capitalism, the bourgeoisie, exploits and oppresses the working class, the proletariat."[3] The result is a working class that has no other means to survive but to work for meager wages.[4] Consequently, oppressed classes may commit crimes under social "duress" and stress—due to their unfortunate circumstances, such as poverty, starvation, and poor living/health conditions. Hence, Marxist theory suggests that extreme conditions of poverty precipitate class alienation and social unrest, resulting in antisocial behavior, violence, and crime.

In modern criminology, Robert Agnew's general strain theory (influenced greatly by Emile Durkheim, Robert Merton, and the works of others) suggests that "poverty" (environmental stressors or stimuli) and social disintegration of society result in violence.[5] This violence may be seen as a partial reflection of the Marxist doctrine. Agnew[6] refers to "strains" as adversity, "events or conditions that are disliked by individuals." He describes three main types of strains: (1) if an individual loses something of value (goods, peoples, relationships, etc.), (2) if an individual experiences emotional or physical injustice/abuse/mistreatment by others, and (3) if an individual has an inability to attain set goals or a desired (social) status/position within society.[7] Agnew[8] suggests that "personal experiences with strains should bear the strongest relationship to crime" rather than "vicarious" (indirect) experiences; for example, on one end of the continuum an individual may witness a friend's or family member's victimization, or on the opposite end they may experience personal interaction with a gang that results in their own gang involvement.

Agnew[9] acknowledges that the original work of Robert Merton (strain theory), Albert Cohen (status frustration), Richard Cloward and Lloyd Ohlin (delinquency opportunity)—all prior to his own work—pioneered the development of strain theory(s) in criminology, and that he was moved to expand the main principles further. The central principle of the above theorists suggests that everyone's goal (in the United States)—poor or wealthy alike—is the pursuit of achieving monetary gains or "middle-class status"[10] and that lower-class individuals experience desire for material goods and a lack of resources, counterbalancing the two variables; the result is that individuals "are unable to achieve monetary success or middle-class status through legal channels. Some of these individuals respond with crime; for example, they attempt to achieve their monetary goals through theft, prostitution, or drug selling."[11]

However, Marxist theory does not necessarily establish full validity in modern times in terms of violence and criminality. The main foundation of Marxism was centered on the production of material goods where human relations/needs/socialization/crime, etc., evolved and came as a secondary attribute of a social theory.[12] Nowadays, people are less conscious and consumed by producing the means of survival—food, clothing, shelter, etc. In other words, technological advancements in science and machinery replaced human labor in most areas, therefore human labor is no longer central and essential as it was in a Marxist paradigm. Since a hundred or more years ago, the hierarchy of needs theory (which was developed in the 1940s) has been indirectly seen as central in the work of many. This includes Charles Darwin (theory on survival of the fittest organisms), Marx (security of employment, improvement of social conditions, etc.), Engels (same as Marx), and even Adolf Hitler (indirectly relevant to survival of the fittest, or supremacy, in humans through development of the Aryan race). In these times, the lowest levels of the pyramid—physiological and safety—were more relevant. In today's society, however, people are conscious of and consumed by human relations; in Abraham Maslow's[13] pyramid this would correspond to love/belonging, esteem, and self-actualization levels.

In Travis Hirschi's[14] control theory, delinquency, or nonconformity of individuals, results when the bond between society and an individual "is weak or broken." He further explains "most forms of aberrant and unusual behavior" by describing four central elements of the bond where "attachment" comes first. However, Hirschi questions validity from a sociological standpoint. If an individual lacks a bond with others or expresses high levels of insensitivity to "the opinion of others," or demonstrates "excessive aggressiveness" and "'lack' of superego control," psychologists tend to label it as psychopathy.[15] Yet, he counterbalances this by saying that the above criteria explain only one part and "the behavior that psychopathy is used to explain often becomes part of the definition of psychopathy."[16]

Hirschi argues that oftentimes practitioners of mental health "tend to tie sensitivity inextricably to other variables, to make it part of a syndrome or 'type,' and thus seriously to reduce its value as an explanatory concept."[17] He believes that by doing so an investigative party handicaps its ability to understand or better evaluate the etiology in the development of aggressiveness and lack of attachment. Further, Hirschi adds, "given that man is an animal, 'impulsivity' and 'aggressiveness' can also be seen as natural consequences of freedom from moral restraints." That the key point of attachment to the norms and/or society lay in man's conscience or superego.[18]

"Commitment" is the second element of the bond; this concept "assumes that the organization of society is such that the interests of most persons would be endangered if they were to engage in criminal acts."[19] Consequently, Hirschi's argument on this element proposes that established individuals would not risk their social status, "goods, reputations, prospects; these accumulations are society's insurance that they will abide by the rules."[20] "Involvement" is the third element of the bond; that "involvement or engrossment in conventional activities is thus often part of a control theory."[21] The last element is "belief"; even if it is an obligatory matter, it will still "to some extent maintain its efficacy in producing conformity."[22]

Another model of understanding human behavior is found in Erich Fromm's theory of freedom, which is a transcendence derived from two theories: Freudian biological drives, the unconscious and repression, and Marx's principle that human beings are perceived by their socioeconomic class. His interest was targeted primarily toward sociopsychological analyses and its components, particularly in the Marxist theory; the initial source of inspirations stems from his religious upbringing and teachings of Talmudic law.[23] He believes that human behavior can be evaluated and understood—from a sociological standpoint—based not upon an individual's personal characteristics but upon society at large, merely because an individual is an extension of society.[24] Fromm's point closely resembles the Marxist perspective that violent human behavior is a result of societal demands and that people's lives and futures are determined by their society, especially their economic level.

For example, in the Marxist theory, it is the oppression and exploitation of the working class by the bourgeoisie (the gap in living conditions) that result in the development of social revolutions or upheavals. Consequently, human response via violent behavior and aggressive acts toward the economic conditions that the government/bourgeoisie/rules/etc. impose is natural and inevitable. Similarly, in Fromm's theory, it is the society at large rather than the individual's innate qualities per se that shape the personal characteristics of the individual.

Thus, both theories underline that society controls, to a degree, human responses, or acts as environmental stimuli. In other words, adversity and poor living conditions of the affected party(s) may be demonstrated later via physical or psychological acts (of one or many individuals). It could be expressed through one medium (as public acts/actions—revolutions, upheavals, strikes, etc.) or via an alternative medium (as personal acts/actions, denials, deviance, and aggression) combining all of the above components into a final product.

Erich Fromm uses Marxist social theory for two reasons: first, to understand irrational human behavior, and second, to underpin the correlation between people's lives/behavior (in particular, social status and their future) and society/government (as one entity). In other words, how an individual (i.e., one alone or multiple members) co-depend(s) and interact(s) with a socioeconomic structure of society and how the two components influence and mold each other. Fromm believes that the above two elements (components) synthesize new behaviors or ideas, individualistic or group; consequently, this relationship is "never static" but rather has a tendency to create "never-ending processes."[25] Fromm further posits that "the character structure . . . and the socioeconomic structure of the society of which he or she is a part are interdependent; the socioeconomic structure of a society molds the social character of its members . . . simultaneously, the social character influences the socioeconomic structure of society."[26]

Fromm's theory of personality is centered on freedom and self-realization; freedom, as his central idea, suggests that individuals have the drive for self-realization and this need comes from the disintegration of traditional authority along with secondary attributes.[27] It is therefore easy to draw a parallel between the Marxist perspective and Fromm's initial source or inspiration in the development of theory on freedom. It is simply because in the theoretical principles laid out by Karl Marx, Fromm sought not only a utopian idea (opposition and struggle of two contrasting masses) but yet wanted to posit an argument for one's freedom and—to a degree—one's salvation.[28] Fromm references Marx's Communist Manifesto as follows: "Communism was not a final goal, but a step in the historical development that was to liberate human beings from those socioeconomic and political conditions that make people inhuman—prisoners of things, machines, and their own greed."[29] Consequently, speaking about Marxism in the 21st century, a social paradigm loses its relevance due to the shift in societal needs—society evolves as do people.

Rainer Funk[30] reflects onto Fromm's work that the latter is able to synthesize and develop further unique ideas of self-fulfillment, relatedness, and happiness. However, for the two theorists, Marx and Fromm, socialism is the only way of life; the two theorists believe that society should be structured and governed this way because "socialism means independence and freedom."[31] Alienation, as a secondary attribute, is seen in Fromm's and Marx's works. Fromm's alienation is from society, self, or the world at large and is the key concept of freedom and self-realization; he suggests that if an individual experiences difficulties in achieving freedom or life goals and struggles with "self-realization," this person is bound to become isolated, alienated, and confused (similar in concept to Agnew's general strain theory). As a final product, an individual tends to reject the idea of freedom because freedom is a challenging thing to handle and not everyone is mentally capable of dealing with it equally successfully.[32]

Fromm's theory goes on further and explains how people would seek ways to escape the burden of freedom via authoritarianism, destructiveness, and automation conformity.[33] The "authoritarian" way or "authoritarianism" explains that an individual either subjects to others (e.g., people/government/ state) or becomes an authority himself; in "destructiveness," one escapes freedom through self-destruction or by inflicting pain on others and becomes a tyrant; in "automation conformity," an individual blends in with society and other people and becomes a social chameleon.[34] (The latter term should not be confused with Robert D. Hare's explanation on psychopathy and social psychopaths: those who do it to manipulate others.)

Fromm also places a great importance on the unity and concordance between the inner—satisfied and content—world of self and the external world—theory of human needs; this is relevant to contemporary studies on crime because these are the needs that are vital for human existence.[35] The five needs are relatedness, transcendence (or creativity), rootedness, frame of orientation (or reference), and sense of identity.[36] Under five human needs, Fromm places "relatedness" first in sequence; he expresses the idea that individuals overcome obstacles in order to achieve unity with other people, which is demonstrated via various forms: submission, power, or love. He argues that "relatedness" is a psychological need that human beings naturally try to achieve, and love, as a medium, enables humans to overcome separateness from each other.[37] Even Charles Darwin commented almost 200 years ago that humans are social animals in whom primal instincts drive and demand the need for socialization—to be with each other. Indeed, we are not meant to live as solitaires; thus, Fromm's references to love demonstrated through desires, needs, and goals of parenting (motherhood/fatherhood) or marriage and partnership—it is a union and simultaneously a connection of oneself with the outside world.

Fromm's second need is "transcendence" or "creativity"; humans do not want to be passive creatures, and they try to find creative outlets in life by becoming artists, musicians, and sculptors—creators of something—as another expression of love. However, if a person cannot find that outlet, he or she may "transcend" passivity into destruction.[38] From this point on we see the indirect relevance to the Marxist perspective, where people or masses would turn hostile or revolt not because they did not find an outlet for love or creativity but out of very basic needs such as shelter, food, or jobs (Maslow's lowest hierarchical levels of the pyramid). The third need is "rootedness"; Fromm believes that we need roots—when we are young, we are cared for by parents, but when individuals grow older they seek another form of connection via marriage, having children, or ties with society.[39] The fourth need is "frame of reference" or "orientation." Fromm argues that people ought to know the world and where they belong, their places in it. He says that religion or philosophy could be a medium to express that need. Consequently, Fromm's conclusion is that those individuals who are unable to fulfill their needs might become anomic and vulnerable to neurotic breakdowns.[40]

Last is a "sense of identity," whereby people have to fulfill the need to stay sane. If an individual experiences an acute need, he or she may go to great length to satisfy the desire, which produces a counter-effect. It also creates discrepancy, dissatisfaction, frustration, and alienation and further disconnects between the person and the outside world.[41] In modern criminology, investigators comment that most serial or mass murderers, psychopaths, and other individuals with behavioral disorders have developed an acute disconnect (during childhood or adolescent stages of development) with their families, then the world, and finally with their victims. This disconnect enables them to commit crimes in cold blood over and over again.

Funk supports the above statement that *entfremdung* (German for "alienation") is one of central themes in Marx's theory on social estrangement.[42] Funk references Fromm's statement on the Marxist perspective that "efforts to deal with alienation must go beyond mere socioeconomic manipulations . . . and the goal of all effort must be to overcome man's estrangement from life, from himself, and from his fellow man."[43]

According to Fromm, with freedom comes the burden of alienation and isolation—from oneself and the outside world. So therefore it is, in a way, a subconscious defense mechanism to escape freedom via radical, extremist ideas and/or violent behavior. He reflects on violence in society by applying a Marxist perspective, suggesting that most political leaders and revolutionaries sought to "change the political and economic structure radically, and that then, as a second and almost necessary step, the human mind will also change: that the new society, once established, will quasi-automatically produce the new human being."[44] Unfortunately, this is a distorted view and skewed thinking of many political leaders of the past and of modern times. As an example, history may recall many extremist political leaders, or dictators, of the past, including Vladimir Lenin, Joseph Stalin, Mao Zedong, Adolf Hitler, and "Che" Guevara, among others.

In retrospect, the main difference between the Marxist and modern theories on deviant and violent behavior, poverty and crime, is that the modern theories analyze and investigate human behavior—in individuals or in groups—where social conditions and environment play rather as secondary (vicarious) stimuli and/or "reinforcers." Comparatively, the Marxist theory looks at SES or class subjectively, and in its entirety; therefore, the theory cannot provide a quality picture or valid analysis of violent behavior in the modern world.

To reiterate, society evolves as do people, along with their needs. Thus, recent research in criminology examines today's human behavior and its possible factors, which consist of multiple elements, in order to deconstruct and explain crime. Disciplines such as neuroscience and biology offer the world a breadth of new theories, facts, and explanations regarding aberrant human behavior. They do not support low SES and alienation/oppression as exclusive agents leading to crime (as it is laid out in the Marxist perspective).

Lastly, the juxtaposition of the Marxist theory in the Communist Manifesto demonstrates central themes that evolve around classes—oppression, exploitation, and alienation.[45] Orrin Klapp argues that the main issue with the Marxist perspective is that it does not examine individual men as a final product, which may be a result of unequal conditions (e.g., class inequalities and market breakdown), potentially leading to social unrest and violence.[46] Even though modern theories, explained above, point out similar factors, yet they go in-depth and provide additional correlates to explain violence. Therefore, a trained professional or researcher needs to consider possible combinations and a multitude of external and internal factors (e.g., biological and sociological) that may play a crucial role in the development of violent behavior in certain individuals.

Notes

1. Clemens Bartollas and Stuart J. Miller, *Juvenile Justice in America* (Upper Saddle River, NJ: Pearson Education, 2011), 72.

2. Leo Panitch and Colin Leys, *The Communist Manifesto Now: Socialist Register 1998* (New York: Monthly Review Press), 1998.

3. Ibid.

4. Ibid.

5. Robert Agnew, *Pressured into Crime: An Overview of General Strain Theory* (Los Angeles: Roxbury Publishing, 1992), 4 –10 .

6. Ibid., 4.

7. Ibid.

8. Ibid., 10.

9. Ibid.

10. Ibid., 7.

11. Ibid., 8.

12. Panitch and Leys, *The Communist Manifesto Now: Socialist Register 1998.*

13. Abraham H. Maslow, *The Father Reaches of Human Nature* (New York: Penguin Group, 1971).

14. Travis Hirschi, *The Craft of Criminology: Selected Papers,* edited by John H. Laub (Piscataway, NJ: Transaction Publishers, 2002), 75.

15. Ibid.

16. Ibid., 76.

17. Ibid.

18. Ibid.

19. Ibid., 78.

20. Ibid.

21. Ibid., 79.

22. Ibid., 84.

23. Kevin Anderson and Richard Quinney, eds., *Erich Fromm and Critical Criminology: Beyond the Punitive Society* (Chicago: University of Illinois Press, 2000).

24. Ibid.

25. Erich S. Fromm, *To Have or To Be?* (New York, San Francisco, London: Harper & Row Publishers, 1976), 134.

26. Ibid., 133.

27. Ibid.

28. Ibid.

29. Ibid., 169.

30. Rainer Funk, *Erich Fromm, His Life and Ideas: An Illustrated Biography*, translated by Ian Portman and Manuela Kunkel (New York: Continuum, 2000), 72.

31. Fromm, *To Have or To Be?*

32. Ibid.

33. Ibid.

34. Ibid.

35. Ibid. More for psychological needs and successful functioning than anything else.

36. Anderson and Quinney, *Erich Fromm and Critical Criminology: Beyond the Punitive Society.*

37. Fromm, *To Have or To Be?*

38. Ibid.

39. Ibid.

40. Ibid. Fromm's idea is also reflected in Horney's work on neurotic personality, as these two authors worked together and influenced each other's theories.

41. Ibid.

42. Funk, *Erich Fromm, His Life and Ideas: An Illustrated Biography*. In other words, people who live in a stratified society are subject to a hierarchical ladder; as a result, they become classes.

43. Ibid., 74.

44. Fromm, *To Have or To Be?*, 134.

45. Orrin E. Klapp, *Models of Social Order: An Introduction to Sociological Theory* (Palo Alto: National Press Books, 1973).

46. Ibid.

Bibliography

Agnew, Robert, *Pressured into Crime: An Overview of General Strain Theory*. Los Angeles: Roxbury Publishing, 1992, 4–10.

Anderson, Kevin, and Richard Quinney, eds. *Erich Fromm and Critical Criminology: Beyond the Punitive Society*. Chicago: University of Illinois Press, 2000.

Bartollas, Clemens, and Stuart J. Miller. *Juvenile Justice in America*. Upper Saddle River, NJ: Pearson Education, 2011, 72.

Fromm, Erich S. *To Have or To Be?* New York, San Francisco, London: Harper & Row, 1976, 133–169.

Funk, Rainer. *Erich Fromm, His Life and Ideas: An Illustrated Biography*. Translated by Ian Portman and Manuela Kunkel. New York: Continuum, 2000, 72–74.

Hirschi, Travis. *The Craft of Criminology: Selected Papers*. Edited by John H. Laub. Piscataway, NJ: Transaction Publishers, 2002, 75–84.

Klapp, Orrin E. *Models of Social Order: An Introduction to Sociological Theory*. Palo Alto, CA: National Press Books, 1973.

Maslow, Abraham H. *The Farther Reaches of Human Nature*. New York: Penguin Group, 1971.

Panitch, Leo, and Colin Leys. *The Communist Manifesto Now: Socialist Register 1998*. New York: Monthly Review Press, 1998.

4

Sigmund Freud

Danica Ivancevich

Sexual behaviors are some of the most interesting, yet complex areas of study to date. Why people engage in sexual deviant behaviors while others do not is a phenomenon that has been widely researched by numerous theorists, including Sigmund Freud, the father of psychoanalysis. Freud is widely known for his controversial theories centered on sexual behaviors and ideation. Freud's interest in sex became apparent when he attended the University of Vienna, where he initially studied zoology. He spent numerous hours dissecting eels in order to locate the testes.[1] After examining over 400 specimens with no indication of the existence of eels' testes, he gave up his search. Later in his career, Freud developed theories based on the findings from his self-analysis. In addition, his fascination with genitalia and sexuality is believed to have influenced his theories on human sexuality and personality. Therefore, historical Freudian theory is employed to explain the etiology of sexually deviant behaviors.

The Life and Career of Freud

One of Freud's best-known psychoanalytic cases occurred during the 1890s when he assisted Josef Breuer, a highly regarded physician, in treating a complicated patient, referred to as "Anna O." Anna suffered from hysteria coupled with a variety of other disorders, such as mental lapses, hallucinations, partial paralysis, and hydrophobia.[2] After observing Anna on several occasions, Freud and Breuer came to the conclusion that Anna's symptoms were due to "residues of sexual feelings and impulses she had felt obligated to suppress, and that reconciliation of such feelings happened only when she spoke freely, uninhibited."[3] Freud and Breuer believed that Anna released her feelings hidden in her unconscious via verbalization, which freed her of further mental disturbance. With this discovery, Freud published *Studies of Hysteria,* which gained much attention. Due to his newfound recognition and praise for the psychoanalytic treatment method, Freud coined the term "psychoanalysis" in

1896. The main component of psychoanalysis was the concept of repression. Freud believed that unwanted feelings, mostly sexual, were denied by the conscious and pushed into the unconscious.[4]

During his time working with Breuer, Freud embarked on a period of self-analysis where he examined his life, especially his childhood. Through his self-analysis, he concluded that he was insecure and viewed his colleagues Ernst Brucke, Jean-Martin Charcot, and Breuer as father figures.[5] Freud revealed to Wilhelm Fliess, a close friend, that "the most important patient for me was my own person."[6] Freud confided in Fliess, who kept numerous letters from Freud that were later turned into a biography. In the letters, Freud stated that as a child he was obsessed with his mother and had hatred for his father, most likely because Freud felt like he had to compete with his father for his mother's attention.[7] Freud's findings through his self-analysis were central to the construction of the Oedipus complex theory.[8] Further, his observations led to the publication *The Interpretations of Dreams*, which suggested that dreams were emotions of the unconscious mind.[9]

Freud developed an addiction to mind-altering drugs, particularly cocaine.[10] He believed that cocaine was helpful for alleviating pain; thus, he prescribed cocaine generously to his patients.[11] His use of cocaine eventually subsided, but his frequent use of cigars did not.[12] Freud described smoking as "ultimately a substitute for that prototype of all addictions, masturbation,"[13] which again demonstrates that he believed every behavior was sexually motivated.

Of his five siblings, Freud was the most spoiled and often got what he wanted, including his own private room in the family residence. Another instance of this favoritism occurred when Freud complained that his sister's piano playing was disturbing him, and his mother immediately had the piano removed. His intelligence became apparent during his childhood, which gave him the status of the favorite child. His mother gave him much attention and referred to him as her "golden Siggie."[14]

This favoritism carried over into Freud's relationships with his own children. For example, Freud had three daughters, but he was fondest of his youngest daughter, Anna.[15] Freud hoped that Anna would continue his legacy by carrying on the psychoanalytic movement, and he felt that she would be the one person to ensure the continuation of his work because she had both the motivation and the mental capacity.[16] As a child, Anna attended Freud's seminars, and, just like his followers, she learned the details of psychoanalysis.[17] Freud psychoanalyzed Anna himself and mandated that she always tell the truth about her thoughts and feelings, even those that were erotic.[18] Thus, she revealed her sexual fantasies and experiences with masturbation to Freud.[19] Anna came out of the psychoanalysis grateful and even more dedicated to Freud.[20] Freud and Anna developed a strong bond that made Freud protective of Anna, especially when it came to sex.[21]

As she began to near her twenties, Anna began to attract men, even one of Freud's followers, but Freud always declared that she was too young to date, contemplate marriage, or leave the family.[22] At one point during Freud's analysis of Anna, she went on a vacation without her parents, which left Freud feeling lonely.[23] He wrote in a letter to his colleague, "I have long felt sorry for Anna for still being at home with us old folks . . . but on the other hand, if she really were to go away, I should feel myself as deprived as I would now if I had to give up smoking!"[24]

Anna practically replaced Freud's wife on an emotional level.[25] She later became his caretaker when his health declined, and in his last days, the two exchanged ideas regarding his psychoanalytic theory.[26] Because Anna appeared to have a closer relationship with Freud than her mother, Freud and Anna's relationship can be explained by Freud's Oedipus complex in which the child has feelings of love for the parent of the opposite sex and exhibits feelings of hostility toward the parent of the same sex.

Theoretical Perspectives

Freud used science and observations to come to conclusions about his theories. Through the use of these techniques, he established concepts that helped explain psychoanalysis. These concepts, or theories, are repression; id, ego, and superego; transference; psychosexual stages; Oedipus complex; dream analysis; the Freudian slip; and sexuality.[27]

Repression

Repression is a psychological defense mechanism that keeps unwanted, disturbing, or stressful thoughts in the unconscious.[28] Randolph Nesse and Alan Lloyd state that "the psychological defenses are the devices that distort cognition in ways that facilitate repression."[29] Repression regulates impulses by decreasing awareness of unwanted memories or feelings and thus, decreasing anxiety.[30] Moreover, Nesse and Lloyd argue that "repression does not just draw attention away from certain mental contents, it actively blocks attempts by the self or others to bring them to the consciousness."[31] Physical symptoms, dreams, Freudian slips, and posthypnotic suggestion indicate that an individual has repressed feelings.[32]

Freud believed that slips of the tongue were not accidental, but rather they had some meaningful underlying cause.[33] James Reason (1984) argues that Freud believed that these Freudian slips "betrayed the presence of some socially unacceptable impulse, and they revealed the failure, at a moment of reduced vigilance, to suppress that impulse."[34] Furthermore, these slips derive from the unconscious, briefly offering a glimpse into the memories or feelings of the unconscious that the individual would have rather kept private.[35] Thus, an individual who wants to conceal something may reveal their true feelings through slips of the tongue.[36]

In order to determine if feelings or memories were being repressed, Freud asked his patients to talk about whatever came to mind, regardless if it was unsettling or irrelevant.[37] This technique was known as the free association method. It is assumed that love masks hatred, anger masks ill wishes, and shamelessness masks guilt. These repressed feelings may appear as physical symptoms; for example, a woman who wishes to kill her husband may experience paralysis of her dominant arm.

Id, Ego, and Superego

One of Freud's key concepts in the psychodynamic-psychoanalytic theory is the structure of psyche: the id, ego, and superego. The id, ego, and superego shape an individual's personality and influence his or her behavior. The id is driven by pleasure and is primarily unconscious, the superego embodies social constraints and is both conscious and unconscious, and the ego is the most conscious system that mediates conflict between the id and the superego.[38]

The id is comprised of unconscious sexual and aggressive instincts.[39] In addition, the id is unconcerned with moral or socially acceptable standards.[40] The goal of the id is to maximize pleasure and minimize pain, also known as the pleasure principle.[41] Further, Nesse and Lloyd explain that "the id seems to motivate behavior that will bring individual satisfaction in the short run, while the superego motivates normative behavior that has short-term costs to the individual and benefits others."[42]

The ego helps control impulses and provides a reasonable direction for an individual's id impulses.[43] Repression is the ego's defense mechanism. Unwanted, stressful, or emotionally painful thoughts are repressed in order to keep the unwanted thoughts away from the conscious system.[44] Richard Ryckman states that the main functions of the superego are to "inhibit the urges of the id, to persuade the ego to substitute moralistic goals for realistic ones, and to strive for perfection."[45] The superego encompasses a set of learned ideals or values much like the ones instilled by parents.[46] For example, parents teach children which behaviors are acceptable or unacceptable in various situations.[47]

Deviant behavior occurs due to an imbalance between the id, ego, and superego, and it is believed to be a meaningful way to fulfill unconscious desires.[48] Conflicts between the id and the ego are too stressful or disturbing for the individual; therefore, the unwanted thoughts are repressed and manifest in the unconscious. Thus, the individual develops defense mechanisms to cope with the conflict, which may lead to problematic, deviant personality traits and behaviors.

Transference

The phenomenon of transferring or displacing feelings about one relationship to another relationship is known as transference.[49] Freud found that during treatment, his patients experienced the conflicts and interactions with authority figures (parents) from their past again with Freud (their therapist).[50] Because patients viewed Freud as a reincarnation of these past authority figures, they transferred emotions and behaviors to Freud that were once directed at these figures.[51] This supports the notion that the relationships during early childhood shape feelings about individuals later in life.[52] According to Nesse and Lloyd, "the conclusion of psychoanalytic studies is that many strong feelings in adult relationships arise, not from current circumstances, but from expectations based on transference."[53] Thus, children's first relationships, usually with parents or caretakers, set the tone for the kinds of relationships children will have in the future.[54] Negative first relationships may lead to negative future relationships and vice versa. For example, a child with positive experiences may think a new acquaintance wants to be friends, while a child with negative experiences may believe that new acquaintances dislike him or her.[55]

Psychosexual Stages

Freud established five stages of psychosexual development: oral, anal, phallic, latency, and genital. Individuals go through each stage during their first 20 years of life and the mastering of each stage aids in the formation of an individual's personality.[56] Normal development consists of pursuing libidinal (sexual) energy through every psychosexual stage.[57] If, during the early stages of childhood, an individual experiences a traumatic event, almost always sexual in nature, abnormal development will occur because the traumatic experience prevents the flow of libidinal (sexual) energy through each psychosexual stage.[58]

During the oral stage, the main focus of pleasurable sensations (sexual) is through the child's mouth. The infant may swallow the food if he/she finds it pleasant or spit it out if he/she finds the food unpleasant.[59] According to Freud, "the original pleasure-ego wants to interject into itself anything that is good and to eject from itself everything that is bad."[60] During the stage, the parents' behavior will affect whether the infant will experience hardships in his/her future.[61] Overindulgence and under-indulgence of the infant's needs could result in problems later on in their life.[62] For instance, if infants are suddenly weaned from breastfeeding, some of their libidinal energy becomes obsessed with this conflict while the rest of the energy moves on to the next stage.[63]

In the anal stage, the mother is no longer the primary caretaker, and the father joins the mother in the caregiving role.[64] Additionally, the child embarks on toilet training during this stage. The main focus of sexual energy is controlling bladder and bowel movements. In this stage, the child will either develop self-control or learn to manipulate those around him/her. For example, if the child does not live up to the parents' standards for potty training, the parents may place more pressure on the child, which could result in the child observing their frustrations over the absence of a bowel movement, thus resulting in the child learning how to manipulate the parents. If the parents deal with the child's refusal to engage in toilet training in a negative manner, the child may later develop feelings of invasion, exposure, and shame. By contrast, if the parents deal with their child's potty training in a positive manner, the child will learn to control his/her bladder and bowels. Freud labeled the release of feces as anal-sadistic and the retention of feces as anal-erotic.

During the phallic stage, the child develops affection for the parent of the opposite sex and holds hostile feelings for the parent of the same sex.[65] Thus, the main focus of sexual energy is on the genitals and the difference between females and males. This rivalry develops because the child feels the need to compete with the parent of the same sex for the attention of the parent of the opposite sex.[66] This concept is also known as the Oedipus complex.[67]

In the latency stage, the sexual development becomes suppressed.[68] This gives the pre-adolescent time to learn more about himself/herself before using his/her strengths in society.[69] According to Freud, "the sexual instinct is humanized during the latency period."[70] Additionally, the pre-adolescent engages more in social interactions with peers and becomes more responsible during this stage.[71]

The main component of the final stage of psychosexual development, the genital stage, is the definite organization of sexuality.[72] During this stage, the onset of puberty begins and individuals develop strong sexual interests toward a desired mate.[73] According to Freud, this symbolizes the "convergence of the affectionate current and the sensual current."[74] The individual embarks on a new journey as an adult, independent of parents and authoritative figures.[75] Once in adulthood, the individual will most likely marry and start a family.[76] Individuals who did not experience traumatic events in childhood with corresponding libido fixations will be able to make adequate adjustments to become successful in various areas of life.[77] Furthermore, these individuals will lead both well-balanced personal and work life, while also becoming secure with their identity, as well as more caring, empathetic, generous, etc.[78] Inadequate adjustments are a result of libidinal fixations and character disorder.[79]

Oedipus Complex

The saved letters of correspondence between Fliess and Freud indicate how Freud came up with the idea of the Oedipus complex.[80] Freud came to this epiphany during his self-analysis.[81]

Jeffrey Masson stated that in their correspondence Freud wrote:

> A single idea of general value dawned on me. I have found, in my own case too, [the phenomenon of] being in love with my mother and jealous of my father, and I now consider it a universal event in early childhood. If this is so, we can understand the gripping power of *Oedipus Rex*. . . . The Greek legend seizes upon a compulsion which everyone recognizes because he senses its existence within himself. Everyone in the audience was once a budding Oedipus in fantasy and each recoils in horror from the dream fulfillment here transplanted into reality, with the full quantity of repression which separates his infantile state from his present one.[82]

Therefore, according to Freud, children develop a love for the parent of the opposite sex and house feelings of hatred and jealousy for the parent of the same sex.[83] Martin S. Bergmann states "it is the repression of the Oedipus complex that separates normal infantile sexuality from adult sexuality and this repression is achieved during the latency period."[84] The Oedipus complex remains a conscious thought during childhood, usually in the phallic stage, but becomes repressed during the latency stage.[85] Even though the Oedipus complex is repressed later in life, it still remains intact and organized in the unconscious. Freud implies that because this fantasy remains intact, it is allowed to become conscious during masturbation.[86] Unconscious fantasies were precursors of hysterical symptoms.[87]

Theory of Sexuality

Sexual instinct and certain mental forces, specifically disgust and shame, serve as resistances to perversions.[88] These mental forces, in addition to education and life experiences, help restrain sexual deviant instincts within normal limits.[89] Freud believed that everyone had a predisposition to perversion.[90] However, deviant sexual instincts and behaviors only become perversions when they are fixated and replace the normal sexual aim (sexual acts).[91] People with and without mental abnormalities lead deviant sexual lives,[92] thus indicating that the intensity of perversion is influenced by life experiences.[93] People with perversions may perform sexually perverted acts while people with neuroticism insufficiently repress their sexual desires, which reappear as symptoms.[94] Those who have successfully repressed these perverted desires are able to lead normal sexual lives but suffer from neurotic symptoms, while those who have not suppressed their perverted thoughts lead deviant sexual lives.[95]

Perversion is the result of the denial of castration anxiety and Oedipal wishes.[96] Freud further explained that masochists retain sexual pleasure by sexualizing castration, compared to fetishists who avoid castration by sexualizing specific objects.[97] According to Freud, every perversion was a defense mechanism against castration anxiety.[98] Individuals who suffer from hysteria or obsessional neuroticism engage in normal sexual behavior rather than sexual deviance.[99] This is because their sexual deviant desires have been repressed and, in turn, manifest in the unconscious, which allows them to lead normal sexual lives.[100] However, these repressed desires do not lose their strength and thus reappear as symptoms of hysteria: tics, paralyses, convulsions, or blindness.[101]

Traumatic childhood experiences greatly influence individuals' sexuality in adulthood.[102] For example, experiencing sexual misconduct in childhood may result in the child becoming polymorphous perverse and engaging in all types of sexual deviance.[103] According to Freud, this demonstrates that an aptitude for perversion is innately present in individuals' dispositions.[104] On the contrary, Freud acknowledged that some individuals who have fallen victim to sexual abuse can and do go on to lead normal sexual lives.[105] Therefore, individuals who experience sexual trauma as a child and have a disposition for sexual irregularities are at an increased risk for engaging in deviant sexual behaviors.

Because children possess innocent views, they are typically without shame in their perverse actions.[106] For example, a child's curiosity may incite them to expose their genitalia to their peers, which for some children may be exciting.[107] Likewise, some children may be interested in the genitalia of their peers.[108] Freud argued that children who engage in this type of behavior might later develop into voyeurs or exhibitionists because behavior of this nature only occurs in the process of satisfying the need for excretion.[109]

Typically, feelings of pity do not develop until later in childhood.[110] Children who are cruel toward animals or peers are likely to engage in deviant sexual behavior in adulthood, specifically masochism.[111] Freud argues that there is an association between cruel and erotogenic (sexual stimulating) forms during childhood and this connection may not be able to be undone.[112] Further, Freud suggests that children who gain a sense of satisfaction from cruelty may enjoy physical punishment, such as spankings.[113]

Children who witness adult sexual intercourse may view the act as harmful or of subjugation.[114] This childhood experience creates a distorted view of sexual intercourse. Therefore, children who witness sexual intercourse at an early age may be inclined to engage in sadistic behavior.

Discussion

Freud destroyed many of his documents with the intent to make it impossible or at the very least difficult to write biographies about his life, memories, and feelings.[115] Likewise, the correspondence between Freud and Fliess was not meant to be public.[116] However, much has been revealed about Freud's childhood, relationship with his daughter, self-analysis, and theoretical perspective through these letters and his own theoretical publications. Freud came to conclusions about psychoanalysis through analyzing his own life; it is with great certainty that Freud's experiences shaped the psychoanalytic theory and method.

Just like his parents, Freud was guilty of treating one of his children with higher regard. The relationship between Freud and his daughter Anna appears to have been unhealthy in that Freud psychoanalyzed Anna and encouraged her to discuss details about her sexual behaviors and fantasies with him. Similarly, Anna virtually replaced Freud's wife by fulfilling his intellectual and emotional needs. Their relationship supports Freud's theory of the Oedipus complex.

One of the main components of psychoanalysis is repression. Through self-analysis and dream interpretation, Freud realized he repressed sexual thoughts and emotions. Through self-analysis, Freud discovered that he repressed thoughts of affection toward his mother and hatred for his father (Oedipus complex). In addition, this discovery helped form the psychosexual stages, especially the phallic and latency stages.

Freud's theoretical perspectives are based on sex. For example, repression serves as a way to rid the mind of deviant sexual thoughts; the id, ego, and superego maintain balance between normal and deviant sexuality; transference suggests that sexual feelings can be transferred to others; and the psychosexual stages explain sexual formation throughout childhood. Freud believed that all behaviors were sexually motivating and that all physical symptoms derived from unwanted sexual ideations. Why some people lead deviant sexual lives while others stay within the normal limits is the result of a sexually perverted predisposition in conjunction with a traumatic sexual experience in childhood. These two factors lead to all types of sexual deviant behaviors and disorders such as voyeurism, exhibitionism, masochism, sadism, and fetishism.

Notes

1. S. Y. Tan and A. Takeyesu, "Sigmund Freud (1856–1939): Father of Psychoanalysis," *Singapore Medical Journal* 52, no. 5 (2011): 322–32. https://fgcu.illiad.oclc.org/illiad/illiad.dll?Action=10&Form=75&Value=129866. This text was used as reference for the entire paragraph.

2. As cited in Tan and Takeyesu, "Sigmund Freud (1856–1939)," 322.

3. Ibid.

4. Tan and Takeyesu, "Sigmund Freud (1856–1939)," 322.

5. Ibid.

6. Ibid.

7. Ibid.

8. Ibid.

9. Ibid.

10. Ibid., 323.

11. Ibid.

12. Ibid.

13. As cited in Tan and Takeyesu, "Sigmund Freud (1856–1939)," 323.

14. Tan and Takeyesu, "Sigmund Freud (1856–1939)," 322.

15. Mark Edmundson, "Freud and Anna," *The Chronicle of Higher Education* 54, no. 4 (2007): para. 8. http://ezproxy.fgcu.edu/login?url=http://search.proquest.com/docview/214646076?accountid=10919.

16. Ibid., para. 7.

17. Ibid., para. 8.

18. Ibid, para. 9.

19. Ibid.

20. Ibid.

21. Ibid.

22. Ibid.

23. Ibid.

24. Ibid.

25. Ibid., para. 10.

26. Ibid.

27. Tan and Takeyesu, "Sigmund Freud (1856–1939)." This text was used as reference for the entire paragraph.

28. Randolph Nesse and Alan Lloyd, *The Evolution of Psychodynamic Mechanisms* (New York: Oxford University Press, 1992), 604.

29. Ibid.

30. Ibid., 605.

31. Ibid., 606.

32. Ibid., 604.

33. James Reason, "The Psychopathology of Everyday Slips: Accidents Happen When Habit Goes Haywire," *Sciences* 24, no.5 (1984): 45. http://web.ebscohost.com.ezproxy.fgcu.edu/ehost/pdfviewer/pdfviewer?sid=f54181fe-3dff-4a7c-9fede106ed36497f%40sessionmgr4002&vid=2&hid=4109.

34. Ibid.

35. Ibid.

36. Nesse and Lloyd, *The Evolution of Psychodynamic Mechanisms*, 604.

37. Ibid. This text was used as reference for the entire paragraph.

38. Dan Segrist, "What's Going On in Your Professor's Head? Demonstrating the Id, Ego, and Superego," *Teaching of Psychology* 36, no.1 (2009): 51. doi:10.1080/00986280802529285.

39. Richard Ryckman, *Theories of Personality*, 9th ed. (Belmont, CA: Thomson, Wadsworth, 2008), 40.

40. Ibid.

41. Ibid.

42. Nesse and Lloyd, *The Evolution of Psychodynamic Mechanisms*, 613.

43. Ryckman, *Theories of Personality*, 9th ed., 40.

44. Nesse and Lloyd, *The Evolution of Psychodynamic Mechanisms*, 605.

45. Ryckman, *Theories of Personality*, 9th ed., 40.

46. Ibid.

47. Ibid

48. Megan Moore, "Psychological Theories of Crime and Delinquency," *Journal of Human Behavior in the Social Environment* 21, no. 3 (2011): 231. doi:10.1080/10911359.20 11.564552. This text was used as reference for the entire paragraph.

49. Nesse and Lloyd, *The Evolution of Psychodynamic Mechanisms*, 616.

50. Ryckman, *Theories of Personality*, 9th ed., 61.

51. Ibid.

52. Nesse and Lloyd, *The Evolution of Psychodynamic Mechanisms*, 616–617.

53. Ibid., 616.

54. Ibid., 617.

55. Ibid.

56. John Garcia, "Freud's Psychosexual Stage Conception: A Developmental Metaphor for Counselors," *Journal of Counseling & Development* 73, no. 5 (1995): 498. http://web.ebscohost. com.ezproxy.fgcu.edu/ehost/pdfviewer/pdfviewer?sid=53a1e2d6-23b4-417d-8213-ed42d9012 e73%40sessionmgr113&vid=4&hid=117.

57. Ryckman, *Theories of Personality*, 9th ed., 45.

58. Ibid.

59. Garcia, "Freud's Psychosexual Stage Conception," 499.

60. As cited in Garcia, "Freud's Psychosexual Stage Conception," 498.

61. Ryckman, *Theories of Personality*, 9th ed., 46.

62. Ibid.

63. Ibid.

64. Garcia, "Freud's Psychosexual Stage Conception," 499. This text was used as reference for the entire paragraph.

65. Ibid.

66. Ibid.

67. Martin S. Bergmann, "The Oedipus Complex and Psychoanalytic Technique," *Psychoanalytic Inquiry* 30, no. 6 (2010): 535–40. doi:10.1080/07351690.2010.518538.

68. Ryckman, *Theories of Personality*, 9th ed., 48.

69. Garcia, "Freud's Psychosexual Stage Conception," 499.

70. As cited in Garcia, "Freud's Psychosexual Stage Conception," 499.

71. Garcia, "Freud's Psychosexual Stage Conception," 499. Ryckman, *Theories of Personality*, 9th ed., 49.

72. Garcia, "Freud's Psychosexual Stage Conception," 499.

73. Ryckman, *Theories of Personality*, 9th ed., 49.

74. As cited in Garcia, "Freud's Psychosexual Stage Conception," 499.

75. Garcia, "Freud's Psychosexual Stage Conception," 499.

76. Ryckman, *Theories of Personality*, 9th ed., 49.

77. Ibid.

78. Ibid

79. Ibid.

80. Bergmann, "The Oedipus Complex," 535.

81. Ibid.

82. Jeffrey Masson, *The Complete Letters of Sigmund Freud to Wilhelm Fliess, 1887–1904* (Cambridge, MA: Belknap Press, 1985), 272.

83. Bergmann, "The Oedipus Complex," 536.

84. Ibid.

85. Bergmann, "The Oedipus Complex," 536. Garcia, "Freud's Psychosexual Stage Conception," 498–502.

86. Bergmann, "The Oedipus Complex," 536.

87. Ibid.

88. Sigmund Freud, *Three Essays on the Theory of Sexuality*, trans. J. Strachey (New York: Basic Books, 1975), 40.

89. Ibid.

90. Freud, *Three Essays on the Theory of Sexuality* (1975), xliv.

91. Sigmund Freud, *Three Essays on the Theory of Sexuality* (1905; repr., London: Imago Publishing, 1949), 34.

92. Freud, *Three Essays on the Theory of Sexuality* (1975), 15.

93. Ibid., xliv.

94. Ibid., 15.

95. Ibid., xlv.

96. A. De Block and P. Adriaens, "Pathologizing Sexual Deviance: A History," *Journal of Sex Research* 50, no. 3/4, (2011): 282. doi:10.1080/00224499.2012.738259.

97. Ibid.

98. Ibid.

99. Freud, *Three Essays on the Theory of Sexuality* (1975), xliii.

100. Ibid.

101. Ibid.

102. Freud, *Three Essays on the Theory of Sexuality* (1949), 69.

103. Ibid.

104. Ibid.

105. Ibid., 68.

106. Ibid., 70.

107. Ibid.

108. Ibid.

109. Ibid.

110. Ibid.

111. Ibid., 71.

112. Ibid.

113. Ibid.

114. Ibid., 74. This text was used as reference for the entire paragraph.

115. Harold Blum, "The Writing and Interpretation of Dreams," *Psychoanalytic Psychology* 17, no.4 (2000): 656. doi: http://dx.doi.org/10.1037/0736-9735.17.4.651.

116. Ibid.

Bibliography

Bergmann, Martin S. "The Oedipus Complex and Psychoanalytic Technique." *Psychoanalytic Inquiry* 30, no. 6 (2010): 535–40. doi:10.1080/07351690.2010.518538.

Blum, Harold. "The Writing and Interpretation of Dreams." *Psychoanalytic Psychology* 17, no.4 (2000): 651–66. doi: http://dx.doi.org/10.1037/0736-9735.17.4.651.

De Block, A., and P. Adriaens. "Pathologizing Sexual Deviance: A History." *Journal of Sex Research* 50, no. 3/4 (2013): 276–98. doi:10.1080/00224499.2012.738259.

Edmundson, Mark. "Freud and Anna." *The Chronicle of Higher Education* 54, no.4. (2007): B8–B9. http://ezproxy.fgcu.edu/login?url=http://search.proquest.com/docview/214646076?accountid=10919.

Freud, Sigmund. *Three Essays on the Theory of Sexuality*. London: Imago Publishing, 1949. First published 1905.

Freud, Sigmund. *Three Essays on the Theory of Sexuality*. Translated by J. Strachey. New York: Basic Books, 1975. First published 1905.

Garcia, John. "Freud's Psychosexual Stage Conception: A Developmental Metaphor for Counselors." *Journal of Counseling & Development* 73, no. 5 (1995): 498–502. http://web.ebscohost.com.ezproxy.fgcu.edu/ehost/pdfviewer/pdfviewer?sid=53a1e2d6-23b4-417d-8213-ed42d9012e73%40sessionmgr113&vid=4&hid=117.

Masson, Jeffrey. *The Complete Letters of Sigmund Freud to Wilhelm Fliess, 1887–1904*. Cambridge, MA: Belknap Press, 1985.

Moore, Megan. "Psychological Theories of Crime and Delinquency." *Journal of Human Behavior in the Social Environment* 21, no. 3 (2011): 226–39. doi:10.1080/10911359.2011.564552.

Nesse, Randolph and Alan Lloyd. *The Evolution of Psychodynamic Mechanisms*. New York: Oxford University Press, 1992.

Reason, James. "The Psychopathology of Everyday Slips: Accidents Happen When Habit Goes Haywire." *Sciences* 24, no.5 (1984): 45–49. http://web.ebscohost.com.ezproxy.fgcu.edu/ehost/pdfviewer/pdfviewer?sid=f54181fe-3dff-4a7c-9fede106ed36497f%40sessionmgr4002&vid=2&hid=4109.

Ryckman, Richard. *Theories of Personality*. 9th ed. Belmont, CA: Thomson, Wadsworth, 2008.

Segrist, Dan. "What's Going On in Your Professor's Head? Demonstrating the Id, Ego, and Super-ego." *Teaching of Psychology* 36, no.1 (2009): 51–54. doi:10.1080/00986280802529285.

Tan, S. Y., and A. Takeyesu. "Sigmund Freud (1856–1939): Father of Psychoanalysis." *Singapore Medical Journal* 52, no. 5 (2011): 322–32. https://fgcu.illiad.oclc.org/illiad/illiad.dll?Action=10&Form=75&Value=129866.

5

Anomie and General Strain Theory

Sarah Norman

Deviance theory cannot be observed in a vacuum. There are many influences that affect all individuals, including those who eventually engage in deviant behavior. While some theorists have focused on the influence of media as a key underpinning of their entire theory, the practical reality is that media plays some role in the lives of all individuals. Even Ted Kasczynski, the recluse who used homemade bombs to kill three and injure 23, took buses and other public transportation to mail his bombs. In his travels, he would have been exposed to media.

The psychological approach to understanding cognitive ability within individuals has been influenced by an abundance of elements. Time has produced research insights. These insights, along with technological advancements, have resulted in new perspectives on cognitive processes. Criminologists have studied the reasoning behind crime, trying to pinpoint the initial break that corrupts the normality of social order. Theories have been analyzed, researched, and studied to map out the path of criminal behavior in an effort to gain insight into justifying criminal action. New theory often fills in the gaps in earlier theorists' thoughts and opinions. Our moral compass is a large-scale depiction of the direction we take both as a society and as individuals. Media has become an exaggerating force regarding societal issues that influence our thoughts and perspectives.

Generational differences have resulted in changes in daily human behavior. One of the biggest changes that have developed in the world is the concept of human patience. Patience appears to be a bygone concept. In today's society, patience has been traded for instant gratification. The majority of the United States has become a nation of greed and selfishness. We covet, we desire, and we are generally less sensitive creatures in relation to the common good. Criminal behavior may be seen as one of the consequences of this decrease in patience and increase in avarice.

Criminal behavior has presented itself throughout history, accounting for the formation of rules and regulations. Criminal activity is deviant based upon the moral standards of the society. Thus, research geared toward the influence of media in relation to criminal behavior may be seen as a line connecting perception, motivation, and behavior. The influence and prevalence of media have changed the way we as a society live and interact.

The development of communication within a society is based on three intentional functions that mandate the basis of internal and external communication, surveillance, correlation, and transmission.[1] "Media is an agent of socialization."[2] It is the volume of expression and communication that leads to social interaction. Media propaganda has influenced the world with its exaggerated impulse of manipulation. Media's focus on criminal behavior, sex, drugs, and violence has overtaken topics such as the economy, politics, and health care reform.[3] Important realities of life have been overlooked and undermined to deliver entertainment and profit without a sense of conscience. The consequence of media entertainment has drastically shifted the paradigm of influence and has desensitized the public to material that once was seen as inappropriate. The article "The News Media's Influence on Criminal Justice Policy: How Market-Driven News Promotes Punitiveness" reinforces the connection of media influence on policy; Sara Sun Beale states, "the news media are not mirrors, simply reflecting events in society. Rather, media content is shaped by economic and marketing considerations that frequently override traditional journalistic criteria for newsworthiness."[4] If media is shaped by the economic and marketing mindfulness, then the socioeconomics and demographics of a society shape the economic and marketing agenda, thus promoting the media's importance and assessment. Research and theory into environmental criminology studies the dimensions in crime.[5] Criminally motivated individuals fit the mold for the dimensions of crime by elements of what Paul Brantingham and Patricia Brantingham describe as "law, offender, target, and place."[6] The purpose of environmental criminology, according to Brantingham and Brantingham, is as follows:

> Geographic imaginations in concert with the sociological imagination to describe, understand, and control criminal events. Locations of crimes, the characteristics of those locations, the movement paths that bring offenders and victims together at those locations and people's perceptions of crime locations all become substantively important objects for research from this shifted perspective.[7]

Environmental criminology can be justified in producing the outcome of the media's position within the economic and marketing forethought of business. Understanding the location not only geographically but also by sociological insight gains a relative basis to control economics and marketing by the media. They form the motivation and program the growth and adaptation of a community's worth and formality.

The inaccurate fallacies of crime and criminals are represented by falsehoods of error and delusion that plague the minds of the public.[8] The public's dependency and trust into the world of media simply adds more fuel to the fire and continues to shadow criminal justice departments. In an existing world, media is the participant within a social organization.[9] According to Nick Couldry,

> Media's role in prescribing social reality is open ended: it is not fully determined in advance. It is based on, in particular, material processes of power that are embedded in everyday practice; those processes are always finite and partial; they allow, at times at least, for rival prescriptive constructions of the world.[10]

Media's effect can be measured by suggestions of influencing violent behavior.[11] Controversy extends its hand in regard to violence and antisocial behaviors. Children and adolescents become influenced by media's cultivation of entertainment that Daniel Derksen and Victor Strasburger explain as having "a powerful effect on the development of unhealthy activities, negative attitudes, and antisocial behaviors."[12] Media's manipulation is vast, in addition to stealing the innocence of well-being. Violence that is observed brings emotional fixations onto issues that yield explanation.

The corruption of media encountered on the criminal level is seen from all angles. From the communication standpoint, it is seen as news, the right, the just for the people to know and understand what is happening within their communities. However, media's initial response to telling a story involves much more than truth and validity. Manipulation for entertainment is the driving vein to sustain life and existence for the entertainment world. Media has now developed into forms of communication that have opened Pandora's box. The evolution of media has developed into a movement that has branded technology into the lifestyles of every generation and has become the foundation of every existence. The concept of "new media" produces Internet and social media, communicative avenues that have overtaken essential concepts of information by evolving through parallel developments within the treatment of criminal behavior.[13] The wave of new media has simply changed the way the world communicates. An instant connection to others has broadened the concept of communication and process of knowledge.

The drastic change in communication within the past decade and beyond is primarily due to new technologies that have overwhelmed the capabilities of people. Our nation has become that of fast and faster. Patience is a virtue of the past and privacy is a historical term. Society has become involved with their smart phones, tablets, and computers. Facebook, Twitter, Instagram, and YouTube have become a social revolution in society today. Thus the media's concept has evolved into a social outbreak that has influenced control, lack of privacy, and a sense of seclusion from reality, thus forming a depiction of false life advertisements. Media logic, social control, and fear all play off the advancements of technology. The obsession of the online fad has become that of control[14]—control to dictate when, where, and how the information is obtained. Power and manipulation have become key ingredients to society's authoritative ways.

Communication Theory published an article in 2013 by David Altheide on "Media Logic, Social Control, and Fear," analyzing communication and logic within the connotation of media and the interaction media played on social control.[15] Society has become fixated on preverbal implications of knowing what others do every second of each day. The knowledge of an individual's every thought and mishap does not have any effect on the social chains of life events; however it's what some want the world to know. Attention becomes a subconsciously submissive link that the mind uses in hope of gaining acceptance and it has become an expression of personality and release. Media has urged citizens to be apart of the *now* rather than the *then*. The Internet has opened a realm of possibilities within the world. Though the Internet brings us logic and knowledge, Altheide suggests it also brings us fear.[16]

The emotional context of fear can be ruthless. In 2011, an Egyptian revolt exploded with protesters. This act was considered to be coordinated by social media. It was said that the overall "effectiveness of the media is judged by the social and political contexts."[17] As the revolt continued, posts, blogs, and information flooded the media circuit. Altheide mentions that though social media gains us access to some parts of the world, certain areas might inhibit the use of social media and use it as a provoking method to falsify certain actions to start a war.[18] It only takes one false post to Facebook or Twitter before outrage explodes among people. Opinions fly from every direction and verbal wars continue for hours over the Web. The links between the technological world and the real world are not far from deviant acts of criminal behavior.

Media is driven by human force and recognition; it is the human prerogative that sets the standard and the foundation for behavior and development. Social media has become a political and marketing ladder that enforces profit and entertainment. Theoretical implications of Emile Durkheim's theory of anomie and Robert Agnew's general strain theory express the connection within sociology and criminology in addition to the effect they play on society. It is here where the integration is made within the relation of media and crime. Media's intentions, focus, manipulation, power, and control are defined by looking at criminal activity due to theory, environmental criminology, social media, generational changes, deviant behaviors, influence, and the political agenda of the many misconceptions media portray to the world. Corruption for entertainment, media's influence on crime is continuing to grow and diverge into a spectacle of what Dersken and Strasburger categorize as displaced healthy activities, disinhibition, modeling inappropriate behaviors, aggressive arousal, association with risk-taking behavior, and desensitizing the public to criminal activity, all of which Dersken and Strasburger define as "the major effects of violence, antisocial behavior, and aggression in the media."[19] Addressing the lack of normality requires an analysis of the confusion and disorder along with a recognition of potential emotional charades. This may help in the research of biological and psychological factors within criminal behavior and their possible connection to the media..

Emile Durkheim's theory of anomie develops two direct theoretical perspectives to describe a theoretical basis of the macro and micro side of anomie. The theory of anomie is the understanding of social knowledge through essential ideologies of exploited social establishments.[20] According to Durkheim in relation to social relationships, "when society is strongly integrated, it holds individuals under its control . . . and thus forbids them to dispose willfully of themselves."[21] The power social media has on a society controls the evolution of thought and in essence does the opposite of Durkheim's thought and becomes a gateway of expression with one's willful views; it exaggerates and sets forth a political agenda of untruths and an outlet for those who are held under the thumb of societal ruling.

Social media has become a tool for all to express their innermost feelings with copious amounts of emotional context that can be addressed without face-to-face contact. It is a way to communicate behind closed doors, without having to face verbal confrontations and tell-tale body language: taking the uncomfortable aura out of the mix, changing the way we communicate, reconfiguring one component of interpersonal communication in the world, drawing a fine line in excessive behavior, and the difference between right and wrong.

Criminal behavior can be addressed by theories that examine psychopathy, narcissistic behavior, mental issues, and the history of aggression that coax and prod an individual to engage in acts of terror upon innocent people. The abundance of mass shootings that have taken place across the world have gained the media's attention, and those responsible for these treacherous acts understood the powers of highlighted media and used it as their channel for ultimate expression.

Virginia Tech shooter Seung-Hui Cho killed 32 people in a mass attack on April 16, 2007.[22] His video package that he mailed to NBC before his rampage was pithy, knowing that the media would consume his vision, thoughts, and perspective and broadcast it to the world. Everyone would finally hear him; media gave him a voice. The media's exploitation of his works gave him power even after death. In

2006, Kimveer Gill shot 20 people in a massive rage, using references to video games and stating his feelings in a Web blog to express his ultimate hatred and despair to the world.[23] Donald Dutton and colleagues' article "Paranoid Thinking in Mass Shooters" quotes Kimveer Gill: "I hate this world, I hate the people in it, I hate the way people live, I hate God, I hate the deceivers, I hate betrayers, I hate religious zealots, I hate everything, I hate so much (I could write 1,000 more lines like these, but does it really matter, does anyone even care)."[24]

Yearning for affection and desiring attention are part of the natural growth of human bonding. Kimveer Gill resolved his emptiness with acts of violent carnage that destroyed the lives of innocent people. Society has no choice but to care, for ignoring a mass destruction like this adds lack of empathy to its members. Kimveer Gill was known, analyzed, and studied and became someone the world would remember forever. The world becomes attentive when media highlights destruction and evil. "To someone who has spent his life in the shadows, a few minutes of fame is worth the risk of violence."[25]

"When society is disturbed by some painful crisis or by beneficent but abrupt transitions, it is momentarily incapable of exercising this influence."[26] In the midst of tragedy, people struggle to reconcile reason with fact, thus media is the magnet and refuge within a storm of abhorrence. Answers and justifications are sought by individuals in society to help serve as a security blanket against increased fear.

Robert Agnew's general strain theory is associated with that of the micro side of anomie; this resonates the breakdown of a society and the increase in deviant behavior. Here, Agnew's formation of the general strain theory is formulated to measure strain on a subjective and objective text.[27] Thus, the overall concept of strain theory contends that with the increase of strain, anger and the often corresponding feeling of irritation and annoyance builds up within the psychological mind frame of the personality and increases the chances of deviant behavior.[28]

Indicative principles of negative relationships communicate the categories of Agnew's continuation of Robert Merton's strain theory. General strain theory accounts for failure to achieve goals, removal of positive stimuli, and the arrangement of negative stimuli.[29] These elements can affect the precision of money, status, respect, and power over oneself within society. In addition to failure, along with the loss of positive influence, one then breeds the general inclination of revenge, consequently being presented with negative stimuli.[30] Life events are crucial in the development of a healthy and understanding life. Children who witness neglect, abuse, or come from an environment that breeds negativity will surely lead to a whirlwind of problematic issues that can increase chances of deviant behavior.[31]

Failure can be a hard burden to bear psychologically. Failure forces people to act. Consistent failures may lead to stress and anxiety. Social media has become a potential weapon of emotional mass destruction. Venting and the expression of oneself can be tweeted, posted, liked, and commented on from literally around the world. "What we want to demonstrate is the fallacy of judging society according to its own standards, because its categories are part of its publicity."[32] Society's standards are based on the traditional norms of a community.

Agnew argued his point in relation to social learning and the impact that it has on the nature of self-interest and social concern. He found that development depends on the circumstance and the people.[33] Agnew states, ". . . it is not the case that people are self-interested or socially concerned or blank slates, but rather that they are self-interested, socially concerned and significantly *shaped* by the social environment."[34] Social environments classify the context of the self-interested and the socially concerned individual. Social media have become an environment where individuals must own up to somewhat of a responsibility of freedom within the media bubble.

Criminal and deviant acts can be analyzed through the biological and psychological factors of human nature. Human nature, nature of society, and nature of reality all encompass the environment in which human beings reside. It is these elements that Agnew describes in relation to criminal activity and the human prerogative.[35] Conflict, oppression with discrimination at its core, and the measure of sources that reduce bias all fall into the categories of the nature of Agnew's theory.[36]

Responsibility of freedom is the unspecified resemblance of being held accountable. Accountability for one's actions is lacking within the borders of societal refuge. Responsibility for actions, words, and decisions need to be well proportioned with the gifts that freedom brings.

Judging by the relationship between theories of anomie and general strain, media can be categorized with the connection of criminal behavior. Socialization is the cornerstone of society's structure. Communication becomes the development of understanding, and how we communicate effectively is the defining factor of our future endeavors. Media is a movement that has caused damage to all areas of interest. Criminal behavior is just one particular scope of study.

In analyzing mass shooters, theory, politics, violence, and social interaction, a crucial understanding of how media plays a part in influencing criminality is displayed. "It helps, however, to look beyond the way reality media writes over the social world and consider other longer established forms of hidden injury that result from media."[37] The perception of crime has been enforced and increased due to the abundant amount of criminal stories that are projected through the media. "Media's regular selection of crime stories for prominence has over many decades 'institutionalized' [the] experience' of crime . . ."[38] Misconceptions and manipulation within the media world have presented the public with wrong ideas of reality within a contextual basis of criminology. It has become the virtue of what will sell and increase ratings for profitable margins and power play in the corporate world of business, while underestimating the significant issues that cause destruction to social norms.

Greed is a significant factor in the deterioration of the moral development of contemporary society. We want more, we want it fast, and we want it now. As stated before, our moral compass is a significant variable influencing the direction we take as a society both as individuals and as a community. Media has become an exaggerated force illuminating societal issues and influencing the thoughts and perceptions of individuals.

Agnew's theory proposes this final thought regarding social interaction, media, and crime: "Individuals are able to intentionally make choices that are not fully determined by forces beyond their control and they are able to act on their choices."[39] The powerful gift of choice resides within us all. The will to do the right thing is based on one's moral development and perception of the situation at hand. The choices within the realm of media do not have to be based on political agenda, money, or power. However, we repeatedly see examples such as the Egyptian revolt, which was instigated by social media, and murderers like Seung-Hui Cho and Kimveer Gill, who were likely motivated by the possibility of excessive media exposure. The traditional theories of anomie and general strain add meaning to the confusion and shed light on possible underlying motivations related to deviant behavior.

Notes

1. Harold D. Laswell, "The Structure & Function of Communication in Society," in *Mass Communications*, ed. W. Schramm (Urbana: University of Illinois Press, 1969), 228.

2. Kimberly A. McCabe and Gregory M. Martin, *School Violence, the Media, & Criminal Justice Responses* (New York: Peter Lang Publishing, 2005), 7.

3. Sara Sun Beale, "The News Media's Influence on Criminal Justice Policy: How Market-Driven News Promotes Punitiveness," *William & Mary Law Review* 48, no. 2 (2006), http://scholarship.law.wm.edu/wmlr/2006, 422–432.

4. Ibid., 397–98.

5. Paul J. Brantigham and Patricia L. Brantingham, *Environmental Criminology* (Beverly Hills, CA: Sage Publications, 1981), 7.

6. Ibid., 7.

7. Ibid., 21.

8. Olga Tsoudis, "Does Majoring in Criminal Justice Affect Perceptions of Criminal Justice," *Journal of Criminal Justice Education* 11, no. 2 (2000), 225.

9. Nick Couldry, *Media, Society, World: Social Theory and Digital Media Practice* (Malden, MA: Polity Press, 2012), viii.

10. Ibid., 65.

11. McCabe and Martin, *School Violence*, 7–8.

12. Daniel J. Derksen and Victor C. Strasburger, "Media and Television Violence: Effects on Violence, Aggression, and Antisocial Behaviors in Children," in *Schools, Violence, and Society*, ed. Alan M. Hoffman (Westport, CT: Praeger, 1996), 61.

13. Beale, "The News Media's Influence," 436–40.

14. Ibid., 439.

15. David L. Altheide, "Media Logic, Social Control, and Fear," *Communication Theory* 23, no. 3 (2013), 223–25.

16. Ibid., 232–34.

17. Ibid., 228.

18. Ibid., 228–32.

19. Derksen and Strasburger, "Media and Television Violence," 71.

20. Emile Durkheim, *Suicide*, translated by John Spaulding and George Simpson (New York: Free Press, 1951), 11.

21. Ibid., 209.

22. Donald G. Dutton, Katherine R. White, and Dan Fogarty, "Paranoid Thinking in Mass Shooters," *Aggression and Behavior* 18, 5 (2013), 549–50.

23. Ibid., 550–51.

24. Ibid., 551. This direct quotation is from Kimveer Gill's blogs (2006) on Vampirefreaks.com. Gill's activity was suspended. For reference to the copies of his blogs, visit http://www.schoolsshooters.info/PL/Original_Documents_files/Kimveer%20Gill%20Online.pdf.

25. McCabe and Martin, *School Violence*, 38.

26. Durkheim, *Suicide*, 252.

27. Robert Agnew, *Pressured into Crime: An Overview of General Strain Theory* (Los Angeles: Roxbury, 2006), 32.

28. Ibid., 13–26.

29. Ibid., 20–26.

30. Ibid., 1–8.

31. Ibid., 173–85.

32. Henri Lefebvre, *Everyday Life in the Modern World* (London: Allen Lane, 1971), 71.

33. Robert Agnew, "Integrating Assumptions about Crime, People, and Society: Response to the Reviews of *Toward a Unified Criminology*," *Journal of Theoretical & Philosophical Criminology* 5, no. 1 (2013), 79.

34. Ibid.

35. Ibid., 89.

36. Ibid., 86–91.

37. Couldry, *Media, Society, World*, 101.

38. Ibid., 103.

39. Agnew, "Integrating Assumptions about Crime," 86.

Bibliography

Agnew, Robert. "Integrating Assumptions about Crime, People, and Society: Response to the Reviews of *Toward a Unified Criminology*." *Journal of Theoretical & Philosophical Criminology* 5, no. 1 (2013), 74–93. http://ezproxy.fgcu.edu/login?url=http://search.proquest.com/docview/1434968839?accountid=10919.

Agnew, Robert. *Pressured into Crime: An Overview of General Strain Theory*. Los Angeles: Roxbury, 2006.

Altheide, David. "Media Logic, Social Control, and Fear." *Communication Theory* 23, no.3 (2013), 223–38.

Beale, Sara Sun. "The News Media's Influence on Criminal Justice Policy: How Market-Driven News Promotes Punitiveness." *William & Mary Law Review* 48, no. 2 (2006), 397–481. http://scholarship.law.wm.edu/wmlr.

Brantingham, Paul J., and Patricia L. Brantingham. *Environmental Criminology*. Beverly Hills, CA: Sage Publications, 1981.

Couldry, Nick. *Media, Society, World: Society Theory & Digital Media Practice*. Malden, MA: Polity Press, 2012.

Derksen, Daniel J., and Victor C. Stransburger. "Media and Television Violence: Effects on Violence, Aggression & Antisocial Behaviors in Children." In *Schools, Violence, and Society*, ed. A. Hoffman. Westport, CT: Praeger, 1996, 61–78.

Durkheim, Emile. *Suicide*. Translated by John A. Spaulding and George Simpson. New York: Free Press, 1951.

Dutton, Donald G., Katherine R. White, and Dan Fogarty. "Paranoid Thinking in Mass Shooters." *Aggression and Violent Behavior* 18, no. 5 (2013), 548–53. http://ezproxy.fgcu .edu/login?url=http://search.proquest.com/docview/1426848334? accountid=10919.

Gill, Kimveer. [Fatality666]. "Messages Posted to VampireFreaks.com" (2006). http://www .schoolshooters.info/PL/Original_Documents_files/Kimveer%20Gill %20Online.pdf.

Lasswell, Harold D. "The Structure & Function of Communications in Society." In *Mass Communications*, ed. W. Schramm. Urbana: University of Illinois Press, 1969.

Lefebvre, Henri. *Everyday Life in the Modern World*. London: Allen Lane, 1971.

McCabe, Kimberly A., and Gregory M. Martin. *School Violence, the Media, & Criminal Justice Responses*. New York: Peter Lang Publishing, 2005.

Tsoudis, Olga. "Does Majoring in Criminal Justice Affect Perceptions of Criminal Justice." *Journal of Criminal Justice Education* 11, no. 2 (2000), 225–36. doi: 10.1080/10511250000084881.

6

Karen Horney

Jessica Vena

The field of psychoanalysis, in its early stages, was a mostly male-dominated school of thought that focused on the human psyche and underlying emotional disturbances.[1] Karen Horney was a progressive woman in an era in which she represented the gender minority. She transformed and expanded this field by challenging many of the prevailing masculine ideologies. Based on her unorthodox approach, she is considered a pioneer in the field of psychoanalysis. Horney's theoretical perspectives focused mostly on neurotic personalities and female psychology; she deviated from the classical Freudian school of thought.

Horney's beliefs on neurotic behavior challenged the thinking that neurotic tendencies were a result of the environment and not an intrinsic manifestation. Some displays of neuroticism could be considered deviant since these behaviors are generally incongruent with what society would consider normal conduct. In addition, the amount of crime committed by women is small compared to men. Horney's concepts of female psychology can be used in understanding crime committed by women, which is a relatively rare occurrence. It is because of her work that deviance can be viewed in gender-neutral terms, as well as the role of neuroticism in analyzing deviant behavior.

Growing up in a house where her brothers received more attention and emotional support,[2] it is little wonder that Karen Horney focused much of her theoretical perspectives on feminine psychology and neurotic behavior. Born in Germany in 1885,[3] Karen Danielson went on to attain her medical degree at the University of Berlin in 1911.[4] While in medical school, Karen married Oscar Horney and had three daughters.[5]

Together, Karen and Oscar raised their daughters in an environment where the father was seen as a strict authoritarian figure, much like how Karen was raised.[6] After practicing medicine for a couple of years, Horney became fascinated with the field of psychoanalysis and studied under the guidance of Karl

Abraham, who happened to be a personal associate and supporter of Sigmund Freud and his theories.[7] This relationship proved valuable for Horney. After researching psychoanalytic theory alongside Abraham, Karen conducted psychiatric work on patients within Berlin hospitals.[8] Her intensive commitment to her work took a toll on her marriage. Karen separated from her husband of 17 years.[9] Her next big decision came when she moved to the United States to hold the title of assistant director of the Institute for Psychoanalysis.[10]

Following her time with the Institute for Psychoanalysis, Karen relocated to New York City to build her own private practice as well as to teach for the New School for Social Research.[11] During her stay, Karen composed two of her major works: *The Neurotic Personality of Our Time* and *New Ways in Psychoanalysis*.[12]

Due to Karen's alternate views regarding psychoanalytic theory and her inability to firmly adhere to the classical Freudian school of thought, she was barred from the New York Psychoanalytical Institute in 1941.[13] Although Karen was invested in the field of psychoanalysis, she believed that a significant amount of personality and personality neuroses were decided by the environment and social contexts rather than the inborn, biological drives of a person.[14] Karen also completely disagreed with Freud's theories on female psychology and instead challenged the idea that female mental issues are a product of the male-dominated world and that Freudian theory originated from the male-centric environment.[15]

Theoretical Perspectives: Neuroticism

Becoming an outcast within her field of study only fueled Karen's desire to prove there is an alternative approach to psychoanalysis. Horney's research on neuroses differed from classical psychoanalytic theory because she believed the environment played a central role in determining which neuroses were present.[16]

In addition, she explained how individuals who suffered from neuroticism had differing reactions to environmental stimuli compared to those who did not suffer from such afflictions.[17] She also believed the root of neurotic behavior arises from an absence of sincere love and care.[18] However, if a child did feel a true sense of love and affection, any negative experiences they were exposed to would not resonate as profoundly because of their resiliency to such events.[19] This included fundamental personality-related problems, such as self-esteem issues. However, if a child were exposed to an environment where parents are unable to express true love and warmth because of their own neurotic tendencies, the child would likely suffer emotionally.[20]

One of the many differences that separated Horney from Freud was her individual stance on jealousy and its influence on neurotic behavior. Horney believed that jealousy of a sibling or even a parent was a significant proponent in neurotic behavior; however, Horney explained how Freud observed jealousy in such a narrow and generalized concept when she stated,

> Freud's observations concerning the Oedipus complex were made on neurotic persons. In them he found that high-pitched jealousy reactions concerning one of the parents were sufficiently destructive in kind to arouse fear and likely to exert lasting disturbing influences on character formation and personal relations. Observing this phenomenon frequently in neurotic persons of our time, he assumed it to be universal. Not only did he assume the Oedipus complex to be the very kernel of neuroses, but also he tried to understand complex phenomena in other cultures on this basis. It is this generalization that is doubtful. [21]

Horney goes on to further explain that the type of children who suffer from extreme jealousy are children who come from parents with their own neurotic personalities and their lack of emotional relations to their child.[22]

The danger of developing neuroses was not found in combating the parent's own neurotic behavior but in the repressing of anger and hostility within the child.[23] Internalizing extreme negative emotions can have two sources: generalized dangers throughout life, and the desire to preserve the love from their parents so it is not lost. [24]

When a child has repressed any feelings of hostility, the result, as Horney believed it, is feelings of extreme anxiety.[25] In addition, even though infantile anxiety is an essential feature, it alone does not account for the development of neuroses in a child; it is the general anxiety of loneliness and isolation that could possibly lead to developing neurotic personality traits.[26]

Karen Horney believed neuroticism was not simply the result of an individual suffering from internal conflicts; it would be unreasonable to assume that an individual did not, at any point, suffer from some private internal issue.[27] Horney further explained that the more frequently individuals confront their inner issues and seek out possible resolutions, the more that person will feel inner freedom and power.[28]

Horney's classification of neuroticism was based on the degree of neuroses present; an individual could be neurotic only to a certain point.[29] She also explained three characteristics of neurotic conflicts: a person suffers incompatibility with the conflict, the conflict remains within the individual unconsciously, and tendencies are compulsive, and in order to alter neurotic behavior, extreme critical thought would be required.[30]

The idea of the unconscious was and still is such an important part of psychoanalytic theory, and it was one of the few topics Freud and Horney agreed upon. Similar to Freud, Horney was committed to the idea that a significant amount of issues within a person lay in the unconscious. In order to identify neuroses, Horney believed in uncovering the conflicts that were intrinsic to him or her. However, uncovering conflicts can be challenging when a person will adamantly deny their presence.[31] Horney explains that in order to uncover the unconscious conflicts, one has to look at the signs when she declares,

> The fact is that every neurotic symptom points to an underlying conflict; that is, every symptom is a more or less direct outgrowth of a conflict. We shall see gradually how they produce states of anxiety, depression, indecision, inertia, detachment and so on. An understanding of the causative relation here helps direct our attention from the manifest disturbances to their source—though the exact nature of the source will not be disclosed.[32]

In an effort to understand personality or personality disorders, Horney clarified that one must look at the motivating forces of the individual's behavior.[33] Additionally, "neurotic trends," as Karen called them, were tools used by individuals to manage mental instabilities that were caused by everyday life.[34]

Neurotic trends contain two main characteristics: indiscrimination when it comes to objectives, such as a neurotic need for affection, and the resulting anxiety that stems from an individual's frustration.[35] These trends are clearly intertwined. The second characteristic defines how anxiety is in direct relation to the compulsive pursuits not being effective; consider a perfectionist who panics when the situation is not perfect or does not live up to their expectations.[36]

One of the main ideas that Karen Horney supported was the idea that personality, including neurotic trends, developed from an individual's temperament as well as from the environment to which they are exposed.[37] Her idea of nature and nurture working in tandem in regard to an individual's personality development varied dramatically from other psychoanalysts during this time period. While most viewed this process as strictly intrinsic, Horney's position on this fundamental concept was that the environment played a more significant role. She believed external factors would either inhibit or expand the growth of an individual. However, if the environment stunted a person's growth, then he or she would not acquire proper self-respect. This would likely result in the person feeling alone and anxious.[38]

Additionally, Horney warns that if there is a lack of solid counteracting factors in a child's life, their personality is in danger of forming neurotic trends.[39] Karen Horney's work on neurotic personalities not only advanced the field of psychoanalysis but also offered a different way of thinking to this seemingly inflexible school of thought.

Theoretical Perspectives: Female Psychology

The idea of feminine psychology was another subject area where Horney deviated from other psychoanalysts and devised her own ideas on the psychology of women and how they develop in the surrounding environment. One of the main concepts Horney expanded on was the masculinity complex in women. She warns that the masculinity complex should not be confused with the masculinization of women, dressing in clothes that resemble those of a man or desiring sexual freedom and expression. In Horney's era, these behaviors were reserved for men and men alone.[40]

Horney believed the reason why it was so easy to determine which traits are clearly feminine and masculine was because of social relations and values of a given environment.[41] However, the masculinity complex was instead a psychological wonder, which dealt with the psychosexual development of a woman.[42] Horney clarified women who suffer from neuroses, such as educated women, and those who are psychologically stable suffered from disorders in direct relation to their sexual functions.[43]

During her time, Horney held that for a woman, the most important consequence of a sexual disorder was frigidity, and how frigid a woman was depended on how much she resisted against her female role.[44] A woman's resistance against her female role or her fear of the female experience was the driving force behind the masculinity complex and is only intensified by an extreme relationship with their father because a woman takes comfort in an illusionary male role.[45]

The reason why Horney was under the assumption females suffered from the masculinity complex was because they were attracted to the male-dominated culture of her time. She states,

The elements that drive a woman away from her female role at a deep instinctual level are paralleled by elements on a conscious level which attract her to the male role. For we live, as Georg Simmel has expressed it, in a masculine culture—that is, government, economic life, the arts and sciences are creations of the male and therefore filled with his spirit. At least until recently, there has been an almost purely masculine influence on value judgments concerning the relative worth of man and woman. The result was that women were measured predominantly according to those traits that make them valuable to men, such as their capacities as wives and lovers, whereas achievements in various fields, worthiness of character, or intellectual abilities have been seen as specifically masculine. Delius declares, "Woman's psychology is the deposit of man's wishes and disappointments." Let me remind you of the Jewish morning prayer, in which the man thanks God that he was born male, while the woman simply thanks God that she was born human.[46]

Due to the strict feminine attitudes toward women, Horney indicated that there were three major effects: a girl will only be seen as a girl, either because of the prestige of the father or the more freedom given to the boys of the family; the idea that boys were given sufficient redirection; and men in general have love lives that are not as severely limiting compared to women.[47] To conclude Horney's idea of the masculinity complex, she added that societal factors strengthen a woman's refusal of their feminine role they are supposed to portray. This ultimately lays a foundation for unconscious masculine fantasies.[48]

How Biographical Data Influenced Karen Horney's Theories

As it has been mentioned before, Karen Horney was a great influence in her field of study, not just for her theories, but also because she offered a different opinion that broadened the scope of psychoanalysis as a whole. However, the greatest difference that most significantly distinguished her from all the others in her field at the time was the simple fact that she was a woman. For topics such as feminine psychology, she offered valuable insight that no man could gain no matter how many books he read or how many women he interviewed. In the time period when Horney grew up, men dominated mostly all aspects of higher education, especially those who held esteemed positions such as doctors and lawyers. Horney's journey in higher education through undergraduate work and on to her doctorate in medicine is both remarkable and outstanding.

What is also noteworthy is that she entered the arena of psychoanalysis with men such as Sigmund Freud, Carl Jung, and Alfred Adler and was able to contend just as well as the men. Receiving a higher education most likely allowed her to gain the respect of her peers but also allowed her to develop her theories based on her experience in medicine and psychoanalysis. Many of Horney's theories were very forward thinking and deviated from the typical theories of psychoanalysis. This was the primary reason for her expulsion from the New York Psychoanalytic Institute. Not only was she advanced in terms of her education, which most women did not have, she was also not adhering to the social norms when it came to her personal life.

A divorced woman in her time was breaking the societal norms and was certainly frowned upon in her era. She did not need a man to define her or provide for her—she did that very well on her own. Being divorced only added more emphasis to her being a contemporary woman, and this can be clearly seen in her theories, especially her theories concerning feminine psychology. She understood that women lived in a male-dominated world, and she interpreted their frustrations with the female role that they are supposed to portray as a reaction to the society that is completely run by the male presence.

Moreover, there is also a dichotomy to her masculinity complex; the name of it alone is frustrating because it adds an acceptance of the male domination within society. At the same time it reflects how even Horney, who was very forward thinking, was bound by the mentality of her time. This only reinforces how much society and culture influence individuals and even research of the era. Yet, despite the strong influence, Horney was not just pioneer of her time but also way ahead of her time. Horney was a woman who pushed boundaries, furthered the field of psychoanalysis, and set the groundwork for future women of the feminism movement.

Conclusion

In order to understand deviance in terms of Horney's theories, a definition needs to be addressed. With all other variables controlled for, deviance is an individual's defiance to adhere to social norms. Social norms are specific to each culture and are guidelines that individuals in a population can follow to function appropriately within a society.

Under this definition, Horney and her theories were inherently deviant. Her work on neuroticism and feminine psychology challenged leading male psychoanalysts in her field and diverged from the typical philosophy, which ultimately led to her expulsion. Even though her theoretical perspectives did not specifically address criminology, she resided outside the boundaries of what was considered normal. Additionally, Horney's mere participation within educated circles was aberrant, given her gender and divorced status. Although her behavior would not be considered deviant by today's standards, it is important to note deviance, in any non-criminal form, is adaptable to the environment given.

Criminal behavior is much more closely linked to the idea of deviance, in that all criminal conduct is by its very nature deviant. While Horney discussed neuroticism in terms of healthy personality development, neuroticism can be connected to criminal behavior. If an individual does not possess the tools for becoming a mentally well-adjusted individual, the result could be not only an individual who suffers from neuroses but one who expresses it in an aggressive and violent way. These expressions can be clearly observed in the pathological woman who does not receive genuine love and affection from her partner.

The neurotic need for affection can potentially create extreme, distorted, and inflated reactions to manifest, coupled with a high degree of difficulty in controlling them. This could produce an extremely unstable character with the slightest provocation or rejection, leaving her partner subject to physical and emotional violence, as seen in domestic abuse situations. A woman with a healthy emotional disposition will not employ tactics that put her at risk at reaching elevated emotional states, while a maladjusted woman fails to recognize healthy coping skills and instead gravitates toward abusive behaviors. Examples of this might be cutting or other forms of self-inflicted harm, when the aggression is directed internally; however, if the aggression is focused externally, a woman might physically and emotionally abuse her children. This forms a connection between Horney's theories on neurotic parenting and several forms of deviant self-expression.

As Horney depicts how conflicts in adolescents, particularly conflicts between father and daughter, contribute to the distrust between men and women, she states,

> The little girl who is badly hurt through some great disappointment by her father, will transform her innate instinctual wish to receive from the man, into a vindictive one of taking from him by force. Thus the foundation is laid for a direct line of development to a later attitude, according to which she will not only deny her maternal instincts, but will have only one drive, i.e., to harm the male, to exploit him, and to suck him dry.[49]

Horney's description identifies several key characteristics of personality disorders such as antisocial and borderline personality disorder. Therefore, when this is applied to a pathological woman, it is a stimulus for all potential manipulation and aggression directed at her partner. Regardless how genuine her partner's feelings and motivations are, the interpretation of the pathological woman is based on her prior negative experiences as a child.

Although personality disorders were not clearly defined in her era, several aspects of Horney's theories addressed neurotic tendencies that can be connected to contemporary personality disorders. The root of neurotic behavior is existent in a significant number of unbalanced and mentally ill individuals who could potentially commit criminal acts.

In summation, the utilization of classical theories enhances insight into understanding motivations for deviant behavior. Although Horney's theories focused mainly on the neuroses of an individual in social frameworks, proper application demonstrates its relevance to other contexts. This provides alternative methods, thus offering more informed and accurate predictions with regard to unlawful behavior in an effort to mitigate criminally deviant conduct within societies.

Notes

1. *Encyclopedia Britannica Online,* s.v. "Sigmund Freud," http://www.britannica .com/EBchecked/topic/272054/Karen-Horney, accessed March 12, 2014.

2. G. Langenderfer, "Karen Horney," http://www.muskingum.edu/~psych/psycweb/ history/horney.htm, accessed March 12, 2014.

3. *Encyclopedia Britannica Online,* s.v. "Karen Horney," http://www.britannica.com/ EBchecked/topic/272054/Karen-Horney, accessed March 12, 2014.

4. Ibid.

5. Langenderfer, "Karen Horney," accessed March 10, 2014.

6. Ibid.

7. *Encyclopedia Britannica Online,* s.v. "Karen Horney," accessed March 12, 2014.

8. Ibid.

9. Ibid.

10. Ibid.

11. Ibid.

12. Ibid.

13. Ibid.

14. Ibid.

15. Ibid.

16. Karen Horney, *The Neurotic Personality of Our Time* (New York: W. W. Norton, 1937), 20.

17. Horney, *Neurotic Personality*, 13.

18. Ibid., 80.

19. Ibid.

20. Ibid.

21. Ibid., 82–83.

22. Ibid., 83.

23. Ibid., 84.

24. Ibid., 86

25. Ibid., 87.

26. Ibid., 88.

27. Karen Horney, *Our Inner Conflicts* (New York: W. W. Norton, 1945), 23.

28. Horney, *Conflicts*, 27.

29. Ibid.

30. Ibid., 28–30.

31. Ibid., 34.

32. Ibid.

33. Karen Horney, *Self-analysis* (New York: W. W. Norton, 1942), 37–38.

34. Horney, *Self-analysis,* 38.

35. Ibid., 39.

36. Ibid., 39–40.

37. Ibid., 40.

38. Ibid., 41.

39. Ibid., 43.

40. Karen Horney, *The Masculinity Complex in Women: The Unknown Karen Horney* (New Haven, CT: Yale University Press, 2000), 28.

41. Ibid.

42. Ibid.

43. Ibid.

44. Ibid.

45. Ibid., 29–30.

46. Ibid., 37.

47. Ibid., 37–38.

48. Ibid., 38.

49. Karen Horney, "Distrust Between the Sexes," in *Feminine Psychology: Papers* (New York: W. W. Norton, 1967), 3.

Bibliography

Encyclopedia Britannica Online, s.v. "Karen Horney." http://www.britannica.com/EBchecked/topic/272054/Karen-Horney (accessed March 12, 2014).

Encyclopedia Britannica Online, s.v. "Sigmund Freud." http://www.britannica.com/EBchecked/topic/219848/Sigmund-Freud (accessed March 12, 2014).

Horney, Karen. "Distrust Between the Sexes." In *Feminine Psychology: Papers*. New York: W. W. Norton, 1967.

Horney, Karen. *The Neurotic Personality of Our Time*. New York: W. W. Norton, 1937.

Horney, Karen. *Self-analysis*. New York: W. W. Norton, 1942.

Horney, Karen. *Our Inner Conflicts: A Constructive Theory of Neurosis*. New York: W. W. Norton, 1945.

Horney, Karen. *The Masculinity Complex in Women: The Unknown Karen Horney*. New Haven, CT: Yale University Press, 2000, 28.

Langenderfer, G. "Karen Horney." Psychology History. http://www.muskingum.edu/~psych/psycweb/history/horney.htm (accessed March 12, 2014).

7

Labeling Theory

Nicholas Zarrillo

The Stanford prison experiment is a widely known study. In this study, which was conducted in the summer of 1971, people were selected to take part in one of two roles: correctional prison officers or prisoners. While this study was more focused on theories such as the Lucifer effect, labeling theory became a prominent component of the experiment. In this experiment, people who had never been prisoners or correctional prison officers conformed to their label simply because other people believed it.

This research experiment and the negative effects showed labeling theory plays a significant role in our contemporary criminal justice system. We see this by people being labeled as sex offenders, sexual predators, career criminals, habitual offenders, and other terms that are widely used in our everyday vocabulary. These labels, legitimate or not, often result in the labeled person conforming to the behavioral parameters associated with that label. As many of the scholars have noted, once that label is placed upon a person the "mirror effect" comes into play. The person starts to see him/herself as that label and finds it easier and easier to adhere to the characteristics of that label. Regardless of the person's desires, labeling theory shows that this person will likely succumb to whatever they were labeled as by society.

Labeling theory has been applied to every aspect of contemporary society. Labels such as job titles, social statuses, and educational titles enable society to "judge a book by its cover." Police officers, doctors, and lawyers are introduced by their career titles, educational achievement initials are placed before or after names, and distinguished titles are given to those in political office.

Scholars embracing the labeling theory of crime warn of the danger of labels. They caution that, rather than diminishing criminal involvement, state intervention—labeling and reacting to offenders as "criminals" and "ex-felons"—can have the unanticipated and ironic consequence of deepening the very behavior it was meant to halt.[1] Labeling theory has always drawn contradictory statements by scholars about whether labeling offenders works or only creates more problems for society. Many scholars believe that labeling a person actually pulls them deeper into the criminal justice system, rather than placing them back out into society avoiding criminal behavior.

Labels are a reality of our existence. Labeling theory has been the start of subcultures, stereotypes, and a characteristic found within the social groups we see in everyday society. Some prominent labels that we see in our everyday lives, ones that have "changed" people include being rich, a police officer, a criminal, a Democrat, a Republican, a liberal, a fighter, a drunk, and countless others. Each of the labels just mentioned is placed upon people, either by themselves or by others, and eventually people will conform to those labels and the characteristics of those labels. Each time a person hears a label of a particular group, they automatically have assumptions about that person and can alter their attitudes and mind-sets to be ready to engage that individual with a particular label.

History of Labeling Theory

Labeling theory has been traced back to as early as 1938, when Frank Tannenbaum started to analyze youths and their identity transformations into adults. Tannenbaum stated that "The first dramatization of 'evil' which separates the child out of his group for specialized treatment plays a greater role in making the criminal than perhaps any other experience. . . . He has been tagged. A new and hitherto nonexistent environment has been precipitated out of him. The process of making the criminal, therefore, is a process of tagging, defining, identifying, segregating, describing, emphasizing, and making conscious and self-conscious; it becomes a way of stimulating, suggesting, emphasizing, and evoking the very traits that are complained of . . . The person becomes the thing he is described as being."[2] Tannenbaum was the first to describe that labeling juveniles, and thus putting them into rehabilitation, can actually be detrimental to their future development, as well as their participation in society.

After Tannenbaum started the driving force to bring labeling theory to the spotlight, Edwin Lemert helped by formalizing many thoughts on the theory. In 1951, Lemert developed two stages of deviance associated with labeling theory. First the "primary deviance" starts when the offender tries to justify their behavior as only being temporary and sees it to actually be socially acceptable. Many offenders do not see themselves as being labeled a deviant, or even an offender. At this point the offender is not conforming to any characteristics of their label. The "secondary deviance" becomes more stressful on the offender, and "the offender becomes stigmatized through name-calling, labeling, or stereotyping."[3] While this tends to evoke reactions and emotions from the offender, they find the easiest way to confront these reactions and emotions is by conforming to their label. They accept the label given to them and organize their life by linking past events to their new identity. Lemert used a mischievous schoolboy to illustrate the process of how the labeling theory can affect a person, specifically a juvenile. A child can become restless and play a practical joke on one of his peers. The teacher will quickly reprimand him, which will be in a semi-public setting. At a later point, the child disrupts class and is again scolded by the teacher. In response to the second infraction, the teacher puts a stigmatizing label such as "trouble-maker" or "bad boy" on the student. The application of this term causes the child to feel resentment toward authority and frustration over the fact that he can no longer assume the role originally expected of him. The child is now tempted to play the role consistent with the deviant label because not only are alternatives blocked but he enjoys the attention he is receiving from his classmates as well as the laughs that are making him stand out.

About 20 years later, labeling theory came into criminology. Howard Becker (1963) started this trend with his famous literature work of "Outsiders: Studies of Sociology Deviance." Becker stated that deviance creates social groups, and thus such groups are labeled as deviant by persons in power. These social groups form a subculture and conform to the label they were given. "Becker recognizes four types of citizens according to the behaviors of those in society and the successful attachment of the deviant label. The members of society that are rule-abiding and free of labels are described as conforming citizens, while those who are labeled without breaking a rule are termed the falsely accused those citizens that exhibit rule breaking behavior and are labeled deviant are referred to as pure deviants, while those that break rules yet avoid labeling are called secret deviants."[4] Becker also stated that there are many types of people who go on crusades to make certain types of events or actions illegal. With this crusade of trying to make something illegal, they therefore make a certain group of people criminals and label them as such. This can be seen with the "war on drugs," which is partially responsible for creating the label of "stoners," the Prohibition era and beyond that created "alcoholics" and "boozers," and even the war on witchcraft back in history that created "witches" and "scapegoats."

Becker coined the term "moral entrepreneur," which was the term for the person who started the crusade to make something illegal, as described above. Becker stated that being labeled as a criminal becomes a person's master status. It takes precedent over any other label such as father, son, wife, teacher, mayor, or doctor. Society is so focused upon the term "criminal" and the moral entrepreneur making that event or action illegal, society fails to see the person for who they really are, not just the label.

With Becker's groundbreaking literature work, many scholars started calling labeling theory a "self-fulfilling prophecy." "The self-fulfilling prophecy is, in the beginning, a false definition of the situation evoking a new behavior which makes the originally false conception come true."[5] When people are labeled, they begin to conform to that label. This will eventually make them become individuals they truly are not, which will then lead them down a different path in life. In regard to the criminal justice system, we see many individuals being labeled after only one offense. Even if an offense was actually committed, a label being placed on that individual makes them a social "outsider." This label will hold back the individual from many activities—even careers and professions. "The meaning of the label 'criminal' in our society leads citizens to make assumptions about offenders that are wrong or only partially accurate. These assumptions are consequential, moreover, because they shape how people react to offenders. Equipped with false definitions or stereotypes of criminals, citizens treat all offenders as though they were of poor character and likely to recidivate."[6] When labeled as such, each individual tends to look back on their past and link their label to past events. They tend to see events that could be associated with their new label and start to believe they truly are, and have always been, that particular label. If an individual does not want to conform to their new label, they try to be included in activities that would eventually help them lose their label or stigmata. This is almost impossible in many circles of society because that label will make it easy for citizens to exclude them. Without losing the label, they feel they are being treated unequally and can slip into other avenues of delinquency, including alcohol, drugs, and other crimes for money due to lack of a steady income.

The 1950s and 1960s were the boom period for the labeling theory and allowed many more studies and research to be conducted due to the works of the founding theorists. After almost 40 years of labeling theory development, one of the most popular and widely known research experiments in criminal justice, sociology, and psychology was conducted by Stanford Professor Phillip G. Zimbardo.

The Stanford Prison Experiment and the Labeling Theory

While the Stanford prison experiment (hereafter referred to as SPE) was not formally conducted to test labeling theory, several key factors of the theory were tested. Twenty-four people were chosen to participate in a paid study that was meant to research the Lucifer effect, human behavior, and prison reform. These 24 people were divided into two very distinct groups: prison guards and prisoners. Each group was given a set of vague rules to which they had to adhere in order to get paid for the study, which was supposed to last two weeks. One morning, the 12 "prisoners" were "arrested," "booked," "sentenced," and placed into a "prison," which was meant to depict the actual process for a true offender. The prisoners had never been arrested in the real world, and the guards had no security, law enforcement, or military training. The prison was made to look as real as possible, and the "guards" were given very little training on how to handle the prisoners. Only certain broad rules and procedures were given for both groups to follow. It should be noted that there were no differences between the volunteers and how they were chosen to be guards or prisoners.

Prisoners were all labeled as prisoners and given identification (ID) numbers, as well as "dresses" or scrubs to identify themselves as prisoners. This was the first step in taking away the identity of the prisoners. The loss of identity allowed them to have a label easily placed upon them. Guards were all given the same uniform to wear—the same mirrored sunglasses and "billy clubs." It took only one full day for both the guards and the prisoners to assume their new identities. The prisoners started to riot, ripping off their sewn-on numbers, refusing to eat, and not adhering to demands of the guards. It took the guards only one full day as well to assume their newly labeled roles, and they took it to the extreme. The guards began to work overtime, and extra shifts were called in to help with the prisoners. Humiliation and borderline torture of the prisoners had begun. Guards used fire extinguishers as weapons, and basic human life privileges such as eating, showering, and bathroom facilities were denied. After only six days, the experiment was called off due to the overwhelming identity crisis that had taken over the guards and the prisoners. Zimbardo stated in his research that one prisoner, prisoner #819,[7] a prisoner who was labeled as a "bad prisoner," had to be taken out of the experiment and given a special immediate session with Zimbardo to convince him he was not a prisoner but a true person. The statements made to prisoner #819 were, "Listen, you are not #819. You are [his name], and my name is Dr. Zimbardo. I am a psychologist, not a prison superintendent, and this is not a real prison. This is just an experiment, and those are students, not prisoners, just like you. Let's go."[8]

While the SPE did not intend to shed light onto the labeling theory, it showed that even a short amount of time with a label placed on an individual can make them conform to the characteristics they are supposed to have and band together to form a social group. This reflected characteristics that are seen in a typical jail or prison setting. The SPE also showed the criminal justice and psychology scholars that a person has the ability to revert back to their old self, a citizen, after the label is lifted from them. Both the prisoners and the guards lived up to their expectations of the label that they were given. The prisoners started calling each other by their numbers, as well as addressing the guards as "Mr. Prison Official," "Sir," and "Mr. Chief Prison Official." One prisoner who was the "hero" of the group made a statement about his identity after the experiment had ended: "I began to feel that I was losing my identity, that the person that I called Clay, the person who put me in this place, the person who volunteered to go into this prison—because it was a prison to me; it still is a prison to me. I don't regard it as an experiment or a simulation because it was a prison run by psychologists instead of run by the state. I began to feel that that identity, the person that I was that had decided to go to prison was distant from me—was remote until finally I wasn't that, I was 416. I was really my number."[9] The loss of identity was a key factor in the study, as it stripped each "prisoner" of who they were and put the label on them. Loss of identity has been associated with drug addicts and those who have experienced traumatic situations such as shootings. Persons will label themselves as a drug addict, or a killer (for deadly force situations) and lose their personal history or identity. "Identity is, for most people, conferred by social recognition of one's uniqueness, and established through one's name, dress, appearance, behavior style and history."[10]

After the experiment had ended, many of the "prisoners" were forced to have weekly sessions with psychologists due to their belief that they had been labeled a prisoner. Many "guards" attributed the experiment with giving them more self-confidence, which does not sound like a bad attribute but it came from the abuse of the power they thought they were given due to their label. Zimbardo himself relives the SPE and documents that he too became embodied by the label of being the prison superintendent. He states that he wanted to make sure he ran his prison to the best of his ability at any costs, and it took the cries for help of one graduate student to help snap him back into reality:

> The powerful jolt of reality snapped me back to my senses. I agreed that we had gone too far, that whatever was to be learned about situational power was already indelibly etched on our videos, data logs, and minds; there was no need to continue. I too had been transformed by my role in that situation to become a person that under any circumstances I detest—an uncaring, authoritarian boss man. In retrospect, I believe that the main reason I did not end the study sooner resulted from the conflict created in me by my dual roles as principal investigator, and thus guardian of the research ethics of the experiment, and as the prison superintendent, eager to maintain the stability of my prison at all costs. I now realize that there should have been someone with authority above mine, someone in charge of oversight of the experiment, who surely would have blown the whistle earlier.[11]

Zimbardo makes an excellent biblical reference to the labeling theory about Lucifer, hence his development of the Lucifer effect. Lucifer was labeled by God as bad and therefore was sent to Hell. Here he was seen as being deviant, was treated as a deviant by all who worshipped God, and thus transformed himself into the label that he was given. As we know, Lucifer never had this label taken off him and thus still holds this label to this day, and depending on your beliefs, still holds the characteristics of a deviant.

The Saints and the Roughnecks

While the Stanford prison experiment was not conducted to directly prove or disprove the labeling theory, The Saints and the Roughnecks research study by William Chambliss (1973) was a participant observation study that included two groups of young adolescent men who had been labeled the Saints and the Roughnecks. Chambliss observed them through their high school years and followed up with the men after the two-year observation, after college, and after their careers had been started. This observation study was conducted based on the labeling theory and principles talked about by Lemert:

> Suppose a student starts to get drunk every day in a particular bar and is eventually banned because of his obnoxious behavior (e.g., swearing at customers). He goes to another bar and is soon banned from that place as well. On top of experiencing this type of social exclusion, the student starts to receive bad grades because his excessive drinking causes him to miss classes and submit assignments after the required deadline. Eventually, he becomes bitter and starts drinking even more, either at bars that allow him entry or at home. To make matters worse, because he spends a substantial amount of money on 'booze,' he is unable to pay his tuition and rent, which causes him to leave school. Lacking a college degree, he can't find a meaningful job and thus resorts to selling drugs to pay for his binges. Following a few arrests, he gradually comes to see himself as a failure, a drunk, and a criminal. He is now a secondary deviant because he self-identifies with the negative labels bestowed upon him.[12]

While this example seems to be set to the most extreme levels of the deviance scale, it is almost what happened with the participants in the Saints and the Roughnecks.

The two groups of participants were those that could be found in any town in America. They were already groups of friends before the observation had started and had grown up together. The first group was labeled the "Saints."

> Eight promising young men—children of good, stable, white upper-middle-class families, active in school affairs, good pre-college students—were some of the most delinquent boys at Hanibal High School. While community residents knew that these boys occasionally sowed a few wild oats, they were totally unaware that sowing wild oats completely occupied the daily routine of these young men. The Saints were constantly occupied with truancy, drinking, wild driving, petty theft, and vandalism. Yet no one was officially arrested for any misdeed during the two years I observed them.[13]

The Saints were continuously involved in delinquent acts, but for the most part they were small. They were known to steal things from construction sites, small pieces of property, and nothing that would be severely detrimental to the person who was losing the property. The Saints drank alcohol on a weekly basis and were almost always involved in some sort of alcohol-related driving, or sober wild driving. Truancy was a constant plan for the boys of the Saints. This was easy for the Saints due to the fact that they had automobiles. With their cars being at the school, they were free to leave school as they pleased and get out of sight quickly of administration. With their vehicles being at their disposal, they would commit most of their delinquent acts far away from the view of their own parents, friends, and police of their town.

The Saints had the ability to show remorse for their delinquent acts and very rarely came into contact with law enforcement. If they did come into contact with law enforcement, they were able to convince the officer that it was a mistake or that they were only being young dumb kids who had good hearts. Only once was a Saint arrested for public intoxication, at which point he paid a $5 fine and was released with no imprint on his permanent record. The Saints also had the ability to get off with their school administrators. Since almost all the boys had "B" averages, and two had "A" averages, they were able to show a different persona if they ever got in trouble at school. They almost always would show remorse and be apologetic for any problems that might have occurred in their presence.

The Roughnecks had a little different situation when it came to their social economic situation—and their delinquent acts. Since the Roughnecks did not have as much money, their clothes were not as nice, they did not have vehicles, and they were always drunk in public because they could not afford to try to drink in bars or taverns. Due to the high visibility of the Roughnecks in their own town, the townspeople had the perception that the boys were always up to no good. The Roughnecks were unable to participate in some of the delinquent acts that the Saints could because of their lower-class status. The Roughnecks' only difference was that they did like to engage in physical altercations, which seemed to gain more attention from the community. While the Saints did commit more frequent acts of deviance, and usually more severe than those acts of the Roughnecks, the Roughnecks' acts were always observed by the community they lived in, as well as by the school and the police.

When it comes to how the Saints and the Roughnecks turned out after the labeling theory observation, the hypothesis was true that labeling youngsters caused them to self-identify with the label they were given:

> Seven of the eight members of the Saints went onto college immediately after high school. Five of the boys graduated from college in four years. The sixth

one finished college after two years in the army, and the seventh spent four years in the air force before returning to college and receiving a B.A. degree. Of these seven college graduates, three went on for advanced degrees. One finished law school and is now in state politics, one finished medical school and is practicing near Hanibal, and one boy is now working for a Ph.D. The other four college graduates entered sub-managerial, managerial, or executive training positions with larger firms.[14]

Of the Roughnecks, two were athletes and did go to college on scholarships but still had some problems that could be referenced back to their Roughneck days. Both continued to fight, had problems in college education, and one even attempted suicide. Both now have graduated college and are married with stable middle-income jobs. Two other Roughnecks were not so lucky and did not even finish high school. Both of these members are serving life in prison, one for second-degree murder and the other for first-degree murder. One other boy became heavily involved in gambling and is now a bookmaker. He is rarely seen around town but is known to have mob connections. The last boy did not go to college, moved out of the area, and was arrested several times after high school.[15]

What we can see from the Saints and the Roughnecks is that the labeling theory can make a permanent effect on a person and allows them to self-identify with that label for the rest of their lives. In comparison, all but one of the Saints is living a very successful life, with prominent careers. Only two of the six Roughnecks are known to be living on stable incomes and have good family lives. The label that was given to each boy stuck with them their whole life, even though each group was equally involved in delinquent acts, and the Saints were probably more delinquent.

Strengths and Weaknesses of the Labeling Theory

When it comes to the labeling theory, there are several strengths and weaknesses, especially in our modern-day society. Labeling can also be seen as other terms, such as stereotyping, which is known to have a negative connotation. Psychology and sociology scholars have all made it clear that people are able to change their pasts, as long as not too severe, with the correct counseling and therapy. By labeling a person, you are giving them another hurdle to overcome. Research has shown that persons who have committed crimes and been given a label are more likely to re-offend. A study of drug offenders who believed they were addicted to various drugs and felt they were labeled as a drug addict had a higher recidivism rate than those who did not believe a label was put on them. This study conducted by William Downs, Joan Robertson, and Larry

Harrison was conducted on only adolescents. The study also showed that the labeling theory affects females in greater numbers than it does males, especially for the age group that was being studied.[16]

> Labeling theory posits that individual deviants who are identified and sanctioned may interpret their "offender" stigma as a master status, thus altering their social identity, and consequently, their behavior. Offenders may also encounter social obstacles that effectively bar them from the benefits of conventional society as a result of serious stigma. Difficulty obtaining meaningful work, earning a high school diploma or post-secondary degree, or building a strong, participatory civic life because of a criminal record severely limits the professional networks open to labeled offenders. Informal sanctions may reinforce the label, weaken the social support of family and friends, and create community expectations of deviant behavior from the individual. Because of this, the offender may withdraw his or her stakes in conformity, reject the institutions that they feel rejected them, and seek out deviant peers who may be seemingly less judgmental and willing to provide a system of social support.[17]

John Braithwaite states in his studies that various cultures have a higher crime rate, which is partially due to how criminals are labeled and how society deals with these criminals. The way a society shames criminals, in this case by placing a label upon them, has a significant impact on the way the criminal and the society interact. If a person is "shamed" by being labeled a criminal, they have a lesser chance of reintegrating into society.[18] Scholar Erich Goode might have been one of the first to speak against the labeling theory, stating that the "theory" is not a theory at all but merely a perspective.[19] In many states there is the ability for an offender to not have a status as an offender or felon placed upon them.

> The state of Florida has a law that allows individuals who have been found guilty of a felony, either by a judge, jury, or plea, to literally avoid the label of convicted felon. Judges have the option of "withholding adjudication" of guilt for convicted felons who are being sentenced to probation. The consequence of this unique labeling event is that offenders who are equivalent in terms of factual guilt can either be labeled a convicted felon or not.[20]

Scholars state that by having laws that withhold adjudication for felons, the individual who is now not labeled a felon will be less like to recidivate. Since they are not labeled a convicted felon, they are still allowed to own firearms, vote, and not have to label themselves as a felon on employment applications (in most states). With civilians being unable to hold back their opinions and stereotypes, this allows persons who do not have the label placed on them to live an ordinary life without the constant degrading thoughts and remarks about that offender. This allows the offender to not slip down into the secondary deviance stage.

Another weakness of the labeling theory is that a label being placed upon a person is most often too generic. For example, a person in Florida who commits the heinous crime of rape is labeled a sexual predator. This is the term used in the state and the person must label themselves as this. This prevents them from living close to certain locations, and they must release this information to law enforcement, homeowners associations, and employers. In retrospect, a young man the age of 18 who has consensual sex with his high school girlfriend who is only 14 or 15 and is caught can be convicted of rape, most likely a lesser offense of the crime, but still have to label himself a sexual predator. This young man will have to adhere to the same guidelines as the offender who had sex with an unwilling person. The justification for the label is not worthy for the young man who got caught up in a legal loophole that was not valid to him less probably less than a couple of months before when he was 17. This young man will most likely fall into the second deviance phase, not as a sexual predator, but as an offender and have to resort to deviant means to survive.

The only positive that has come from the labeling theory is that it allows persons who have been labeled to be identified and thus can help the criminal justice professionals, as well as other professionals, change their tactics in how to deal with that offender. In law enforcement, many different labels are given to offenders, including habitual driving offenders, sexual predators, habitual drug offenders, labeled felons, gang members, violent offenders, susceptible runaways, and more. These labels usually take the law enforcement community and court systems several contacts in order to have that label adhered to them. Law enforcement agencies will usually leave these labels attached to the individual for quite some time due to the ability of the offender to revert back to their old ways in times of stress.

Labeling Theory for Law Enforcement

As a law enforcement officer, this chapter's author has extensively studied what has been known as the "police subculture." The police subculture entails different theories, definitions, and labels regarding law enforcement officers, their actions, and thinking. When a person holds a party to which guests are brought, they are usually introduced by their first and last name. In almost every situation, when a law enforcement officer is introduced, it usually sounds something like, "This is my friend John Smith, he is a cop." With this introduction, the flashback to the previous days, "tour of duty," flashes for that law enforcement officer. He/she begins to wonder why they are being introduced as a "cop," and whether they have negatively encountered the person they are being introduced to. The label of "police officer" makes it almost impossible for the officer to lose his working personality:

> The process by which this "personality" is developed may be summarized; the policeman's role contains two principal variables, danger and authority, which should be interpreted in the light of a "constant" pressure to appear efficient . . . as a result the policeman is generally a "suspicious" person.[21]

The reason that the policeman's working personality cannot be dropped is due to the label that is placed upon them. This label makes them conform to a generalization about law enforcement officers, even if they are unlike the rest of the officers they work with. A law enforcement officer always has a negative connotation due to the generalization and stereotype that has been placed behind the label.

In law enforcement, labels are used for the types of citizens that they come in contact with. These labels help the law enforcement officer look for certain characteristics, which helps keep them safe, as well as the community they serve. Certain labels such as drug user, violent offender, gang member, weapon offender, burglar, and habitual traffic offender help the law enforcement officer when investigations occur. These labels are only attached once a confirmation of the offender's arrest and tendencies are known.

Conclusion

There are many ways in which labeling theory is relevant to the contemporary criminal justice system. Many of these ways are used by law enforcement officers as ways to differentiate citizens, and these labels given to people help law enforcement officers figure out the best ways to deal with them. A gang affiliation label is one that is often used. Personally, as a law enforcement officer I have seen a label of "blood gang member" placed on a juvenile who year after year refused to admit his affiliation. In each encounter with this juvenile, more delinquent behaviors were observed, as well as more "flags," or red-colored pieces of clothing. This is a prime example of how the labeling theory can make a person conform to the label that society has placed upon them.

Some other contemporary program policies that run in correlation with labeling theory are the way states are now running their sexual predator and sexual offender programs. Many states now place the label of "sexual predator" or "sexual offender" on a person once they commit a crime that fits them into that category. That label then sticks with the offender, which places certain limitations on the person, such as where they can live, where they can visit, and even the ways they register their addresses. Many persons feel that placing this kind of label on a person does not fully allow them to rehabilitate—it places the negative stigma on that offender.

Labeling theory has been stated to "create criminals" due to the fact that people will eventually see themselves as that label. Many scholars and theorists have now evolved the labeling theory into many other theories for crime and have used it as a building block. While labeling theory is still very prevalent in today's society, I believe that the negative aspects of the theory have created criminals, and have even ruined lives. This is particularly true in cases of people who truly have been falsely labeled, or have only committed one criminal infraction in their entire life. The labeling theory has had its time in history to shine and has now moved over for more prevalent criminal theories.

Notes

1. Frank Tannebaum, *Crime and the Community* (New York: Columbia University Press, 1938), 19–20.

2. Edwin Lemert, *Social Pathology* (New York: McGraw-Hill, 1951), 76–77.

3. Cecil E. Greek, "Using Active Learning Strategies in Teaching Criminology: A Personal Account," *Journal of Criminal Justice Education* 6, no. 1 (1995).

4. Cecil Greek, "Howard Becker's Labeling Theory" (2005). http://www.criminology.fsu.edu/crimtheory/becker.htm.

5. Robert Merton, *Social Theory and Social Structure* (New York: Free Press, 1968), 477.

6. Robert Lilly, Francis Cullen, and Richard Ball, *Criminological Theory: Context and Consequences* (Washington, DC: Sage Publishing, 2011), 146.

7. Prisoners were given numbers and these numbers were used in place of their names. In many states incarcerated inmates use their prison inmate numbers as a form of identification.

8. Phillip Zimbardo, "Stanford Prison Experiment" (1972). http://www.prisonexp.org.

9. Ibid.

10. Craig Haney, Curtis Banks, and Phillip Zimbardo, "Interpersonal Dynamics in a Simulated Prison," *International Journal of Sociology of Law*, 2 (1973), 96.

11. Phillip Zimbardo, "Revisiting the Stanford Prison Experiment: A Lesson in the Power of Situation," *The Chronicle Review* 53, no. 30 (2007).

12. Walter DeKeseredy, Desmond Ellis, and Shahid Alvi, *Deviance and Crime: Theory, Research and Policy* (New York: Matthew Bender, 2005), 10.

13. William Chambliss, "The Saints and the Roughnecks," in *Down to Earth Sociology*, ed. J. M. Henslin (1973), 24.

14. Ibid., 28.

15. Ibid., 28–30.

16. William Downs, Joan Robertson, and Larry Harrison, "Control Theory, Labeling Theory, and the Delivery of Services for Drug Abuse to Adolescents,"*Adolescence* 32, no. 125 (1997), 1–24.

17. John Braithwaite, *Crime, Shame and Reintegration* (New York: Cambridge University Press, 1989).

18. Ibid.

19. Erich Goode, "On Behalf of Labeling Theory," *Social Problems* 22, no. 5 (1975), 570–83.

20. Ted Chiricos, Kelle Barrick, and William Bales, "The Labeling of Convicted Felons and Its Consequences for Recidivism," *Criminology* 45, no. 3 (2007), 548.

21. Jerome Skolnick, *A Sketch of the Policeman's "Working Personality"* (New York: John Wiley & Sons, 1966), 45.

Bibliography

Becker, Howard. "Outsiders; Studies in the Sociology of Deviance." New York: Free Press, 1963.

Braithwaite, John. *Crime, Shame and Reintegration*. New York: Cambridge University Press, 1989.

Chambliss, William. "The Saints and the Roughnecks." In *Down to Earth Sociology*, ed. J. M. Henslin, 1973.

Chiricos, Ted, Kelle Barrick, and William Bales. "The Labeling of Convicted Felons and Its Consequences for Recidivism." *Criminology*, no. 3 (2007): 547–81.

Davis, Nanette. "Labeling Theory in Deviance Research: A Critique and Reconsideration." *The Sociological Quarterly*, no. 4 (1972): 447–74.

DeKeseredy, Walter, Desmond Ellis, and Shahid Alvi. *Deviance and Crime: Theory, Research and Policy*. New York: Matthew Bender, 2005.

Downs, William, Joan Robertson, and Larry Harrison. "Control Theory, Labeling Theory, and the Delivery of Services for Drug Abuse to Adolescents."*Adolescence*, no. 125 (1997): 1–24.

Goode, Erich. "On Behalf of Labeling Theory." *Social Problems*, no. 5 (1975): 570–83.

Greek, Cecil. "Howard Becker's Labeling Theory." Last modified 2005. http://www .criminology.fsu.edu/crimtheory/becker.htm.

Greek, Cecil E. "Using Active Learning Strategies in Teaching Criminology: A Personal Account." *Journal of Criminal Justice Education* 6, no. 1 (1995).

Haney, Craig, Curtis Banks, and Phillip Zimbardo. "Interpersonal Dynamics in a Simulated Prison." *International Journal of Sociology of Law* (1973): 96.

Lemert, Edwin. *Social Pathology*. New York: McGraw-Hill, 1951.

Lilly, Robert, Francis Cullen, and Richard Ball. *Criminological Theory: Context and Consequences*. Washington, DC: Sage Publishing, 2011.

Merton, Robert. *Social Theory and Social Structure*. New York: Free Press, 1968.

Skolnick, Jerome. *A Sketch of the Policeman's "Working Personality."* New York: John Wiley & Sons, 1966.

Tannebaum, Frank. *Crime and the Community*. New York: Columbia University Press, 1938.

Zimbardo, Phillip. "Lucifer Effect." (July 28, 2007). http://www.abc.net.au/radionational/ programs/allinthemind/when-good-people-turn-bad---philip-zimbardo-in/3249802

Zimbardo, Phillip. "Revisiting the Stanford Prison Experiment: A Lesson in the Power of Situation." *The Chronicle Review*, no. 30 (2007).

Zimbardo, Phillip. "Stanford Prison Experiment." Last modified 2014. http://www .prisonexp.org.

8

Jean Piaget

Shauna Stoeger

While Jean Piaget's theories on childhood development would not likely be the first to come to mind when examining theories of deviant behavior, they are immensely helpful in grasping aspects of different stages of development. The experiences of an individual who is progressing through these stages provides great insight to the health, or lack thereof, of their development. When an individual's experiences and behaviors through these stages are examined, significant early signs may be detected. It may be possible to correlate early behavior patterns observed within these developmental stages with subsequent deviant behavior. Piaget's expertise was not found in exclusively deviant behavior but rather in developmental behavior itself.

Piaget's work in the realm of moral development is particularly revealing as it relates to behavior that deviates from the societal norms. His work connecting cognition and morality sheds light on developmental aspects of an individual's life that may lead to deviant behavior.

Childhood

Jean Piaget was the first-born son of Arthur Piaget and Rebecca Jackson on August 9, 1896, in the town of Neuchatel, Switzerland.[1] Piaget came from a middle-class family and was one of three children. His father was a respected academic historian who believed immensely in valuing systematic work, even when it came to small issues.[2] His father's systematic outlook is thought to have influenced the way Piaget looked at the world and issues in life a great deal. Piaget's mother, while said to have been warm and nurturing, was also said to be quite neurotic and made issues in the family difficult.[3] To escape his strained relationship with his mother, he started working at the age of 10 as an after-hours assistant at the Neutchatel Museum of Natural History, where he was introduced to the scientific process.[4] While working at the museum, he became interested in the adaptation of mollusks, which led him to question greater evolutionary processes. He published his first paper very early in his adolescence on his observations of an albino sparrow, showing his early interest and talent for observation in the scientific realm.

During Piaget's adolescence, he came to accept science as the only way to gain knowledge; however, this led to an emotional, philosophical, and spiritual crisis in his beginning years in university and he had a difficult time reconciling science with religion, as religion was the accepted view of the day.[5] However, he still spent this time publishing on mollusks and social reform and writing a philosophical autobiography, which helped him work through this crisis.[6] At the young age of 22, Piaget obtained his PhD in natural sciences, focused on zoology, but was already bored with studying and writing on mollusks. Therefore, he traveled to France, where he worked for a year in a boy's institute created by Alfred Binet, in which he worked with growing children to standardize Burt's test of intelligence.[7] This is when he first started working in psychometric testing and was first exposed to the way children reason, as he would render them to different tasks and analyze their responses.[8] In 1923, he married Valentine Chatenay, with whom he had three children. Together, he and his wife intensely observed their children, from which Piaget formed the theories for some of his most influential writings.[9]

Cognitive Development Theory

Piaget is known for various theories in childhood development, although he did not think of himself as a psychologist but rather an epistemologist, or one who studies the theory of knowledge.[10] One of Piaget's best-known theories is in developmental psychology: his cognitive theory and model of development in children. In this theory, Piaget outlines four stages of development in children; the sensory-motor stage, the preoperational stage, the concrete operational stage, and the formal operational stage.[11] In the first sensory-motor stage, an infant is developing practical knowledge upon which to base later knowledge.[12] In this stage, infants are learning about the physical world around them. They learn about spatial recognition and learn to construct the world around them. An example Piaget gives is that infants early in this stage do not have a sense of object permanence. If something disappears from their sight, they believe it to be gone. However, throughout this stage, they eventually learn to physically look for it by locating it in the space around where it was. By using past experiences they develop the ability to structure the thought of object permanence.[13]

In the second stage of Piaget's theory, the preoperational stage, a child still cannot form logical thoughts, although they do develop language skill during this time.[14] It is the beginning of operational thoughts, although there is still an absence of solid rationalization. Piaget gives the example that if one pours liquid from a glass into another glass of a different shape, a child in this stage will not be able to comprehend the rational thought that it is the same amount of liquid; they will think one glass has more liquid than the other, when really they are equal.[15]

The concrete operational stage is the stage in which children first start to have the ability to understand the permanence, reversibility, and spatiality of objects.[16] Piaget expresses that this stage is named concrete operations because in this stage children are not yet able to work through hypothetical problems expressed verbally; rather, they are just learning to navigate objects spatially and temporally.[17] This is the stage in which elementary levels of relations and logic begin to develop.[18]

Finally, the fourth stage is the formal operations stage. In this stage a child can finally work through hypothetical issues and does not need just to think in terms of concrete objects.[19] Abstract and more complicated thought patterns develop.[20] By the end of this stage, if everything develops normally, children find themselves in adulthood with all necessary cognitive tools, having passed through the four stages of cognitive development.

Moral Development Theory

Along with the development of children, Piaget also studied the moral development of children, as he believed cognition and morality to be closely related. In his theory of moral development, he believed that the first moral acts of child are external and come from simply obeying one's parents and authority figures.[21] Piaget observed that after this initial stage in childhood comes a stage of respect for the actual rules parents and authority figures give, rather than a simply blind following of parents and authority figures themselves. He also associated this stage with lying, in both the respect that children start to lie because they are not simply blindly following their parents and they realize lying is wrong even if they are not punished for it.[22] Piaget generally classified this as the first stage of moral development that lasts up until the age of seven or eight.[23]

According to this theory, a second period of moral development takes place between ages eight and 11 years, in which children begin to value equality over authoritarianism.[24] In this stage, children are said by Piaget to accept only punishments they see as just; if a punishment is not fair or equal, a child will no longer accept it as the ultimate rule as they would have before.[25] For instance, if a parent does something they tell a child not to do, the child will no longer accept the punishment for doing the same, as they no longer see it as equal treatment to the adult. In the final Piagetian stage of moral development, which occurs around 11 to 12 years old, Piaget theorizes that children no longer value straight equality for all but rather start considering the individual circumstances of each person when deciding how to treat others.[26] In this sense, a child would not look to punish an infant the same way they would an older child or an adult. Therefore, in this stage, if a parent does something they tell a child not to do and the child does it anyway, the child will first think about the fact that the parent is an adult and the circumstances are different for the parent when given a punishment, unlike in the previous stage.

Piaget's Clinical Method

Not only were Piaget's theories groundbreaking for his time but the methods and techniques he used to study his theories were original. Piaget combined naturalistic observation, psychometrics, and psychiatric clinical examination.[27] He learned these techniques throughout his life starting at a young age. He learned naturalistic observation very young, watching his father and working at the museum. Next, he learned about psychometric testing right after he earned his university degree and went to work in Binet's lab. Finally, after he had published his first papers, he decided his methods were not thorough enough and adapted his own form of psychiatric clinical examination from other clinicians. In his first works, Piaget discussed his methodology in detail, as well as his struggles with finding an adequate method to understand the thought process of children.[28] Eventually he came to combine these three methods, intensely observing children, engaging them in tests, which often consisted of games, and his version of examination, which included asking the children to explain something and being prepared to listen and not interrupt.[29]

Childhood Influence on Theoretical Work

Perhaps Piaget's childhood played a more obvious role in his clinical methods than his actual theories, although his childhood influences are present in multiple aspects of his work. In his methodology it is quite obvious that he grew up in a household where his father placed value on systematic work, no matter how small the issue. This is manifested through Piaget's obvious respect for systematic investigation into seemingly unsystematic issues such as cognition and morality. Piaget took something that was previously unscientific and based it more in science, at first by simply making observations, something he learned to do at a young age.

Looking deeper at Piaget's cognitive development theory, it seems that perhaps he started questioning the development of his own childhood, which carried over into questioning the development of all children. With his academic father being his role model, it is no wonder he grew up to be a stellar academic.

However, there is still the question of his mother. His mother was said to be mentally unsound, causing family problems and having an effect on Piaget and his two siblings.[30] This not only had an effect of Piaget's clinical method, as this most likely caused him to escape for hours to the museum, where he developed his first scientific writings and observations, but most likely made Piaget question his mother's effect on his siblings and his own development.

Furthermore, Piaget began studying mollusks already at the age of 10 when he worked at the natural history museum in his hometown. He became deeply interested in the adaptation of mollusks and questions of evolution because of these studies.[31] His interest in adaptation is evident in his theories, as is his interest in evolution. His two most pronounced theories, on cognition and morality, are both outlined in steps as a child ages. He took evolution and scaled it down to the development of a child, to see how they evolved and adapted from infant to adult. This is evident in all of his work and earned him a name as a famous developmental psychologist, even though he did not consider himself as such. However, the basis for this interest can be seen in his childhood interest in mollusks and their adaptation and evolution, as a majority of his theories view humans as an evolutionary process from infant to adult.

When it comes to his theory on morality, Piaget was seeking to find a more biological basis for morality.[32] This most likely comes from his early adolescent struggles trying to reconcile religion and science. In Piaget's case, morality was thought to come from an Immaculate God.[33] As Piaget came to accept early in his life that science was the only way to obtain knowledge, he struggled with this explanation, which is presumably a trigger of his early adolescent crisis. This struggle to understand sparked his studies to find the biological basis of cognition, which he believed to be connected to morality. It is hard to doubt that if he did not have this early internal struggle, he would not have tried to reconcile this issue and these theories may not have come about.

Application of Piaget's Theories on Deviance

Several academics have applied Piaget's theories, especially on morality, to the topic of deviance in contemporary literature. Lonn Lanza-Kaduce and Mary Klug applied the reformed morality theory of Piaget to social learning theory to see if social interactions had an effect on an individual's tendency to cheat. The researchers found that the less developed one's sense of morality, the more likely an outside social factor would influence them to cheat.[34] However, the more developed and autonomous one's moral development, the more likely no outside social factor would influence their desire or will to cheat.[35]

Furthermore, Harvey Milkman and Kenneth Wanberg used Piaget's moral and cognitive theory to explain and discuss criminal conduct and irresponsible behavior in adolescents, such as substance abuse.[36] These researchers discuss the idea that normal cognitive and moral development results in normal moral behavior. However, if at any time there are deficits in cognitive development, a child or adolescent can fail to understand how their behavior impacts others around them, resulting in a lack of morality.[37] Essentially, they used Piaget's cognitive theory to explain a potential reason for a lack of empathy, and thus morality. If one has a cognitive deficit in this particular area, they may not understand how their actions impact others, ultimately ending up in immoral and criminally delinquent acts. Elaine Cassel and Douglas Bernstein also theorize that cognition and morality are linked and that developing faulty schemas, or ideas about one's surroundings, as a young child can cause one to misunderstand the world around them and commit deviant acts.[38]

As is evident, Piaget's seminal works laid the groundwork for future research in various disciplines, including deviance research. His work on cognitive development and morality is seen as strikingly original and demonstrated to the scientific community that these topics could be studied in a systematic manner, which may be just as great a contribution as his actual theories. Showing the scientific and academic community that these topics could have a basis in biology was indubitably a turning point in science and psychology and provided a basis for behavioral studies today. However, without Piaget's childhood escape to the museum, systematic nature learned from his father, curiosity regarding his mother's effects on himself and his siblings, and internal struggles to reconcile science and religion, this research and methodology may never have been manifested.

Notes

1. Leslie Smith, "A Brief Biography of Jean Piaget," *Jean Piaget Society*, last modified March 12, 2014, http://www.piaget.org/aboutPiaget.html.

2. Kerry Duffy, "Jean Piaget: The Man Behind the Lab Coat," *Miami University*, last modified December 13, 1996, http://www.users.muohio.edu/shermalw/honors_2001_fall/honors_papers_2000/duffey.html.

3. Faith Presnell, "Jean Piaget," *Psychological History*, last modified May 1999, http://muskingum.edu/~psych/psycweb/history/piaget.htm.

4. Kerry Duffy, *Miami University.*

5. Ibid.

6. Ibid.

7. Leslie Smith, *Jean Piaget Society.*

8. Faith Presnell, *Psychological History.*

9. Debbie Carter, "Jean Piaget (1896–1980)," *Great Thinkers,* no. 64 (2006).

10. Ibid.

11. Jean Piaget, "Cognitive Development in Children," *Journal of Research in Science Teaching,* no. 2 (1964): 177–78.

12. Ibid., 177.

13. Ibid.

14. Ibid.

15. Ibid.

16. Ibid.

17. Ibid.

18. Ibid., 178.

19. Ibid., 179.

20. Jean Piaget, *The Moral Judgment of the Child* (New York: Free Press Paperbacks, 1997), 193.

21. Ibid., 194.

22. Ibid.

23. Ibid., 314.

24. Ibid., 315.

25. Ibid.

26. Ibid., 316.

27. Susan Mayor, "The Early Evolution of Jean Piaget's Clinical Method," *History of Psychology* 8, no. 4 (2005): 362–72, doi:0.1037/1093-4510.8.4.362.

28. Ibid.

29. Ibid.

30. Ibid., 365.

31. Kerry Duffy, *Miami University.*

32. Susan Mayor, *History of Psychology,* 362–72.

33. Ibid.

34. Lonn Laza-Kaduce and Mary Klug, "Learning to Cheat: The Interaction of Moral-Development and Social Learning Theories," *Deviant Behavior* 7, no. 3 (1986): 256, doi:10.1080/01639625.1986.9967710.

35. Ibid.

36. Harvey B. Milkman and Kenneth B. Wanberg, *Criminal Conduct and Substance Abuse Treatment for Adolescents: Pathways to Self-Discovery and Change* (Thousand Oaks, CA: Sage Publications, 2012), 37–38.

37. Ibid.

38. Elaine Cassel and Douglas A. Bernstein, *Criminal Behavior Second Edition* (Mahwah, NJ: Lawrence Erlbaum Associates, 2007), 88–89.

Bibliography

Carter, Debbie. "Jean Piaget (1896–1980)." *Great Thinkers,* no. 64 (2006).

Cassel, Elaine, and Douglas A. Bernstein. *Criminal Behavior Second Edition.* Mahwah, NJ: Lawrence Erlbaum Associates, 2007.

Duffy, Kerry. "Jean Piaget: The Man Behind the Lab Coat," *Miami University,* last modified December 13, 1996. http://www.users.muohio.edu/shermalw/honors_2001_fall/honors_papers_2000/duffey.html.

Lanza-Kaduce, Lonn, and Mary Klug. "Learning to Cheat: The Interaction of Moral-Development and Social Learning Theories." *Deviant Behavior* 7, no. 3 (1986): 243–59, doi:10.1080/01639625.1986.9967710.

Mayor, Susan. "The Early Evolution of Jean Piaget's Clinical Method." *History of Psychology* 8, no. 4 (2005) : 362 – 372, doi: 0.1037/1093-4510.8.4.362.

Milkman, Harvey B., and Kenneth B. Wanberg. *Criminal Conduct and Substance Abuse Treatment for Adolescents: Pathways to Self-Discovery and Change.* Thousand Oaks, CA: Sage Publications, 2012.

Piaget, Jean. "Cognitive Development in Children." *Journal of Research in Science Teaching,* no. 2 (1964): 176–86.

Piaget, Jean. *The Moral Judgment of the Child.* New York: Free Press Paperbacks, 1997.

Presnell, Faith. "Jean Piaget," *Psychological History,* last modified May 1999. http://muskingum.edu/~psych/psycweb/history/piaget.htm.

Smith, Leslie. "A Brief Biography of Jean Piaget," *Jean Piaget Society,* last modified March 12, 2014. http://www.piaget.org/aboutPiaget.html.

9

B. F. Skinner

Cynthia Penna

The seminal theories of B. F. Skinner theories are behaviorism, operant conditioning, and the schedules of reinforcement. He was not only an American psychologist but he was also an inventor and a behaviorist. He published several books and articles related to his research. He had also won multiple awards for his work in the field of psychology prior to his death in 1990.

Skinner's research has opened the door to look at new ways to explain and answer contemporary research criminal and societal problems. Possible answers lie in the theory of operant conditioning and how some people are conditioned by their environment and the behaviors that they see every day.

Biographical Data

Burrhus Fredric Skinner was born in Susquehanna, Pennsylvania, on March 20, 1904, to his parents, William Skinner who was a lawyer and his mother Grace Skinner. Skinner also had a younger brother named Edward. Susquehanna was a small town with a "population of around two thousand people and because of the town residing on the rising hills that flanked the narrow Susquehanna river valley it was also known as the city of stairs."[1]

At a young age, the behaviors of local animals interested him greatly. Skinner enjoyed catching bees in different flowers, "watching cows being milked, and looked on while bulls or dogs copulated."[2] With one of his good friends he experimented and tried to get pigeons drunk with beer-soaked corn to observe their behavior. A young Skinner was inspired by "learning how to make money in furs, so he purchased and set up traps and never caught anything, but on a few occasions returned home with turtles and various local animals that his mother did not enjoy."[3]

At a very young age Skinner's parents knew he was a very creative and imaginative child. He enjoyed using boxes to build a private fort as a place where he could read in peace and quiet. Unlike the other boys in his neighborhood who built shacks, for the young Skinner "his box building was more sophisticated. He added curtains and had small shelves to hold his books and his writing materials. He also had smaller shelves for candles."[4] This was like a private study for him to go and be alone.

Upon graduation from high school, Skinner went on to attend Hamilton College in Clinton, New York, in 1926. Entering Hamilton College as a freshman was a huge change from the rural life back home in Susquehanna. He went on to discover "that he was not nearly as sophisticated with language as he thought himself to be back in Susquehanna."[5] It was the following year that tragedy struck his family when his younger brother Edward passed away. The initial autopsy determined that he died due to a heart attack caused by acute indigestion that caused inflammation in his heart. Later on, Skinner "would show the autopsy report to a physician, who concluded that Edward died at the age of sixteen from a massive cerebral hemorrhage."[6]

It was in the summer of 1926 that Skinner became interested in different writers who studied the behavioristic philosophy side of science. Skinner began to read about "John B. Watson in the spring of 1928, Watson was the founder of American behaviorism."[7] He graduated from Hamilton College and then attended Harvard University.

It was in late 1928 that Skinner started his graduate education in psychology at Harvard University in Cambridge, Massachusetts. Skinner decided to "focus on the field of psychology and psychology at a moment when historical developments had paved the way for new behavioral science."[8] It was during his time as a graduate student at Harvard that he came up with an idea to develop a modified box to start studying the reflexes of rats. This would be the turning point in his future research on operant conditioning. He ended up graduating from Harvard University in 1930 with a master of arts degree in psychology. He would end up back at Harvard to pursue his PhD in psychology. He graduated with his PhD in psychology in 1931.

While he was a graduate student at Harvard Skinner invented an apparatus that would later be known as the operant conditioning chamber, or the "Skinnerian box." The box consisted of "lights, a loudspeaker, a response lever, the food dispenser, and in some cases an electrified grid. When the subject correctly performs the behavior, the chamber mechanism delivers food or another reward."[9] The operant conditioning chamber was able to help Skinner explore the rate of response to the given stimulus.

It was during Skinner's last year as a "junior fellow that a friend introduced him to Yvonne Blue, and it was after their first date that he was able to convince her to go back to Cambridge with him to meet his family."[10] They had a whirlwind summer romance and fell in love. He believed that because they both had similar backgrounds, it helped with their compatibility. They were married on

November 1, 1936, and had two children. Their first daughter, Julie, was born in 1938 and their second daughter was born in 1944.

His career began when he took an instructorship at the University of Minnesota in 1937. He was then promoted to the position of associate professor in 1939 and worked at the school until 1945. During this time, World War II broke out and, because of Skinner's work with reinforcement and conditioning with rats, the war gave him the opportunity to try something new. He decided to try to apply "operant conditioning to weapons systems to try to improve missile guidance. This gave him a chance to take operant conditioning outside the box and work with a government-funded research program called the Pigeon Project."[11]

Skinner wrote a book published in 1948 titled *Walden Two*. It was written from an interesting and unconventional perspective. The book did not seek to focus on or rely on human reasoning to bring good to a person's life. Skinner notes that an important thing to remember with *Walden Two* is that "to say that human nature cannot be changed means that human nature is something in itself and there is at least the possibility that part of this is something valuable."[12]

During this research Skinner noticed that there were various behaviors that the pigeons could perform if they were "held by hand and reinforced after pecking."[13] Skinner was able to develop a variety of behaviors for the pigeons to attempt. As a consequence of his observation of the behavior of pigeons, he decided to switch his research focus from rats to pigeons and from keys to levers. The Pigeon Project helped strengthen his ideas for the future of operant conditioning and how it would apply to human behaviors. In 1943, the government "rejected Project Pigeon and involved more of a disagreement of the technical reliability over the veracity of the data."[14]

Skinner also went on to publish several books on behavior and on his theory of operant conditioning. In 1938, Skinner published his dissertation *The Behavior of Organisms: An Experimental Analysis*. In 1953, he published *Science and Human Behavior*. In 1957, he published *Verbal Behavior* and also *Schedules of Reinforcement*. In 1969, he published *Contingencies of Reinforcement: A Theoretical Analysis*. In 1971, he published *Beyond Freedom and Dignity*. In 1989, a year before he died, he published *The Origins of Cognitive Thought: Recent Issues in the Analysis of Behavior*.

During his career, Skinner won several awards and medals. In 1942, he received the Howard Crosby Warren Medal from the Society of Experimental Psychologists. In 1958, he received the Distinguished Scientific Contribution Award from the American Psychological Association. In 1968, Skinner received the National Medal of Science from the National Science Foundation. In 1972, Skinner received the Humanist of the Year Award from the American Humanist Society. Then in 1990, after his death, he was awarded the Lifetime Achievement Award from the American Psychology Association.

One of his most notable and most popular books was the aforementioned *Walden Two*, which was a continuation in a way of Thoreau's classic *Walden*. For Skinner, this novel was "an imaginative expression of his hopes for behavioral science as a social invention."[15] Writing this also gave Skinner a chance to examine his very own problems, including how he viewed himself. The book was published in 1948 but sales did not start soaring until the 1960s. It appears the book was ahead of its own time. The biggest controversy surrounding *Walden Two* is that it abandoned the idea of free will and focused more on the idea that human behavior was controlled.

Skinner was a brilliant man with exceptional skill in the area of developing theories to explain human behavior in its simplest form: that we are able to be conditioned to act a certain way based on various types of reinforcements in our environment.

Theoretical Perspectives

Skinner is still recognized as a major contributor to behaviorism, and his view of radical behaviorism became known as Skinnerian behaviorism. The theory maintains significant popularity in the field of psychology today. As Skinner put it, "Skinnerian behaviorism is the belief that all of the behaviors of animals, including humans may be explained in terms of prior stimulation and contingencies of reinforcement. All behavior may be reinterpreted in terms of the animal's reinforcement history and natural selection."[16]

One of Skinner's most widely known theoretical perspectives is operant conditioning. His work on this theoretical perspective started during his graduate studies at Harvard University. The term "operant conditioning" was coined by Skinner, which is why it is sometimes referred to as Skinnerian conditioning. Operant conditioning is "when a response occurs and is reinforced, the probability that it will occur again in the presence of a similar stimuli is increased."[17]

This method of learning occurs through the process of rewards and punishments. Operant conditioning consists of various consequences that impact behavior. Those consequences are reinforcement, punishment, and extinction of the desired behavior or behaviors. There is an experimental "procedure in operant conditioning which is straightforward. We arrange a contingency of reinforcement and expose an organism to it for a given period of time. We then explain the frequent emission of the response by pointing to this history."[18]

There are five categories within operant conditioning. The first category is positive reinforcement, which "happens when a behavior is followed by some form of stimuli that is rewarding, thus increasing the behavior's frequency."[19] The second category is negative reinforcement, which "happens when a behavior is followed by the removal of aversive stimuli, thus increasing that behavior's frequency."[20] The third category is positive punishment, which "happens when a behavior is followed by a stimuli, such as a loud noise, and results in a decrease of that behavior."[21] The fourth category is negative punishment, which "happens when a behavior is followed by the removal of the stimuli, such as taking away a video game from your significant other, after an undesired behavior, thus the behavior will decrease". The fifth category is extinction, which "happens when a behavior that has been reinforced is no longer effective."[22]

Another of Skinner's theoretical perspectives is his schedules of reinforcement. The first type of reinforcement is continuous reinforcement, which is the desired behavior being reinforced every single time that it occurs. This type of learning is best used in the early stages of learning development. A great example of this is when a child is learning to do new things, such as pronouncing a new word. When the child talks and has learned a new word, the parent reacts by giving a hug, a kiss, or giving some form of praise. The second type of reinforcement is partial reinforcement. This is when the desired behavior is reinforced only part of the time. With this type of reinforcement, learned behaviors are acquired more slowly, yet the response is still resistant to extinction. Also within the aspects of the schedules of reinforcement are the four types of partial reinforcement: variable ratio, fixed ratio, fixed interval, and variable interval.

Variable ratio reinforcement is a type or reinforcement where the schedule, or number of incidents of reinforcement, is varied rather than consistent. A good example would be a person playing the lottery.

Fixed ratio reinforcement "occurs when every nth response produces a reinforcing stimulus. This type of schedule produces a high and steady rate of responding with only a brief pause after the delivery of the reinforcing behavior."[23] A good example of this would be someone playing a video game and attempting to collect all the items in order to receive a reward or prize.

Fixed interval reinforcement is "when the first response after a designated amount of time is followed by a reinforcing stimulus. This type of reinforcement causes high amounts of responding near the end of the interval, but much slowed responding after the delivery of the reinforcing behavior."[24] A good example of this would be someone receiving his or her paycheck at the end of the week. The employee is reinforced every seven days or every two weeks with a paycheck for their work.

Variable interval reinforcement "occurs when the intervals between reinforcements vary in a random or nearly random order. The response occurs when the reward is given at unpredictable various times. This type of reinforcement produces a slow, steady rate of response."[25] An example would be playing a casino-style slot machine.

Within the idea of schedules of reinforcement there are also two other basic types of reinforcement. There is "continuous reinforcement in which every response produced is reinforced and then there is extinction which is when there is no response reinforced."[26] Aside from the basic levels of reinforcement, there are also three additional levels of the rate of reinforcement based on the number of responses and the interval time between the responses.

The first main level is alternative, which is when a "reinforcement is programmed by either a ratio or an interval schedule, whichever is satisfied first."[27] The second level is conjunctive, which is when a "reinforcement occurs when both a ratio and an interval schedule have been satisfied."[28] The third level is interlocking, which is when "an organism is reinforced upon completion of a certain number of responses, but the number changes during the interval which follows the previous reinforcement."[29]

A single reinforcement is one that is received after two different conditions has been satisfied in tandem order. For this type, tandem is where "a single reinforcement is programmed by two schedules, the second of which begins when the first has been completed with no corresponding change in stimuli."[30] Another single reinforcement is chained. This is when a conspicuous change to the stimuli happens upon completing the first component of the schedule.

Skinner also identified a type of reinforcement he called adjusting reinforcement. This is when the value of the rate of the interval or the ratio is changed "in a systematic way after reinforcement as a functioning of the immediate preceding performance."[31]

The final component of schedules of reinforcement is called a complex program. This program "may be composed of two or more of these schedules arranged in any given order."[32] The first type is multiple, and this is when the reinforcement is "programmed by two or more of these schedules alternating usually at random."[33] The last one is mixed, which is somewhat similar to multiple with the exception there is no stimuli that is correlated with the schedule. It should be noted that reinforcement schedules can occur in small blocks over a given period of time.

Another key aspect of operant conditioning and reinforcement is aversion, avoidance, and anxiety. Aversive behavior tends to be the type of behavior you casually, but not aggressively, seek to avoid. This is the "kind of stimuli, which is usually unpleasant or annoying."[34] Avoidance is just like it sounds; it is a stimulus that the person or animal just wants to avoid altogether. When it comes to anxiety, it is a stimulus "that is preceded by a strong negative reinforcement that causes a very unwanted result."[35]

Skinner's Theory and Deviance

Early in life, Skinner had a fascination with the behaviors of animals and humans. He also had a fascination with coming up with new, creative ideas. Skinner and his idea of Skinnerian behaviorism led to his doing experiments in his graduate education to see if animal behavior could be controlled. Through the use of rats and the research into Project Pigeon, he discovered that animals could be conditioned to a certain response.

One of the biggest developments that appeared to influence his interests in operant conditioning and reinforcement occurred during his graduate education at Harvard University. During his second year at Harvard, he started to become more invested in his research and decided to start using rats in his experiments. Skinner "became interested in finding a way to measure and record the rats' changing postures."[36] This started his research into animal reflexes.

In 1929 Skinner decided to look into the study of a single rat and to record its reflexes as it entered a modified box. It was during this study that he started his work on operant conditioning and reinforcement. He was able to study the effects of trying to control the "rat's movements in and out of the tunnel by clicking an old telegraph receiver key. The first click sent the rat scurrying and then it would appear again a short time later. Skinner had hoped to plot a curve that would show the process of adaptation."[37] His operant conditioning chamber helped better understand the importance of how various stimuli have an effect on the test subject.

Skinner's operant conditioning and the different reinforcements may be effective in modifying the behavior of criminals. A child who misbehaves in turn is either punished or has a toy taken away. This is reinforcing that said behavior is not acceptable, and if it happens, a desired stimulus is removed or an undesired stimulus occurs.

It was during many trials and flaws that Skinner finally had an amazing discovery in his experiments. Skinner discovered that

> The instantaneous sound of the magazine combined with the immediate appearance of food resulted in reinforcing conditioned behavior. This was neither a learning curve nor a learning process, only the effect of reinforcement on rate of response. If you give an animal food, that isn't instantaneous. When you push the lever down and it goes BANG, that BANG is the thing. It is absolutely instantaneous with the movement, and that is what makes it possible.[38]

It was because of this series of observations that Skinner accidentally discovered immediate reinforcement.[39] Skinner found out that no hypothesis was needed and that the rat would "continue to push the lever at a different rate if fed on different schedules prompted by the scarcity of pellets."[40] It was this basic research and experiments that helped Skinner better understand his theory of reinforcement and operant conditioning. Skinner's experiments and research have clearly advanced the field of behaviorism and understanding and provided evidence of what he termed operant conditioning and the various schedules of reinforcement.

Operant conditioning and the schedules of reinforcement may be used in various forms of research related to criminal behavior in our society. It is because of psychologists like Skinner and many others that we can develop treatment plans and various experiments to come up with a way to deal with criminal behaviors. The theory may also be applied to some of our social problems. We are conditioned from a very young age on how to behave and how to act. We also mirror the environment that we live in and model the behavior of those around us. Skinner's theories are just one of many that we can look at to develop a plan to fix current problems.

B. F. Skinner was able to devise a theory and apply it to human behaviors. What makes us think that we will not be able to apply it to current problems? In some ways we presently use operant conditioning as a means of dealing with criminal behavior. When someone commits a crime, they are arrested and charged, may serve time in jail and possibly pay a fine. This might be a way of using reinforcement to extinguish the undesired behavior with an undesirable stimulus or punishment.

Operant conditioning and reinforcement is clearly present in how we deal with children. A child who misbehaves generally experiences negative reinforcement. For example, a healthy 10-year-old child knows that painting on the wall is wrong. She paints on the wall and the parent sees the behavior. The parent puts the child in time out, which is a negative reinforcement. The child's negative behavior is reinforced with a punishment, thus the little girl realizes that if she paints on the wall, she will get in trouble.

Deviant behavior it its own right does go hand in hand with the different levels of reinforcement. Skinner's theory shows us that these behaviors can be reinforced in different ways and by different people. Deviant criminal behavior can be reinforced by various ideas and systems. Look at gangs. Gangs reward new recruits with money, sex, drugs, and other things as a promise for their commitment to criminal deviant behavior. Without this reinforcement, gangs and drug cartels might even have a hard time functioning.

Skinner's lifetime body of work is remarkable. His theories have evolved from his early curiosity as a small child. That work resulted in multiple written works regarding the subject. It also included the creation of a fictional novel that proved to be ahead of its time. Skinner himself was ahead of his time, and his theories are now at the forefront of behavioral analysis.

Notes

1. Daniel W. Bjork, *B. F. Skinner: A Life* (Washington, DC: American Psychological Association, 1997), 3.

2. Ibid., 20.

3. Ibid.

4. Ibid.

5. Ibid., 33.

6. Ibid., 37.

7. Ibid., 62.

8. Ibid., 78.

9. Ibid., 87.

10. Ibid., 116.

11. Ibid., 122.

12. Ibid., 157.

13. Ibid., 158.

14. Ibid., 123.

15. Ibid., 125.

16. Ibid., 130.

17. Ibid., 149.

18. Ibid., 151.

19. Ibid., 219.

20. James T. Todd and Edward K. Morris, *Modern Perspectives on B. F. Skinner and Contemporary Behaviorism* (Westport, CT: Greenwood Press, 1995), 180.

21. B. F. Skinner, *Contingencies of Reinforcement: A Theoretical Analysis* (Englewood Cliffs, NJ: Prentice Hall, 1969), 133–34.

22. B. F. Skinner, *Science and Human Behavior* (New York: Macmillan, 1953), 68.

23. Mark A. Mattaini and Bruce A. Thyer, *Finding Solutions to Social Problems: Behavioral Strategies for Change* (Washington, DC: American Psychological Association, 1996), 51.

24. Ibid.

25. Ibid.

26. Ibid.

27. Charles B. Ferster and B. F. Skinner, *Schedules of Reinforcement* (Acton, MA: Copley Publishing Group, 1997), 391.

28. Ibid., 39.

29. Ibid., 133.

30. Ibid.

31. Ibid., 326.

32. Ibid., 5.

33. Ibid.

34. Ibid., 6.

35. Ibid., 5.

36. Ibid., 6.

37. Ibid.

38. Ibid., 7.

39. Ibid.

40. Skinner, *Science and Human Behavior*, 171

Bibliography

Bjork, Daniel W. *B. F. Skinner: A Life*. Washington, DC: American Psychological Association, 1997.

Ferster, Charles B., and B. F. Skinner. *Schedules of Reinforcement*. Acton, MA: Copley Publishing Group, 1997.

Mattaini, Mark A., and Bruce A. Thyer. *Finding Solutions to Social Problems: Behavioral Strategies for Change*. Washington, DC: American Psychological Association, 1996.

Skinner, B. F. *Contingencies of Reinforcement: A Theoretical Analysis*. Englewood Cliffs, NJ: Prentice Hall, 1969.

Skinner, B. F. *Science and Human Behavior*. New York: Macmillan, 1953.

Todd, James T., and Edward K. Morris. *Modern Perspectives on B. F. Skinner and Contemporary Behaviorism*. Westport, CT: Greenwood Press, 1995.

10

Abraham Maslow

Sarah Norman

Embedded in the existence of societies are individual elements for successful experiences regarding personal relationships, subjugation, and achievement. Our fortitude of existence relies on choice and the will to achieve ultimate life goals. Social order, societal influence, and culturally significant methods of achievement can define our existence and the contributions we put forth in society. We face adversity through our experiences, and our decisions are based on our potentials from within. However, when one is faced with the behavioral regulations that dictate morality and societal standards, the decisions become a desirable connection of acquiring both self-worth and needs to survive. In attaining these desirable connections, one might sway from the accepted standards of social behaviors. This action may cause them to depart from the conventional status of formality, thus constructing essential elements that breed deviant behaviors.

In such an example, shifting the paradigm of historical ways of thinking, humanistic psychologist Abraham Maslow is considered one who challenged the wayward thinking of society and founded the principles of humanism, known as the "Third Force," resting behind the basic ideologies of Freudianism and behaviorism.[1] Humanism can be seen as an act of rebellion, a contrast in relation to Sigmund Freud and J. B. Watson's psychosocial advances in theory and human understanding.

Deviant behaviors show a disregard of social norms. This research focuses on the main influences of Abraham Maslow and his theory of humanism in regard to perspectives on conformity. It also examines Robert Merton's mode of adaptations through strain theory. The simplicities of deviance are likely related to shortcomings. If one lacks in attaining what one needs, then one finds the way to get what one needs regardless of what societal parameters of acceptable behavior are set. This lack creates a potential personal and societal dilemma. Do we conform if we covet what we lack?

The founder of humanistic psychology is best known for his theoretical principles of the hierarchy of needs and self-actualization. Both give measure to how concepts of human motivation drive the force in conceptual features of behavior. Historical perspectives of theories fall into an array of academic standpoints. Humanism takes the approach of being related to the social aspects of life by integrating motivation as a factor. Maslow states,

> Human life will never be understood unless its highest aspirations are taken into account. Growth, self-actualization, the striving toward health, the quest for identity and autonomy, the yearning for excellence (and other ways of phrasing the striving "upward") must by now be accepted beyond question as a widespread and perhaps universal human tendency.[2]

Philosophers of the past enriched the world with their beliefs and theories on basic concepts, principles, and schools of thought. Philosophers Alfred North Whitehead, Henri Bergson, Thomas Jefferson, Abraham Lincoln, Plato, and Baruch Spinoza acted as inspirations to Maslow's development in the process of human behavior, development, and the main focus of human behavior: motivation.[3] These men deposited the groundwork to the process of philosophy, higher learning, rights of man, and the concepts of self.[4] Maslow found stimulation and motivation in their works, shaping his mold into that of a psychologist. Maslow felt that his contributions to the school of psychology were based on all the knowledge that he learned from all those around him, especially those who had made an impact on the discipline. He never wanted to become a clone of past and present psychologists; he educated himself on what not to do and gained influence on other insights of theory so he could create his own.[5]

The Northern Blackfoot Indian tribe was an example of Maslow's depiction of the differences between his studies in heredity and behaviorism. He found that the reason for hostile environments is not a trait passed down from generation to generation but rather a cultural difference that resides within all societies.[6] Realization within his research and study of Native Americans revolutionized his personal views from what he had originally identified with the human mind. Maslow channeled this change to reclaim the answers through the people. Cultures have their traditions, rituals, and beliefs; mentalities ridicule difference and the Blackfoot Indian tribe opened Maslow's eyes to the psychological well-being of the human mind and his transition from behaviorism to something new.

Maslow's influences prepared him for a dynamic shift in changing his foundation of psychological principles through theoretical interpretations. He would change the forward thinking of the world with the introduction of human behavior in hope of contributing to the extensive amounts of societal issues.[7]

Maslow's hierarchy of needs identifies the importance of biological needs as motivators in a systematic arrangement that designates a sense of priority for accomplishment.[8] Growth in motivation drives insight into the importance of the basic needs one must obtain. The absence of a basic need is what Maslow explains "produces illness."[9] Human nature is a force of the inherent position that drives the basic needs of motivation. Maslow devised a system of characteristics that define if, in fact, a basic need is present: "1. Its absence breeds illness, 2. its presence prevents illness, 3. its restoration cures illness, 4. under certain (very complex) free-choice situations, it is preferred by the deprived person over other satisfactions, 5. it is found to be inactive, at a low ebb, or functionally absent in the healthy person."[10] Basic need characteristics lay the foundation for the elements of Maslow's hierarchy of needs. Basic needs become the fundamental movement in acquiring human motivation and achieving self-actualization. Physiological, safety, love and belonging, esteem, and self-actualization all emanate what Maslow refers to as a "holistic-dynamic theory."[11]

"For the man who is extremely and dangerously hungry, no other interests exist but food. He dreams food, he remembers food, he thinks about food, he emotes only about food, he perceives only food, and he wants only food."[12] The needs for survival outweigh all other needs, for they are the essential elements that individuals must obtain for survival. Physiological needs are the most influential and significant of all the needs in Maslow's hierarchy and fall under the essential components of breathing, drinking, shelter, sex, and sleep.[13] These primitive urges of physiological needs are the foundation of existence and crucial in advancing up the hierarchy.

Security, health, protection, stability, and order—once physiological needs have been met, safety needs such as these can be placed within the forward thinking of advancement.[14] This stage articulates the course of order and stability. Safety needs depend on the importance of engagement within an individual. Security becomes a category that attaches its meaning to those individuals who best dominate its practice.[15] From a child's dependency to an adult's consistent need for security, safety needs are necessary within the components of life.

"We must understand love; we must be able to teach it, to create it, to predict it, or else the world is lost to hostility and to suspicion."[16] Achieving reason into motivation is the basic concept of love and belongingness. Love and belongingness approach as a unit, falling in line after initial needs of physiological and safety needs have been met. This craving brings forth a desire for what Maslow calls "affectionate relationships."[17] Maslow thought that human beings have the drive and want for a connection far beyond the reach of their own happiness: for one to be complete, the need for affection is a true statement of the human prerogative. The direction Maslow found within the elements of love is defined in his book *Motivation and Personality*: ". . . the love needs involve both giving and receiving love."[18]

It takes years to build one's reputation and only seconds to destroy it. Respect of others, respect by others, admiration, confidence, responsibility, and ego define Maslow's esteem needs.[19] Maslow affirms: "The most stable and, therefore, the most healthy self-esteem is based on *deserved* respect from others rather than on external fame or celebrity and unwanted adulation."[20] Thoughtfulness and admiration are values that people find comforting and warming to the soul. These feelings of esteem needs are motivations that drive behaviors.

The theory of motivation is founded on principles of the need for self-actualization. It is here that all the other needs set the foundation for an individual's desires. Individual differentiation expresses that desire into self-actualization.[21] Morality, problem solving, acceptance of facts, self-fulfillment, and personal growth define the development of self-actualization. Maslow emphasizes, "What a man *can* be, he *must* be, He must be true to his own nature."[22] This is the goal of theorist Abraham Maslow's hierarchy of needs, truth within an individual to reach their true potential.

Self-actualization drives motivation to its peak of existence, one that can address itself as a human being adjusted to the realities of the world. Some-one who is at peace, creative, natural, positive, holds appreciation for life and is perceptive to others' needs.[23] The wanting for more, the desired addiction to continue with motivation becomes a continuous plight for improvement and development. Becoming a self-actualized individual brings forth a capti-vated sense of development, psychological development, and accomplishment within a healthy context of reaching one's peak in life experiences.[24] Maslow found that, in essence, "*Being* a human being—in the sense of being born to the human species—must define also in terms of *becoming* a human being."[25]

Basic needs are the basis of thought and motivation and become the drive associated with accomplishments within individuals in a society. What we seek to find is based on the simple ideologies of psychology and human nature. The essence of goals and acceptance motivate and captivate our attention in the pursuit of our true state of being, our true nature.

Why does one fall short of potential? The unpredictable relationships between goals and how those goals are achieved are based on social structures, standards, environments, and/or lack of accountability. With motivation as the defining factor within humanism and the study of human behavior as an anchor, one must produce the answer to the foundation of the social equation. Evaluating pressures of culturally defined goals and the accepted approach of achieving those goals define the inconstancies that individuals obtain through societal structures.[26] Calculating motivation and achievement expresses a direct correlation between Robert Merton's theory of strain in relation to deviance and the founding principles of humanism, thus tying the hierarchy of needs and self-actualization to modes of adaptation. Addressing elements of motivation between individuals keeps social deviance and the conflict of discrepancies within the conceptualized ideas of social order.

Social structures are, in essence, configuring the elements that have a significant role in manipulating and changing social behavior. Humanism is founded on the drive of motivation. True potential regarding Merton and his five modes of adaptation define the acceptance and rejection of social structures within societal measures by addressing complications of how one obtains Maslow's hierarchy of needs and the ultimate goal of self-actualization. Merton's modes of adaptation consist of five elements: conformity, innovation, ritualism, retreatism, and rebellion.[27] To achieve self-actualization, the acts of rejection and acceptance of a society can work off each other to maintain balance within an individual. Merton sought to describe these modes of individual adjustments by expressing: ". . . categories refer to role behavior in specific types of situations, not to personality. They are types of more or less enduring response, not types of personality organization."[28] Merton links these adjustments to the "the production, exchange, distribution, and consumption of goods and services in our competitive society."[29] However, addressing these amendments to the hierarchy of needs procures a figurative example to the motivation or the lack of motivation one has.

Conformity is a fundamental aspect of a civilized society found within the basic development of its structure. A society is maintained by key principles that accept goals and means of a given culture. Accepting defined goals and means is an essential component of Merton's perspective. While a minority of individuals in a society dismiss said goals and means, the majority fall under the title of what Merton describes as conformists.[30]

Innovation proceeds to describe the acceptance of goals, however the rejection of means. Deviant behavior according to Merton binds to innovation by expressing the statistics of criminal activity.[31] Components of a society that lack in needs and available structures of education, employment, and economical means find it hard to successfully achieve these elements, for they are not available to achieve them within their own structures.[32] So, in turn, they accept what society has to offer them, however they reject the ways in which they attain them—in essence, the origin of criminal activity. I will achieve what I need through my own rules and regulations.

Ritualism is going through the motions of life without having the aspirations to achieve more. Merton describes this as individuals "playing it safe."[33] Merton characterizes this as "the theme threaded through these attitudes that is high ambitions invite frustration and danger whereas lower aspirations produce satisfaction and security."[34] Flying under the radar, becoming lost in the shuffle, hiding from critical analysis, and thinking outside the box are easier to endure than the expected implications of strains on society. This becomes the comfortable way to adjust and maintain within society when one cannot advance up the hierarchy.

Retreatism is the rejection of both elements of adaptation. Individuals within a society that reject both ideologies of adaptation stand to reason by Merton that the "escape" method is perceived as the best option. Such behaviors are manifestations of overwhelming resignations from society. Merton addresses, "the conflict is resolved by abandoning *both* precipitating elements, the goals and the means."[35] Disowned from society, these individuals are classified by Merton as drug dealers, prostitutes, and mentally ill individuals who cast off the normality of social integration and reject all principles of community and community-driven goals.

Rebellion incorporates communication and equivalence amid elements of values, attempts, and remuneration.[36] Subjective isolations from societal endeavors of attaining goals and principles drive rebellion into individual adaptations. By rejecting both goals and means of society and replacing them with one's own personal inspiration of belief in how the society should be structured can create the extremist. Merton describes that this method can be confused with the concept of resentment.[37]

Applying adaptations to social structures in essence recognizes the inhibitions and drives of motivation, thus defining humanism. Maslow sought hostile environments through the study of the Blackfoot Indian tribe. Correlation within his study maintained the philosophy that hostility and aggression are not traits but cultural differences. Societies are devised of numerous cultures that maintain their own traditions, rituals, and beliefs. They establish their basic needs with respect to their culture. Self-actualization is sought after lifetimes of change and adaptation; however, when varieties of cultures are blended together, deviance can ensue. Modes of adjustments delineate in reference to the motivation and personality within cultures. Societies incorporate all the typologies of individual adjustments. Deviance is settled within the conformist, the innovator, the ritualistic, the retreater, and the rebellious. Inflation of deviant behavior is seen directly in some cases more than others; however, its stance takes on that of acceptance, rejection, and substitution.

If the absence of a basic need "produces illness," then deviance can be defined in association with Maslow's humanistic approach as the reason for such behaviors that defy social norms. If individuals lack within the needs of dependency, affection, giving and receiving love, respect both gained and received, and understanding that *can* and *being* require *must* and *becoming*, then humanism defines a valid statement, without needs, to build on self-actualization; one becomes lost and when one is lost, their motivational behaviors change.

Do we conform to what we have? We conform to the foundations built by our society based on our initial being. Who we are and what we are can suffocate our true nature when we are expected to conform to certain rules and regulations that do not fit our culturally stimulated existence. We travel through the hierarchy of needs in hope of attaining self-actualization; however, we are bombarded with realities of life. Personalities, motivations or the lack thereof, cultural beliefs, inspirations, learned behavior, and the absence of important entities in our life can direct our path to accept or reject the pressures of societal influence. Deviant behavior will proceed to manifest into societal structures because of the individual adaptations that derive from the basic needs of humanism.

Notes

1. Abraham H. Maslow, *Motivation and Personality* (New York: Harper & Row, 1954), xxvii.

2. Ibid., xii–xiii.

3. Frank G. Goble, *The Third Force* (New York: Grossman Publishers, 1970), 10.

4. Andre D. Irvine, *Alfred North Whitehead, The Stanford Encyclopedia of Philosophy*, ed. Edward N. Zalta (2013), http://plato.stanford.edu/archives/win2013/entries/whitehead. Please see F. Freidel and H. Sidey, "The Presidents of the United States of America," White House Historical Association (2006), WhiteHouse.gov.; R. Kraut, *Plato, The Stanford Encyclopedia of Philosophy*, ed. Edward N. Zalta (2013), http://plato.stanford.edu/archives/fall2013/entries/plato; L. Lawlor and L. V. Moulard, *Henri Bergson, The Stanford Encyclopedia of Philosophy*, ed. Edward N. Zalta (2013), http://plato.stanford.edu/archives/win2013/entries/bergson.

5. Goble, *The Third Force*, 11–12.

6. Ibid., 12–13.

7. Ibid., 18–21.

8. Maslow, *Motivation and Personality*, 38.

9. Abraham H. Maslow, *Toward a Psychology of Being* (New York: Van Nostrand, 1962), 21.

10. Ibid., 22.

11. Maslow, *Motivation and Personality*, 35. Holistic-dynamic theory: integration of theories from other psychologists.

12. Ibid., 37.

13. Ibid., 36–37.

14. Ibid., 39.

15. Ibid., 38.

16. Ibid., 181.

17. Ibid., 43.

18. Ibid., 45.

19. Ibid.

20. Ibid., 46.

21. Ibid.

22. Ibid.

23. Maslow, *Toward a Psychology*, 97.
24. Ibid., 97.
25. Maslow, *Motivation & Personality*, xviii.
26. Robert King Merton, *Social Theory and Social Structure* (Glencoe, IL: Free Press, 1957), 132–41.
27. Ibid., 140.
28. Ibid.
29. Ibid., 140–41.
30. Ibid., 141.
31. Ibid., 141–49.
32. Ibid., 144–45.
33. Ibid., 150.
34. Ibid.
35. Ibid., 153–54.
36. Ibid., 155.
37. Ibid., 156.

Bibliography

Goble, Frank G. *The Third Force: The Psychology of Abraham Maslow*. New York: Grossman Publishers, 1970.
Irvine, Andrew. D. *Alfred North Whitehead*, *The Stanford Encyclopedia of Philosophy*, ed. Edward N. Zalta (2013). http://plato.stanford.edu/archives/win2013/entries/whitehead.
Maslow, Abraham H. *Motivation and Personality*. New York: Harper & Row, 1954.
Maslow, Abraham H. *Toward a Psychology of Being*. New York: Van Nostrand, 1962.
Merton, Robert King. *Social Theory and Social Structure*. Glencoe, IL: Free Press, 1957.

11

Albert Ellis

Ashley Veasy

Albert Ellis, the oldest of three children, was born on September 27, 1913, in Pittsburgh, Pennsylvania, to Hettie and Henry Ellis. In the hope of finding better business, Henry Ellis moved his family to New York City in 1917, when Albert was four years old.[1] During his childhood, Ellis faced several challenges that greatly impacted his ability to make the best of disadvantageous situations as well as the development of his innate problem-solving skills—two characteristics that define the man and psychologist he became.

When discussing his childhood, Ellis described himself as a "semiorphan"[2] because both of his parents were neglectful in his and his siblings' upbringing. Ellis's father was a traveling salesman, which required Henry Ellis to be away from home for prolonged periods of time. When Henry was home from business, he was more concerned about his next business endeavor and his personal nighttime interests and he spent no more than a few minutes in passing with his children each day.[3] Henry and Hettie divorced when Albert was 12, ensuring even far less time was spent with his father as a child, despite Henry's living only a few miles away from Hettie's house in the Bronx.[4] Ellis's mother, Hettie, was described as so self-absorbed that she immersed herself in her own desires rather than in her family. Her day typically consisted of busying herself with temple functions and playing bridge or mah-jongg with her friends, with minimal attention to cleaning, cooking, child-rearing, and shopping.[5] Hettie was very uninterested in tending to her children, often leaving her children unattended at night while she spent time with her friends.[6]

Since his mother was too busy to raise her children and his father was not present, Ellis took the responsibility of making sure his brother and sister were woken up, dressed, and fed before walking to school by themselves through a dangerous area of the Bronx.[7] Ellis saved up his own money and purchased an alarm clock so he could be sure that he and his siblings would be ready in time for school, often waking before his mother.[8] When the Great Depression hit the United States in late 1929, Ellis's family was no exception to the financial woes through which most Americans were suffering. Henry Ellis was still living fairly lavishly, considering the Depression, yet refused to pay Hettie Ellis the thousands of dollars he owed in alimony, which almost forced Hettie and her children to live on welfare.[9] Despite neglectful parents, Ellis used this challenge as an opportunity to develop autonomy and self-reliance rather than dwell on the negatives.

During his early childhood, Ellis suffered from a number of health-related issues that placed him in the hospital for long periods of time. At the age of five, Ellis almost died from a case of tonsillitis that progressed into a serious strep infection and led to life-saving emergency surgery.[10] This surgery ended up leading to acute nephritis, an inflammation in the kidney preventing the filtering of blood to make urine.[11] Between the ages of five and seven, Ellis was hospitalized another eight or more times for a variety of reasons, but mostly due to the acute nephritis, with some of these hospitalizations lasting almost an entire year.[12]

These hospitalizations prohibited Ellis from taking part in typical childhood activities such as sports, preventing him from fully experiencing the prime years of social development, which can be said to have taken a toll on his social behavior. "I was unusually shy and introverted, and particularly shy and afraid of any kind of public presentation during my childhood and adolescence."[13] Ellis often avoided any anxiety-provoking situations, including speaking in front of a group of people and even avoiding social and sexual advances with girls he would develop feelings for in fear of rejection.[14] Instead of measuring his self-worth by social interactions, Ellis maintained high self-esteem by measuring his self-worth based on his achievements in his intelligence and success in school.[15] While he never fully overcame is shyness, Ellis was "able to structure his world so that it didn't cause him too much trouble."[16] To overcome his shyness toward women, Ellis applied in vivo desensitization techniques, approaching women over and over again, even if his advances were rejected, to challenge and overcome his anxiety-provoking belief that rejection leads to low self-worth.[17] These three challenges that Ellis overcame are the events that allowed him to enhance his problem-solving abilities that later helped develop his rational emotive behavioral therapy.

Despite these obstacles, Ellis was very successful in his later academic endeavors, getting a bachelor of business administration degree at the Baruch School of Business and Civic Administration of City College. During his time at Baruch, he started off as an accounting major but, finding that too easy, instead majored in English.[18] Becoming a psychologist crossed the mind of Ellis early on in college and, as a result, he developed a relationship with Alexander Mintz, the head of the psychology department and professor of applied psychology. However, because of his love of writing, Ellis decided to instead write psychological novels rather than pursue a career in psychology. Ellis realized becoming an author was not meant to be when he wrote more than 20 manuscripts to no avail, and instead focused on nonfiction writing.[19] Many of his later nonfiction writings were focused on sex, love, and marriage, leading him to counsel many friends on personal sexuo-amative, or love and sex, problems. Ellis realized his love of counseling and decided to revisit his notion of becoming a psychologist, with his focus on clinical work in the field of sex, love, and marriage.[20]

After several obstacles getting into Columbia University, Ellis joined the clinical psychology department at Teachers College at Columbia in September 1942.[21] After receiving his master's degree with honors, Ellis pursued his PhD at Columbia University.[22] Like the time he was earning his MA, Ellis again focused on love, sex, and marriage for his PhD thesis; however, due to the methodology of personally asking women about intimate details of their love life, several professors within the department voted against his thesis on love.[23] Instead of publishing this research within the university, Ellis branched out to various psychological and sociological journals. To prevent further censorship of his dissertation, Ellis chose a safe topic on personality questionnaires and finally earned his PhD from Columbia University in 1947.[24]

Much of his postgraduate work focused on both sex and personality testing, but Ellis also focused very heavily on revising the original psychoanalysis framework developed by some of psychology's greats such as Sigmund Freud, Alfred Adler, and Karen Horney. By 1953, Ellis began identifying himself as a psychotherapist rather than a psychoanalyst after rebelling so much against psychoanalysis.[25] As a psychotherapist, Ellis took from his personal experiences as well as a variety of currently established psychotherapeutic techniques, rejecting the most prominent form of psychology at the time—Freudian psychoanalysis—which explores how the unconscious influences thoughts and actions.[26] This new direction taken by Ellis led him to rational emotive therapy at the beginning of 1955.[27]

Rational emotive therapy (RET), later known as rational emotive behavior therapy (REBT), focuses on how rationality can lead to an enjoyable and happy life and was developed as a way to help people who suffer from emotional misery and interpersonal problems seek a more positive and happy life.[28] The most basic assumption of REBT is that feelings and behaviors result from rational and irrational beliefs about a particular event. Naturally, all humans have innate desires or preferences they wish to happen, but when humans decide that these desires *must* happen, an irrational belief is created that will lead to feelings and behaviors associated with this irrational belief.[29] For example, if a student says that they *must* always succeed academically, the alternative to not always achieving success is failure. If that student fails, they believe themselves to be idiots, incapable of ever succeeding again, which develops a sense of great anxiety subsequently leading to dissatisfaction and unhappiness with their life.

To best explain how people create their own disturbances, and subsequently un-create these disturbances, Ellis outlined his clinical theory through an A-B-C framework. A is the activating experience or event, such as failing an exam.[30] C, Ellis and R. Grieger (1977) explain, is the emotional and/or behavioral consequence from the activating event or experience.[31] Continuing with the example of failing an exam, the student may feel depressed about the grade and may avoid studying for the next exam. However, the common misconception is that the activating event or experience *causes* the emotional and/or behavioral consequences when in fact there's an entire factor missing—a person's original belief about the activating event or experience, or the B of the A-B-C framework.[32] The student may have believed that they must pass this exam and will feel absolutely awful if they do not do so, therefore when they do in fact fail the exam, the resulting consequences are despair and depression. REBT holds that it is

not the activating event that makes a person have emotional and/or behavioral consequences but, rather, it is the person who causes these feelings because of holding onto strong beliefs. "The things that occur do not upset you—but your *view* of those things does."[33]

The final two components of REBT outlined by Ellis and Greiger (1977) expand upon and seek to solve the disturbances developed in the A-B-C framework: they are D, or disputing irrational beliefs; and E, a new effect and emotive. One must identify the irrational beliefs that create negative emotions in order to get to components D and E—both of which are part of the actual therapy. Disputing irrational beliefs involves methods that attempt to "demonstrate to people the irrationality of their thinking" and help them develop a more sound, logical, and overall realistic view of the world.[34] Once a person rejects the irrational beliefs they have developed, they are able to develop new, rational beliefs that provide a happy emotion whereby they can enjoy life.[35]

If it is irrational beliefs that lead to irrational emotions and/or behaviors, how does someone identify these beliefs? Irrational beliefs are some sort of unrealistic statements made about the world, typically in a commanding or demanding fashion such as "this *must* or *should* happen" or that it is a *necessity* that you get what you desire.[36] They also generally result in inappropriate and disturbed emotions and do not help attain goals.[37] By asking yourself what standards you hold yourself to and what should or should not happen in your life, it is fairly easy to detect irrational beliefs; however, if you are not as conscious or aware, it is easier to look at the inappropriate behavioral and emotional consequences as well as the activating experience or event and analyze your thought process of why you feel a certain way.

Ellis described three general irrational beliefs that can most likely explain most irrational thinking. The first is "I must do well and win approval or else

I am an inadequate, rotten person."[38] This irrational belief is created because people set such high standards and expectations, and if they do not live up to them, they are a failure at life. The second is "others must treat me considerately and kindly in precisely the way I want them to treat me; if they don't, society and the universe should severely blame, damn, and punish them for their inconsiderateness."[39] Egocentricity is a part of being human, but sometimes this "center of the universe" belief leads people to feel despair, anger, etc., when others are not catering to their every need and desire. The third and final general irrational belief is that "conditions under which I live must be arranged so that I get practically everything I want comfortably, quickly, and easily and get virtually nothing that I don't want."[40] Again, egocentricity is human nature. We live in a society where the belief that everything comes easily is prominent and everything should be handed to us. When this does not happen, negative emotions emerge, leading to irrational beliefs.

It is the primary responsibility of an individual, not outside factors such as other people and conditions, to create and subsequently un-create problems. Based on this premise, there are three main insights of REBT. The first is that "you choose to disturb yourself about unpleasant events" because "you mainly feel the way you think,"[41] meaning that it is up to the client as a free-acting agent to reject the irrational beliefs and replace them with rational ones. The second is that no matter how or why the original irrational beliefs were established, you choose to maintain them, which is why you are now troubled.[42] This insight means that it is not external factors that are causing distress and neurotic believes but the individual. Therefore, the client can choose to view their problems as something they can change. The final is that there is no magical cure for irrational beliefs and no remedy that will quickly relieve your troubles—it will take time, patience, and a lot of work.[43]

Ellis' original rational emotive therapy was the first of the major cognitive behavioral therapies, and by the end of the 1960s, REBT was the leading form of cognitive behavioral therapy (CBT).[44] Many newer schools of CBT continue to use Ellis's A-B-Cs of REBT as the basis of their theories.[45] Up until his death in 2007, Ellis continued to modify and improve his theory of REBT, pushing the limits of CBT as far as he could, making great advancements in the field.[46] In his autobiography, he acknowledged himself as the father of REBT and also noted he is the grandfather of CBT.[47]

The primary goal of cognitive behavioral therapy, based on the theory of RET, is to get the client to give up their irrational beliefs and behaviors and to then maximize their rational thinking and believing to allow the client to live a happy life by eliminating anxiety, guilt, depression, and anger.[48] A therapist practicing REBT must be active-directive, meaning the therapist disputes the client's irrational beliefs through a forceful manner, modeling the disputing process so as to allow the client to reproduce the process on their own.[49] Clients are also given homework assignments to encourage clients to work independently, outside therapy, in order to prevent a reliant relationship between the therapist and client. These homework assignments vary case by case but can range from something like dating a girl whom the client was too afraid to ask out or to go looking for a new job.[50] The first few sessions require the therapist to be very active and verbal, rather than passively listening to the client. These verbal interactions are trying to persuade the client out of their strongly held irrational beliefs. These sessions are to serve as educational tools—to educate the client about the irrational beliefs they have and how to eradicate them.[51]

The therapy derived from REBT is very cognitive based, meaning that a great deal of time is spent eradicating irrational beliefs that lead to negative emotions; however, Ellis recognized that "cognitive change is very often facilitated by behavioral change"[52] and therefore uses several behavioral methods to support his cognitive focus.[53] His behavioral methods consisted of shame-attacking, risk-taking, "stay in there" activities, and antiprocrastination exercises, but the most common, and usually the most effective of these methods, was risk-taking. Risk-taking exercises get clients to push themselves to take calculated risks in areas of their lives they are interested in changing.[54] An example from Ellis's life that he most often cited to his clients was when he forced himself to approach and talk to women, despite his fear of rejection. The goal of this method is to show clients that the outcomes of their actions are not all negative and that, in fact, some good can come from it.[55]

Cognitive behavior therapy (CBT) is the most widely accepted therapy used in correctional facilities and has shown great strides in reducing recidivism in a majority of major crimes. In a structured cognitive behavioral model, it is believed that the offender is in full control of their thoughts and behaviors and that the offender is a rational actor with the potential to change these thoughts and behaviors.[56] According to a study done on sex offenders and their responses to cognitive behavioral therapy, the reason someone offends in the first place is due to a cognitive distortion, or maladaptive/irrational thoughts and beliefs that cause distress. These behaviors are acted out due to these irrational beliefs.[57] The main goal of these therapeutic treatments, in the case of sex offenders, is not exactly rehabilitation, as there is a long-standing belief that sex offenders can never be rehabilitated, but rather reducing their risk to society. By teaching an offender how to control his emotions and behaviors by transforming cognitive distortions, like Ellis suggested in his REBT, future offending can be reduced.[58] Similar beliefs are held for other categories of criminals, hence why Ellis's work is seen as so important today.

There is no denying that Albert Ellis was one of the most influential psychologists in the development and advancement of not only his theories on rational emotive behavior therapy but the field of cognitive behavioral therapy as a whole. *Psychology Today* described Ellis as the "greatest living psychologist" prior to his death in 2007, and in a survey issued in 1982 to approximately 800 American clinical and counseling psychologists, Ellis was seen as more influential and detrimental to the field of psychology than Sigmund Freud, who is considered one of the best-known psychologists to any layman.[59] The practical applications of Ellis's REBT are overwhelming and his therapy has helped thousands of people with many difficulties ranging from addictions to anger management to depression. Cognitive behavioral therapy is the most widely accepted treatment for adults and juveniles in the prison system today.

What influenced Ellis to come up with one of the most influential psychological theories of all time? "I do not believe that the events of my childhood greatly influenced my becoming a psychotherapist, nor oriented me to becoming the kind of individual and the type of therapist that I now am."[60] Ellis may have claimed that his childhood experiences had absolutely nothing to do with the development of REBT, but it is hard not to see many connections to the way in which he dealt with the challenges he faced in life to his theory of REBT. Ellis does accredit his childhood for his development of incredible problem-solving skills because, despite all of the troubles he grew up with—neglectful parents, many childhood illnesses that prevented him from having a normal childhood, and his unusual shyness towards others—he was still able to come up with solutions for how to deal with them and make the best out of his childhood.[61]

Since Ellis spent a majority of his childhood in and out of the hospital and was unable to play sports like most of the children his age, he took an interest in academia. He began reading ancient philosophers and early psychologists at a young age, heavily influencing his critique and rejection of psychoanalysis in the 1950s, which later led to his development of psychotherapy and the development of REBT. Ellis based his theory not only within psychology but he also had influences from the ancient philosophers that he grew up reading as a young adult.[62] Clearly, Ellis thought like a cognitive behavioral therapist early in his life, as he treated himself for his fear of making advancements toward women. Instead of continuing to have irrational beliefs that every woman will reject him, he took a risk and went to talk to 100 or more women in the Botanical Gardens in order to desensitize himself of that fear and the anxiety he would get from talking to women.[63] While he was not fully cured of his shyness, he was already making great strides toward cognitive behavioral therapy before he had even pursued the field of psychology. Ellis used his own personal life example to explain to his clients what it meant to take a risk and how it benefited them to do so within the realms of his therapy.

While assumptions can be made about whether Ellis would have ever taken such a profound interest in the advancement of academia that led him to pursue psychology had he not experienced his kind of upbringing, it is evident that his childhood experiences and the way in which he learned to deal with adversity heavily influenced the development of his theory. Acceptance of life's realities is one of the most defining characteristics of Ellis's REBT, and the first major step toward his development of the rational living theory was the acceptance of his own personal struggles and overcoming them in a rational manner. Ellis was developing his theory all his life, right up to the day he died, and it is no wonder he is by far the most influential psychologist of all time.

Notes

1. Joseph Yankura and Windy Dryden, *Key Figures in Counseling and Psychotherapy: Albert Ellis* (London: Sage Publications, 1994), 1.

2. Albert Ellis, "My Life in Clinical Psychology," ed. C. E. Walker (Pacific Grove: Brooks/Cole, 1991), 2.

3. Yankura and Dryden, *Albert Ellis*, 2.

4. Ellis, "My Life," 2.

5. Ibid.

6. Yankura and Dryden, *Albert Ellis*, 2.

7. Michael Bernard, *Rationality and the Pursuit of Happiness: The Legacy of Albert Ellis* (Sussex, UK: Wiley-Blackwell, 2011), 4.

8. Yankura and Dryden, *Albert Ellis*, 4.

9. Ellis, "My Life," 3.

10. Yankura and Dryden, *Albert Ellis*, 3.

11. Charles Silberberg, Medline Plus, "Acute Nephritic Syndrome," Last modified September 8, 2013, http://www.nlm.nih.gov/medlineplus/ency/article/000495.htm (accessed December 1, 2013).

12. Yankura and Dryden, *Albert Ellis*, 3.

13. Ellis, "My Life," 2.

14. Yankura and Dryden, *Albert Ellis*, 3.

15. Ibid., 5.

16. Ellis, "My Life," 4.

17. Yankura and Dryden, *Albert Ellis*, 6.

18. Ellis, "My Life," 5.

19. Ibid., 6.

20. Ibid., 7.

21. Ibid., 8.

22. Ibid., 9.

23. Ibid., 10.

24. Ibid., 11.

25. Ibid., 15.

26. American Psychoanalytic Association, "About Psychoanalysis," Last modified 2014, www.apsa.org/about_psychoanlysis (accessed March 1, 2014).

27. Ellis, "My Life," 19.

28. Bernard, *Rationality*, 43.

29. Ibid., 25.

30. Albert Ellis and R. Grieger, *Handbook of Rational-Emotive Therapy* (New York: Springer, 1977), 6.

31. Ellis and Grieger, *Handbook*, 6.

32. Ibid.

33. Ibid., 8.

34. Bernard, *Rationality*, 52.

35. Ellis and Grieger, *Handbook*, 31.

36. Ibid., 9.

37. Bernard, *Rationality*, 25.

38. Ibid., 28.

39. Ibid.

40. Ibid., 29.

41. Yankura and Dryden, *Albert Ellis*, 48.

42. Ibid.

43. Ibid.

44. Ellis, "My Life," 21.

45. Ibid., 22.

46. Yankura and Dryden, *Albert Ellis*, 57.

47. Ellis, "My Life," 15.

48. Ellis and Grieger, *Handbook*, 189

49. Yankura and Dryden, *Albert Ellis*, 63.

50. Ellis and Grieger, *Handbook*, 194.

51. Ibid., 195.

52. Yankura and Dryden, *Albert Ellis*, 87.

53. Ibid., 89.

54. Ibid., 88.

55. Ibid., 90.

56. C. Friestad, "Making Sense, Making Good, or Making Meaning? Cognitive Distortions as Targets of Change in Offender Treatment," *International Journal of Offender Therapy and Comparative Criminology* 56, no. 3 (2012): 465–82, doi:10.1177/0306624X11402945 (accessed March 27, 2014).

57. Friestad, "Making Sense," 468.

58. Ibid., 473.

59. Albert Ellis Institute, "Homepage," Last modified 2013. http://albertellis.org (accessed December 1, 2013).

60. Ellis, "My Life," 1.

61. Ibid., 3.

62. Ibid., 30.

63. Yankura and Dryden, *Albert Ellis*, 88.

Bibliography

Albert Ellis Institute. Albert Ellis Institute Homepage (2013). http://albertellis.org (accessed November 2013).

American Psychoanalytic Association. "About Psychoanalysis." www.apsa.org/about_psychoanalysis.aspx#top (accessed March 20, 1014).

Bernard, Michael E. *Rationality and the Pursuit of Happiness: The Legacy of Albert Ellis.* Sussex, UK: Wiley-Blackwell, 2011.

Ellis, A. "My Life in Clinical Psychology." In *The History of Clinical Psychology in Autobiography*, vol. 1, by C. E. Walker. Pacific Grove, CA: Brooks/Cole, 1991, 1–37.

Ellis, A., and R. Grieger. *Handbook of Rational-Emotive Therapy.* New York: Springer, 1977.

Friestad, C. "Making Sense, Making Good, or Making Meaning? Cognitive Distortions as Targets of Change in Offender Treatment." *International Journal of Offender Therapy and Comparative Criminology* 56, no. 3 (2012): 465–82.

Silberberg, Charles. Medline Plus (September 8, 2013). http://www.nlm.nih.gov/medlineplus/ency/article/000495.htm (accessed December 2013).

Yankura, Joseph, and Windy Dryden. *Albert Ellis.* London: Sage Publications, 1994.

12

Clifford Shaw and Henry McKay

Christina Molinari

Deviant behavior demonstrated by children is, to some extent, expected. However, if this behavior manifests as criminal conduct, social tolerance is withdrawn. When viewed as a continuum, crime is the most extreme form of deviancy. Therefore, a large quantity of data has been compiled on juvenile delinquency in an effort to better understand why certain youths go to such deviant extremes. Some of the most influential research in this area comes from the work of Clifford Shaw and Henry McKay. Their research focused on exploring the social and environmental characteristics associated with the delinquency rates of Chicago-area juveniles. Although almost a century old, many of their concepts still apply to the fields of criminology and sociology today.

Clifford R. Shaw

As a passionate scholar, Clifford R. Shaw took on the administrative aspects of the research and was outgoing, persuasive, and charismatic.[1] He sympathized and built relationships with many juvenile delinquents he encountered through the course of his research, becoming long-term friends with several of them.[2] Shaw's personality was so dynamic and compelling, "[f]riends often jested that it was a pity he became a sociologist, for the world thereby lost one of its ablest con-men."[3]

Shaw grew up in an area that starkly contrasted with the urban and socially disconnected neighborhoods he eventually studied. The Shaw family were hard-working, deeply religious Scottish-Irish Protestants who, for many generations, lived in the rural farm community of Luray, Indiana. Born in 1885, Shaw came from a large family of 10 siblings. During adolescence, he spent more time working on the family farm than attending school.[4]

Although a diligent worker, Shaw still found time to get into trouble. Later in life, he would sometimes reflect publicly and warmheartedly on these memories. One particular example Shaw detailed was a time when he was caught stealing bolts from a blacksmith's shop. Instead of turning him in to the authorities, the blacksmith helped Shaw fix the wagon for which he had stolen the parts. Shaw told this story as a way of demonstrating the response to delinquent behavior that was characteristic of small-town communities.[5]

Despite his intermittent acts of youthful rebellion, Shaw went on to achieve his graduate degree in 1924 from the University of Chicago's renowned sociology department. In 1926, he became the director of Chicago's Institute of Juvenile Justice, where he and Henry McKay eventually conducted their collaborative research.[6]

Henry D. McKay

In terms of personality, Henry D. McKay was, in many ways, opposite from Shaw. McKay was a more introspective individual who preferred to focus most of his time on the quantitative aspects of research. As an invested scholar, McKay was determined to use empirical evidence to establish a niche in academia.[7] He ". . . plotted the maps, calculated the rates, ran the correlations and described the findings which located empirically and depicted cartographically the distribution of crime and delinquency in Chicago."[8]

While their personalities differed greatly, Shaw's and McKay's rural childhoods were more congruent. McKay grew up on a vast area of farmland in Hand County, South Dakota. His grandfather was a Scottish immigrant who migrated to Minnesota in 1873. They were a religious family and, like Shaw, McKay spent most of his time as a child working on the family farm.[9]

McKay first met Shaw when he enrolled in graduate school at the University of Chicago. Four years behind Shaw, he stayed at the university for only one year before leaving to continue his studies at the University of Illinois. It was there that McKay met and became close friends with Edwin Sutherland. Shaw and McKay began their research together in 1927 when McKay became employed as a clerical research assistant under Shaw at the Institute for Juvenile Research.[10]

The Chicago School

At the beginning of the 20th century, biological theories on criminal behavior were becoming less popular. During this time, criminologists witnessed dramatic economic changes that resulted in extreme population expansions and, consequently, oversaturated and run-down urban neighborhoods.[11] Viewing criminal acts as a side effect of poor social and economic conditions indicated that criminal behavior was circumstantial and not necessarily a static intrinsic characteristic.

The "Chicago School" refers to the cohort of criminologists who concentrated on this ecological approach. The University of Chicago's sociology department was headed by Ernest W. Burgess and Robert E. Park and promoted the use of empirical data and fieldwork in the examination of social dynamics within urban areas.[12] As Shaw and McKay met and studied there, their theoretical development relied heavily on the Chicago School's belief that society played a much bigger role in criminality than individual influences alone. This methodological emphasis worked well for Shaw, the activist, and McKay, the statistician.

Theoretical Perspectives: Juvenile Delinquency

Shaw and McKay's research explicated connections between delinquency distributions and corresponding physical and social organization. Building on Burgess's concentric zone theory[13] and his resulting concept of social disorganization,[14] Shaw and McKay were successful in identifying specific geographical patterns of juvenile crime. Although they also conducted their research in other cities,[15] Shaw and McKay were most known for their Chicago findings.[16]

Before they analyzed their findings, Shaw and McKay needed to get a general sense of Chicago's interpersonal dynamics. They began by studying the growth trends of Chicago to better understand the developmental differences in cultural values, social influences, and community organizations that characterized the city.[17] They found that areas closest to the center of industry were undesirable and, therefore, had the lowest housing rates. Since, at the time, immigrants were mostly employed as unskilled laborers who received the lowest wages, they inhabited these unstable and aesthetically unpleasant areas. Traveling outward from the central area of the city, housing costs increased. As immigrant groups thrived, many eventually moved farther from the city's center. They concluded that the main reasons for such differences in values and organization stemmed from economic segregation.[18]

Next, Shaw and McKay focused on evaluating court records in order to measure the number of delinquent youths living in certain areas of Chicago. Another pattern emerged.[19] As the researchers explain:

> Most of the areas characterized by high rates of delinquents, as well as by a concentration of individual delinquents, are either in or adjacent to areas zoned for industry and commerce. This is true not only for areas close to the central business district but also for outlying areas. . . . On the other hand, the areas with low rates [of delinquency] are, for the most part, those zoned for residential purposes.[20]

Shaw and McKay acknowledged that this pattern did deviate in some areas;[21] however, the strong connection between juvenile criminal activity and its proximity to commerce supported their theoretical perspectives.

Although areas with high juvenile delinquency rates were mostly populated by immigrant groups, Shaw and McKay did not believe that certain race and nationality groups were more criminal or deviant than others. Instead, they theorized that it resulted from the impoverished ecological and social conditions these groups were subjected to. They pointed out that immigrants had limited access to life's necessities and, as a result, were unable to organize themselves socially.[22] Criminal (deviant) behavior in these Chicago "slums" was the product of weakened social controls produced by systematic economic seclusion. As these groups converged and diverged in their attempt to prosper and survive, crime—not legitimate endeavors—provided quicker access to higher socioeconomic status.

Shaw and McKay also found that delinquency rates remained generally static over time despite a complete change in nationality and racial demographics within many of the disadvantaged neighborhoods.[23] This was a significant finding for the researchers. Crime rates did not follow these groups as they moved out of the slums. Instead, delinquent behavior disseminated within newer groups as they moved into the disorganized neighborhoods. Shaw and McKay had strong evidence to support that crime was not environmentally precipitated because "[j]ust as [older immigrant groups] were being replaced in their old areas of residence by more recent immigrants, so their sons were replaced in the dockets of the court by the sons of new arrivals."[24] Otherwise, over time, delinquency rates would have distributed more equally between each of Chicago's zones.

In addition to outlining the unique environmental and economic characteristics of high and low crime areas of Chicago, Shaw and McKay were also interested in delineating the "subtle differences in values, standards, attitudes, traditions, and institutions" that differentiated them.[25] They found that the early-20th-century Chicago communities that demonstrated the lowest rates of juvenile delinquency put a strong emphasis on values and were generally consistent. Attitudes relating to child rearing and social conformity were stable and reliable among most families residing in these areas. Parents placed a high emphasis on education and engagement in productive free-time activities. Likewise, institutions and associations designed to reinforce social controls also existed within schools, churches, and other community organizations.[26] These social structures strategically left little room for even the mildest forms of deviant behavior.

Shaw and McKay also found these children were generally isolated from conflicting values and behaviors. Therefore, they were only exposed to belief systems that disapproved of criminal and unconventional conduct.[27] However, the researchers asserted that individuals residing in higher economic neighborhoods were not always law abiding because "any unlawful pursuits are likely to be carried out in other parts of the city, [so these] children . . . are, on the whole, insulated from direct contact with these deviant forms of adult behavior."[28]

While children may have been aware that alternative values and attitudes existed, these options were not experienced as fundamental aspects of their daily lives.[29] By ensuring that deviancy was not modeled to their youth, no reinforcement of prestige or economic gain was attached to delinquency. Furthermore, if a boy did decide to deviate from these stringent communal standards, such behavior would have been difficult to conceal and maintain for any length of time.

The long-term, stable residencies of these outer Chicago zones made it possible to develop this type of high-functioning social organization. This allowed for values, attitudes, and morality to develop and disseminate universally. This consistency assured that children did not experience, for example, internal conflicts between what was held in high esteem at school and what was taught at home.

While areas of high economic status were able to organize, assimilate, and reinforce values, the opposite was true for low-income neighborhoods. Shaw and McKay explained that areas of low socioeconomic status and high delinquency rates did not experience the shared attitudes of suburban communities. Belief systems varied greatly and ranged from conventional to unlawful. What was taught in churches and at home tended to be in complete contrast to what individuals learned elsewhere.[30]

Deviant and legitimate values vied within the same space; gangs and organized crime coexisted alongside legitimate businesses that attempted to make an earnest living.[31] Shaw and McKay believed these conflicts increased the rates of juvenile delinquency, as they state:

Within the same community, theft may be defined as right and proper in some groups and as immoral, improper, and undesirable in others. In some groups wealth and prestige are secured through acts of skill and courage in the delinquent or criminal world, while in neighboring groups any attempt to achieve distinction in this manner would result in extreme disapprobation. Two conflicting systems of economic activity here present roughly equivalent opportunities for employment and for promotion. Evidence of success in the criminal world is indicated by the presence of adult criminals whose clothes and automobiles indicate unmistakably that they have prospered in their chosen fields. The values missed and the greater risks incurred are not so clearly apparent to the young.[32]

This quote highlights how these dichotomies encourage criminal behavior. It also explains how an overexposure to the glamourous aspects of unlawful activities prevent children from experiencing the potential benefits of practicing conservative values.

It was this type of intimate exposure to crime, they believed, that caused juvenile delinquency and not through contact with impersonal mediums such as television, radio, and magazines. In Chicago's low-income neighborhoods, boys were constantly exposed to deviancy and, as a result, were keenly aware of the benefits and prestige associated with various types of illicit behavior. They knew where to find stolen merchandise and could easily identify the criminals who were openly engaged in the sale of such goods.[33] In contrast to the wealthier Chicago areas, the convenience and proximity of crime and other deviant behaviors were a fundamental part of life in the slums.

Unlike children in suburban communities, the researchers believed youths living in slum neighborhoods were presented with many alternative values and attitudes. The line between conflicting ideologies was often blurred. According to Shaw and McKay, habits and values formed primarily around the belief systems of the specific group the child engaged with the most or whom he or she became associated with.[34] Therefore, boys who ran around with other delinquents during the week and attended church with their family on Sundays would have been more likely to adopt deviant rather than conventional attitudes.

Shaw and McKay also found that deviant behavior was primarily executed in group settings. They theorized this occurred because of exposure to heavy concentrations of pressure to conform to group deviancy. For youths residing in the suburbs, widely dispersed delinquency rates meant it was relatively uncommon for them to ever come into contact with, or be directly influenced by, other juvenile delinquents.[35] Moving outward toward the suburbs separated delinquent boys from their criminal peer groups. Subsequently, they were involved in less deviant behavior. This highlights a clear connection between environmental and social influences on crime and deviancy.

The concept of juvenile delinquency as a tradition was also of great interest to Shaw and McKay. They regarded the presence of segregated and unique criminal protocols as proof that crime was handed down generationally.[36] They observed that certain crimes, and the procedures used to commit them, were characteristic of specific slum neighborhoods since "[t]he execution of each type [of crime] involves techniques which must be learned from others who have participated in the same activity."[37] In addition, Shaw and McKay believed that crime was socially hereditary based on the evaluation of juvenile court records because "some members of each delinquent group had participated in offenses in the company of other older boys, and so on, backward in time in an unbroken continuity as far as the records were available."[38]

Although criminal traditions were sometimes, but not exclusively, passed down through family members, Shaw and McKay examined other domestic dynamics that may have influenced delinquency rates. They identified that in low-income communities, a family's set of conventional values often conflicted with outside pressures to conform and survive. In many circumstances, families who subscribed to conservative values also had some sort of association with one or more career criminals. In these situations, the family's condemnation of deviancy was neutralized.[39] Conversely, in higher socioeconomic communities, uniformity of values protected families and youths from experiencing these double standards of morality.

They also believed that European-born parents faced additional struggles. They explained that "Old World" interests, attitudes, and solutions were not effective or applicable in urban America. In many situations, this weakened parental controls and caused the family's influence on a child to be limited against more appealing and exciting deviant activities. Also, excessive free time for urban youth created more opportunities to engage in delinquency. They highlighted the fact that children from rural America and European countries were typically kept preoccupied by working and contributing to their households and communities at an early age. This was not the case for children living in lower socioeconomic neighborhoods. Instead, many of these boys used their leisure time to commit crimes.[40]

Shaw and McKay's theoretical framework illustrated the causal effects of socially disorganized neighborhoods on juvenile crime frequencies during the first few decades of the 20th century. In communities where shared conventional values represented the moral minority, many individuals adapted to criminal lifestyles that met their immediate needs for esteem and prosperity. This concept provided hope because it argued that delinquency was a situational adaptation, therefore, criminal (deviant) behavior would eventually be replaced by conventional conduct when families improved their social positions by moving outward toward Chicago's suburbs.

Influences on Theoretical Development

Shaw and McKay were both raised in rural farm towns. It is reasonable to assume that both researchers experienced some degree of culture shock as they migrated to the city in pursuit of their degrees. The dramatic shift in lifestyle, economy, and values would have been immediately observed. Also, the new perspective they inevitably gained while adjusting to city life likely contributed to their social and ecological curiosities as sociologists. It also directly impacted their theories. For example, their beliefs regarding rural and European parents who kept their children out of trouble by limiting free time and expecting active contribution to the household described their own childhood experiences in many ways.

Shaw's story of the blacksmith who helped him fix his wagon rather than judge or consequence him illustrates the juxtaposing realities of rural and urban life. In a small town where crime was not common, business owners were not likely wary of youths stealing or causing mischief. As in Shaw's case, a patient and paternal response to juvenile crime would have been common.

However, Shaw observed the opposite was generally true for the urban areas he and McKay studied. The transient and disconnected lifestyles that were typical of these neighborhoods would have made it unusual for personal relationships to exist between individuals and business owners. The concentration of deviance complicated and exacerbated even the smallest incidents of unlawful behavior, resulting in angry and reactionary attitudes toward juvenile crime.

Shaw also had an empathetic insight toward the delinquents he studied. His theoretical development was more than just a linguistic explanation for quantitative findings. The life histories he wrote on several juvenile delinquents demonstrated his emersion in their personal experiences and culture. Perhaps Shaw saw these youths as having the potential to grow up more like he did, had they experienced social control, shared values, and adults who responded to crime with compassion rather than admonishment.

McKay was preoccupied with finding out what, if any, effect race and ethnicity had on criminal propensities.[41] This academic curiosity was likely influenced by his own experience growing up in an immigrant family. His isolation from criminal and deviant values at home would explain his interest in the causal relationship between high crime rates and immigrant demographics. Moreover, as a second-generation Scottish American, McKay would have had an intimate understanding and appreciation for the immense struggle immigrant families experienced while adapting to American culture in disorganized communities.

In addition to Shaw's and McKay's childhoods, their roots in the Chicago School also impacted their future research and theories. The Chicago School's influence is identifiable by the presence of other Chicago theorists' ideals found in Shaw and McKay's writings. Burgess, Park, and Sutherland, for example, are referenced several times in *Juvenile Delinquency and Urban Areas*. Many of Shaw and McKay's theoretical perspectives incorporate principles from Sutherland's differential association theory. Since McKay and Sutherland happened to be close friends, it is understandable that his ideologies shine through in Shaw and McKay's interpretations and beliefs.

The development of influential, accurate, and enduring theories of crime often require that theorists consider their past life experiences and apply those viewpoints to the phenomena they are currently researching. In this case, Shaw and McKay's experiences as rural boys turned urban men likely impacted their process of critically assessing the communities they studied and the interpretations of their findings. Whether it was conscious or subconscious, how and where Shaw and McKay were raised, their social interactions, and the people they met along the way supplemented their theoretical perspectives of juvenile delinquency.

Conclusion

Shaw and McKay's conceptualizations of crime were progressive and influential in their time and, in many ways, continue to remain strong today. Many youths, especially those living in the inner city, still find that the value systems of their family, church groups, and social clubs are incongruent with the attitudes of other influential community members, such as neighborhood gangs. Furthermore, many children observe their parents work tirelessly at legitimate jobs and struggle to pay bills while, at the same time, they witness older peers show off expensive clothes and cars purchased through the sale of drugs or stolen goods. Conflicts between morality and prosperity still exist today.

There are some aspects, however, of Shaw and McKay's observations that no longer represent current social and community dynamics. Changes in industry and commerce distributions no longer follow the strict concentric layout created in the wake of the Industrial Revolution. This diversity has worn away the boundary that once shielded suburban households from unwanted influences that disparage conformity. Today's youth are far less protected from deviant behavior as a result.

Also, Shaw and McKay asserted that deviancy is primarily learned through intimate exposure. This concept cannot be maintained in today's society since most people, especially children, consciously seek out impersonal sources for guidance in the development of their sense of self and value system. While it cannot be argued that close proximity to adverse behaviors is extremely influential, our current culture reinforces the emulation of behavior viewed remotely.

In particular, current access to technology has increased exposure and tolerance to deviant beliefs and lifestyles. Television shows regale young viewers with stories of celebrity role models getting caught driving drunk or doing drugs. Music that glorifies the use of violence and objectification of women inundates radio stations. Within seconds, pornography, violent images, or plans to make homemade bombs can be accessed online. As a result, deviance and criminal conduct is much more diversified now than it was in the 1920s and 1930s when Shaw and McKay made their observations.

Notes

1. Jon Snodgrass, "Clifford R. Shaw and Henry D. McKay: Chicago Criminologists," *British Journal of Criminology* 16, no. 1 (1976): 3.
2. Snodgrass, "Shaw and McKay," 8. According to Snodgrass, Shaw became best friends with the subject of his well-known book, *The Jack Roller*.

3. Ibid., 7.

4. Ibid., 3.

5. Ibid.

6. Ibid., 4–5.

7. Ibid., 2–3.

8. Ibid., 2.

9. Ibid., 5.

10. Ibid.

11. Robert J. Lilly, Francis T. Cullen, and Richard A. Ball, *Criminological Theory: Context and Consequences*, 5th ed. (California: Sage, 2011), 40–41.

12. Snodgrass, "Shaw and McKay," 2.

13. Ernest W. Burgess, "The Growth of the City: An Introduction to a Research Project," in *The City: Suggestions for the Study of Human Nature in the Urban Environment*, ed. Robert E. Park et al. (Chicago: University of Chicago Press, 1925), 50–54. Burgess's theory of concentric zones stated that there is a radial pattern to urban development. Burgess illustrated this pattern by using a map of Chicago, distinguished by five zones. Each zone expanded centrifugally and grew larger over time. Zone I was identified as the business and industry part of town, which Burgess called "the Loop." Moving outward, Zone II was referred to as the transition zone. This zone was represented as being in a constant state of encroachment by Zone I. As the businesses of downtown Chicago constantly expanded, individuals living in the "slums" of the transition zone were dislocated. This zone was of special interest to Burgess as he described it as being marked by deterioration, crime, disease, and disorganization from the constant displacement of residents. On the outskirts of this deteriorated area was Zone III, which was inhabited by the industrial workers who were able to eventually escape the unstable housing of the transition zone. Zone IV was mostly residential neighborhoods comprised of expensive apartments and single family homes. Lastly, and least affected by crime, was Zone V. Burgess described this zone as the commuter's zone, which was located approximately 30 to 60 minutes from Zone I.

14. Ibid., 57. Burgess explained that social disorganization was the product of diverging economic, social, cultural, and recreational groups, formed within the transition zone, who failed to harmonize because of the continuous and cumbersome expansion of industry. This perpetual process broke down the ability and desire of communities to become cohesive so, in turn, they remained in a state of constant isolation and chaos.

15. Clifford R. Shaw and Henry D. McKay, *Juvenile Delinquency and Urban Areas*, Rev. ed. (Chicago and London: University of Chicago Press, 1969). Shaw and McKay extended their research to cities such as Philadelphia, Boston, Cincinnati, Cleveland, and Richmond. Due to limited space, findings for these cities were not included in this chapter. More information can be found in this book.

16. Shaw and McKay, *Juvenile Delinquency*. It should be noted that the following findings covered data collected by Shaw and McKay between 1900 and 1933. They also conducted longitudinal research in later years; however, their theoretical framework was developed on the heels of their 1900–33 research analysis. Consequently, it is only these findings that are examined in detail in this chapter.

17. Ibid., 17–18.

18. Ibid., 19–21.

19. Ibid., 45.
20. Ibid., 55.
21. Ibid.
22. Ibid., 155.
23. Ibid., 153–55.
24. Ibid., 157–60. Shaw and McKay also explained that no constant, distinguishing rate of delinquency was associated with any specific race or ethnic group in Chicago.
25. Ibid., 170.
26. Ibid., 170–71.
27. Ibid., 171.
28. Ibid.
29. Ibid.
30. Ibid., 171–72.
31. Ibid., 172.
32. Ibid.
33. Ibid., 172–73.
34. Ibid., 172.
35. Ibid., 173–74.
36. Ibid., 174–75.
37. Ibid., 174.
38. Ibid., 175.
39. Ibid., 183.
40. Ibid., 184.
41. Snodgrass, "Shaw and McKay," 5.

Bibliography

Burgess, Ernest W. "The Growth of the City: An Introduction to a Research Project." In *The City: Suggestions for the Study of Human Nature in the Urban Environment*, ed. Robert E. Park, Ernest W. Burgess, and Roderick D. McKenzie. Chicago: University of Chicago Press, 1925, 47–62.

Lilly, Robert J., Francis T. Cullen, and Richard A. Ball. *Criminological Theory: Context and Consequences*. 5th ed. Thousand Oaks, CA: Sage, 2011.

McKay, Henry D. "Introduction." In *Juvenile Delinquency and Urban Areas*, by Clifford R. Shaw and Henry D. McKay. Rev. ed. Chicago and London: University of Chicago Press, 1969, xix–xxi.

Shaw, Clifford R., and Henry D. McKay. *Juvenile Delinquency and Urban Areas*. Rev. ed. Chicago and London: University of Chicago Press, 1969.

Snodgrass, Jon. "Clifford R. Shaw and Henry D. McKay: Chicago Criminologists." *British Journal of Criminology* 16, no. 1 (1976): 1–18.

13

Albert Bandura

Kimberly Ortiz

Albert Bandura was born the youngest child of six on December 4, 1925, to immigrant parents. His father was of Polish descent and his mother Ukrainian. His parents had both immigrated to Canada as teenagers. Bandura's father worked for the trans-Canada railroad as a laborer and his mother worked in the small-town general store. Neither of Bandura's parents had a high level of education; however, they were able to save enough money to buy a plot of land in Mundare, Canada, where they had to clear most of the land of boulders and trees by hand in order to make it tillable and fertile enough to grow crops. Bandura's father also taught himself to read three foreign languages. Bandura's father's self-teaching abilities earned him a position on the school board.[1]

During his childhood, Bandura experienced many accounts of losing life. His town was hit with a severe flu pandemic that claimed the life of one of his sisters; then, shortly after, he lost a brother due to a hunting accident. These incidents took their toll on Bandura's father, who went from a person full of life to someone just going through the daily activities needed to survive. Toward the end of the Great Depression, when Bandura's father had the ability to expand the farm, he noticed a change for the better in his father. He became yet again the happy-go-lucky and high-spirited person Bandura thought had disappeared for good.[2]

Even though his father's spirits had picked up, there was nothing that could be done about the education problem facing the small town in which they lived. There was only one school to facilitate the education for every child in that town—from kindergarten through high school. By the time Bandura reached high school, there were only two teachers handling the entire high school–level curriculum for the town. The lack of resources and personnel able to teach led the children to be left to their own devices in order to expand their knowledge base. The children within the town turned to the local library and took it upon themselves to further their education beyond the limited resources of the school. Bandura was not alone in his endeavors at this time;

most, if not all, of the kids from his school took this approach when it came to obtaining an education in this small town.[3]

Even though the school produced many students who would attend universities across the world, including Bandura himself, the credit for this accomplishment is not given to the school board or teachers who were in charge of overseeing the education. Rather, the lack of resources and teachers able to help and guide a child in learning seemed to be the enabling factor for persons in this small town to achieve well scholastically.[4]

Social Learning Theory

The most known theory related to Albert Bandura is his social learning theory. It is within this theory that Bandura focuses more on what motivates a person to act a certain way as well as what self-regulatory mechanism does a person possess or lack that would contribute to exhibited behaviors. Bandura's work went beyond the thinking that biological or emotional factors were the key influences to a person's behavior; he looked into the social surroundings a person was placed in that could hold information as to why a certain behavior would be acceptable in a specific society yet unacceptable in others, such as crime within urban city living.[5]

According to this theory, Bandura believed that a person's behavior is a pure manifestation of behaviors observed in other persons. When a person sees that a certain behavior allows him/her to acquire something they wish to obtain, the person will modify their behavior to mimic that which they have seen to bring others the end result they wish to achieve. This theory highly emphasizes the importance of how observational research leads to imitation and modeling of behavior in order to obtain certain goals in life. Bandura stated that "Learning would be exceedingly laborious, not to mention hazardous, if people had to rely solely on the effects of their own actions to inform them what to do."[6]

In order to learn through observations, it was thought by Bandura that there are four phases of behavior modeling that occur in order for behaviors to truly be labeled as learned from society. These phases are attention, retention, reproduction and motivation.[7]

The phase of attention pertains to Bandura's belief that if a person is to learn anything, he/she must pay special and specific attention to the features of the modeled behavior. There are many reasons a person would pay attention to the molding activities: take the earlier scenario about crime in an urban setting being acceptable within that society but not in an upper-class area. When a child is shown that a person has large sums of money, the best cars, and the newest fashions, it catches their attention. Also think of how a child would view a teenager having so much authority that persons would go out of their way to give them anything they want. This kind of behavior catches the attention of the youth, and the youth starts to pay attention to how this is achieved.[8]

After seeing the behavior they wish to model, a person goes through Bandura's retention phase. It has been found that this is the period of modeling behavior in which a person is influenced the most.[9] The reason for this is that in order to achieve reproduction of the behaviors that are noted to give the person the desired outcome, the person will go above and beyond to retain all aspects of how to reproduce the circumstances they deem necessary to achieve the outcome they want. Memories of the behaviors that have been observed, such as how to handle a drug sale, are stored in the brain using mental images and verbal descriptions, creating the ability to reiterate verbally to other persons the behavior that they have seen. If a child sees a drug dealer in his local neighborhood in possession of everything they desire in life, the child will take note of how the drug dealer acts and will memorize the places, times, and mannerisms that are displayed by the drug dealer. When this child talks to friends about things he has seen in order to give himself status, he is recalling these images and using verbal descriptions to solidify the memory. The aspect of regurgitation of the behaviors observed over and over again allows the child to maintain the effectiveness of the memory, as it is those exact observed motions that will lead the child to obtaining the things that he wants.[10]

The third phase is reproduction. The child has now seen what the behavior can get him, has witnessed and recounted exactly which behaviors need to be present in order for him to obtain the things he desires, so now the child will reproduce the behaviors.[11] As this child grows and understands further that his behavior may need some modification to conform to the fulfillment of his personal needs, he will adjust as needed. Through reproduction, the modeled behavior becomes a reality and the person attempting to re-create it adds his/her own personal touch to overcome personal obstacles, or adds adjustments to better suit personal needs in order to reproduce the behavior flawlessly—after all, practice makes perfect.

The last and final phase, according to Bandura, is motivation.[12] If a child has a perception of grandeur about the lifestyle of a dope-slinging gang member, such as status, money, cars, and so forth, and does not see any negative repercussions, then there is reinforcement that the behavior to achieve these things is justifiable. On the other side of the argument, if a child sees that person who has the above-mentioned things obtained through drug deals and sees that the person has been sent to jail numerous occasions, or has witnessed the actual arrest and the effect it had on family members, this would serve as a deterrent to the behavior as the child would not believe the selling of drugs to be justifiable means to obtain the status and wealth they still desire from the attention phase. The person will then readjust things in order to achieve everything their mind is telling them they need to be successful on the streets in their neighborhood another way.[13] This simply ties into positive and negative rein-forcement. If the person that the behavior is modeled on receives nothing but perceived positive outcomes, the behavior will be copied to achieve the same things. If the person whose behavior is modeled receives negative outcomes from their actions, then those who are attempting to model the behavior will stop or recalibrate their own behaviors to prevent the negative effects from happening to them. The motivational factor is basically positive and negative reinforcement. If you see a positive outcome of an action, then you are moti-vated to mimic the action as long as it helps you obtain the things you want. If you see a negative outcome of an action, then your motivation is to adjust your actions or not exhibit the behavior at all in order to achieve your goal.

Bobo Doll Experiment

This experiment was pertinent to the theory that Bandura held about observa-tional learning being the major basis for behavioral manifestations within per-sons. In this experiment, Bandura took 72 children who ranged in age from 37 to 69 months.[14] There were an equal number of male and female test subjects, 36 boys and 36 girls, who were divided into eight groups. Bandura, Dorothea Ross, and Sheila Ross[15] give an explanation of the testing method and control measures:

> Subjects were divided into eight experimental groups of six subjects each and a control group consisting of 24 subjects. Half the experimental sub-jects were exposed to aggressive models and half were exposed to models that were subdued and nonaggressive in their behavior. These groups were further subdivided into male and female subjects. Half the subjects in the aggressive and nonaggressive conditions observed same-sex models, while the remaining subjects in each group viewed models of the opposite sex. The control group had no prior exposure to the adult models and was tested only in the generalization situation.[16]

During the experiment, the children who were shown aggressive behavior imitated the same aggressive behavior and sometimes went further than the shown behavior.

Perhaps the most notable part of the experiment is that while no gun was used in the demonstration of aggressiveness, a toy gun was placed with the children. Once the adult left the room, the children started to hit the doll in the manner they had seen in the demonstration and eventually escalated to use of the gun, most specifically noted among the male subjects. It was also noted by Bandura et al.[17] that females tended to be less physically aggressive but more verbally aggressive toward the doll. This experiment was found to show in great detail that behaviors are learned and in a way self-taught, as a person will mimic behaviors that they feel are best suited for the situation in which they find themselves in. In the Bobo doll experiment, it just so happened that the children believed they were expected to act that way; adults are modeled as influential persons in a child's life and children are expected to act as the adults do.

Childhood Influence on Theoretical Work

In Bandura's childhood it is seen that in order to obtain an education worth having, the children had to go beyond their limitations at school and find resources that were available through libraries in the area. It was not just one child who did this but the entire school. It has been documented by N. Sheehy, A. J. Chapman, and W. A. Conroy[18] that all of the students who attended this school went on to academic success at universities, even though they were not given the best education in their hometown. It is thought that because it was seen that going beyond the confines of the school resources and teachers and reaching out to other community resources would allow for the expansion of knowledge, a person was able to obtain a university-level education; this behavior was replicated by each generation and soon became a common fixture in everyday life of the school-aged child in Bandura's small town. Just by seeing the actions that were displayed in the social group with which Bandura was affiliated and knowing that if he followed the same course of action he too could be afforded the education that his parents were never able to achieve, Bandura modified his behavior to mimic that of persons who expanded their academic goals to include continuing education at or beyond the university level.

Bandura's parents were intelligent, yet never finished high school. It can be said that perhaps Bandura noticed that his parents wanted better in life than for their family to be considered just mere immigrant children and saw the opportunities available to those who had an education. In order to obtain the status they desired, by seeing it occur through others' actions, Bandura's parents changed their behaviors; they taught themselves the things necessary to achieve a higher status within their community. When talking about the school resources and children reaching out to other areas or taking other avenues of approach to learning, it is quite possible that seeing not only the persons from their school doing so and getting into universities but also what his parents were able to do by educating themselves that drove Bandura and, through him, his schoolmates to want to achieve a higher level of education, so they took it upon themselves to educate themselves in any manner that was possible.

When Bandura's father changed his outlook on life during the Great Depression to be bleak instead of optimistic, it can be thought that his father fell into his somber stay not only from the deaths of his children but also from seeing the behaviors of those around him as the economy failed to thrive. It was stated by Sheehy et al. (1997) that around the time the economy started to pick up, so did Bandura's father's spirit come back to life. It seems too coincidental that at the time when everyone else was most likely cheering up about their life status, so was his father. Bandura could have noticed this and seen what an influence society can play, not only on behavior, but on the outlook on life as well.

It is safe to assume that throughout his childhood, Bandura saw his social learning theory affect many lives, including his own. Perhaps the changes he saw in others that were coincidentally a result of their affiliations and interactions with the society in which they lived led Bandura to understand how behaviors can be shaped by seeing them enacted by others, which is how social learning theory was incorporated by Bandura. Seeing the training of oneself to act in a certain way to obtain something they covet another person having is the essence of his childhood. This is seen in his parents' behavior as well as the behavior surrounding the self- teaching concept adopted by Bandura and his peers for educational aspirations.

Notes

1. N. Sheehy, A. J. Chapman, and W. A. Conroy, eds., *Biographical Dictionary of Psychology* (London: Routledge Press, 1997).
2. Ibid.
3. Ibid.
4. Ibid.
5. A. Bandura, *Social Learning Theory* (New York: General Learning Press, 1977).
6. Ibid. p.22.
7. Bandura, *Social Learning Theory*.
8. Ibid.
9. Ibid.
10. Ibid.
11. Ibid.
12. Ibid.
13. Ibid.
14. A. Bandura, D. Ross, and S. A. Ross, "Transmission of Aggression through Imitation of Aggression Models," *Journal of Abnormal and Social Psychology*, 63 (1961), 575–82.
15. Ibid.
16. Ibid., 576.
17. Bandura, Ross, and Ross, "Transmission of Aggression."
18. Sheehy, Chapman, and Conroy, *Biographical Dictionary of Psychology*.

Bibliography

Bandura, A. *Social Learning Theory*. New York, NY: General Learning Press, 1977.
Bandura, A., D. Ross, and S. A. Ross. "Transmission of Aggression through Imitation of Aggression Models." *Journal of Abnormal and Social Psychology*, 63 (1961), 575–82.
Sheehy, N., A. J. Chapman, and W. A. Conroy, eds. *Biographical Dictionary of Psychology*. London: Routledge Press, 1997.

14

Lawrence Kohlberg

Lindsey Page

Throughout history, the criminal justice system, as it is organized, gives a predominantly objective comprehension to deviance and criminal behavior. Unfortunately, given the social construction and relativity of deviance, there is no cut and dry understanding as to how and why deviance originates. Deviants are not products of inevitable processes that they cannot control. There is a significant degree of subjectivity to the process of becoming deviant. Lawrence Kohlberg and his theory of morality microscopically dissect this subjectivity and, to an extent, allow for determination of the stage of morality at which the deviant has essentially "fallen off track," "lost their way," or "crossed over to the dark side."

The journey of Lawrence Kohlberg began on October 25, 1927. He was born into a significantly wealthy family in Bronxville, New York. He was the youngest of the four children of Alfred Kohlberg and Charlotte Albrecht, with Jewish and Protestant backgrounds, respectively. Kohlberg's parents separated when he was four and finally divorced when he reached the age of 14. The financial stability of his family was evidenced by his attendance at Phillips Academy in Andover, Massachusetts, well known for being a prestigious, highly selective boarding school.

Contrary to one's expectations, Kohlberg established an infamous reputation for himself as the typical high school adolescent, consistently on probation for smoking and drinking and just as frequently caught visiting girls at a nearby school. He was considerably better known for his sense of mischief than his interest in academics and theory. During his high school career, one of his teachers suggested that he read Fyodor Dostoevsky's *Brothers Karamazov*.[1] This manuscript proved to have a significant effect on his later personal development and fueled his theoretical development as well. Outside high school his life consisted of vacationing with friends and working on farms, road gangs, and in an airplane factory.[2] This experience in physical labor and developing working relationships with his coworkers reinforced the importance of American democracy that his parents had initially presented to him.[3]

Travels to Europe in the fall of 1945 as a merchant marine significantly expanded Kohlberg's "real life" experiences. Having a Jewish father, the impact of witnessing the physical destruction and chaos caused by war, exacerbated by the traumatic experience of the survivors of the Holocaust and mass genocide, was immeasurable. After completion of his service, fueled by his experience as a merchant marine, Kohlberg began volunteering to illegally transport shiploads of Jewish refugees through the British blockade to Palestine. During this process, Kohlberg's ship was captured and taken to a concentration camp in Cyprus in the Eastern Mediterranean Sea. The Haganah, or Jewish Defense Force, provided Kohlberg and his crew with false papers and facilitated their escape from the camp.[4] Until they could safely leave the country, they inhabited a kibbutz, or collective settlement community. Kohlberg's experience at the Israeli kibbutz had a significant influence on his overall development.

In 1948, Kohlberg began his collegiate studies at the University of Chicago. Kohlberg's undergraduate studies provided him with the fuel for his fundamental interest in morality. Studying the likes of Plato, John Dewey, John Locke, John Stuart Mill, and Thomas Jefferson awakened Kohlberg to the ideas of cultural relativity and individualism in relation to morality, human rights, and human welfare.[5] He became aware that his own personal moral structure was relevant in his current societal and cultural environment. He was still in search of that universal principle that would serve as the foundation for all moral situations, regardless of the culture or society. Kohlberg reached the conclusion that Immanuel Kant's perspective on treating every human being as an end in and of him/herself was the most applicable starting point.[6] He viewed equal respect for human dignity as the core of justice. It was at the postgraduate level that, torn between his interests in morality and justice, he had difficulty deciding between the routes of psychology or law. A summer spent as an attendant at a mental hospital witnessing the interaction between psychology and legal justice was enough to clarify his direction.

After earning his bachelor's degree in just one year, he expanded his education with graduate psychology work and acquired his PhD in psychology from the University of Chicago in 1958. Kohlberg studied psychoanalysis under Bruno Bettelheim, humanistic psychology under Carl Rogers, and behaviorism under Jacob Gewirtz.[7] He felt that none of these areas were adequately appropriate in dealing with morality and the application of justice. Intrigued by Jean Piaget's foundation in moral development, he focused his doctoral dissertation on the moral development of adolescent boys. Kohlberg's teaching career began in 1959 at Yale University as an assistant professor of psychology and continued to develop from there. In 1962, he returned to the University of Chicago as an assistant professor in psychology and simultaneously directed the Child Psychology Training Program. By 1968, Kohlberg had married Lucille Stigberg, fathered two children, and found himself working as a professor of education and psychology at Harvard University, where he spent the remainder of his teaching career.

Kohlberg has been deemed by some a "model of graceful suffering," as he never complained about the pain and suffering he endured during the final years of his life.[8] In 1971, while in Belize conducting cross-cultural work, he contracted a "parasitic infection" and spent the last 16 years of his life suffering in silence. On a day pass from the hospital on January 19, 1987, Kohlberg, age 59, drove himself to Winthrop, Massachusetts, and walked right into the frigid Boston Harbor, committing suicide.

Piaget was the first to explore the issue of moral development. Lawrence Kohlberg looked to extend the work on moral development that Piaget had established and follow moral judgment and reasoning into and through adolescence. The fact that adolescents had their own distinct patterns of thinking was of significant interest to Kohlberg. It was notably similar to those patterns that Piaget had found in children. He added three more stages to the three preexisting stages that Piaget had already constructed and presented on moral development. Step-by-step progression through a strict sequence to the final stages has been extremely rare. He made a significant effort to follow up with his original subjects every three years, which provided him with reliability in refining his theory and revision of his stage descriptions.[9]

Kohlberg was not closed-mindedly interested in the moral development of American culture; rather he had a personal interest in universal morality. He traveled to places such as Taiwan and China to replicate the American moral development study after making culture-sensitive alterations to the study. After numerous cross-cultural moral stage development studies, Kohlberg summarized his findings as "the first four stages being found in almost all cultures while the fifth stage is found in all complex, urban cultures and elaborated systems of education such as Taiwan, Japan and India."[10]

For Kohlberg, morality was to be understood to include feelings, thoughts, and actions, however; it was moral reasoning that gave the moral quality to these aspects.[11] Moral reasoning is what guides the determination of what is "right to do." Kohlberg was concerned that in order to study moral behavior, it is necessary to determine an individual's judgments as well as provide criteria for classifying the actions within the moral domain.[12] Moral understanding is the major facilitator of moral action. To some degree, the motives that fuel our behavior remain active through life. They progressively transform and evolve as we expand our cognitive development; however, they only acquire moral meaning if they are integrated with our moral understanding.[13] Each of his six moral stages is characterized by the decline of some motives and increase in other motives.[14]

Kohlberg believed that moral understanding needed to be effective in controlling the innate human desire for social acceptance because when it produces behavior that the individual judges to be immoral, this leads to unfair solutions for someone involved.[15] For a cognitive theory of morality to actually be viable, reasoning must be fueled by a motivating power.[16] Morality must be a matter of evaluation and justification, fueled by moral understanding. There is a universal language of morality comprised of norms, modal elements, and value elements. These norms and modal and value elements play a crucial role in morality, as they provide the "bones" for Kohlberg's six stages of moral development.[17]

Norms are used to justify moral decisions and include the following:

1. Life
   a. Preservation
   b. Quality and quantity
2. Property
3. Truth
4. Affiliation
5. Erotic love and sex
6. Authority
7. Law
8. Contract
9. Civil Rights
10. Religion
11. Conscience
12. Punishment[18]

"Moral norms are highly important as they (1) regulate human claims, (2) define basic human rights, (3) are culturally universal, (4) are subject to sanctions, and (5) are nonreducible."[19] Modal elements function to express the moral mood or modality of the moral language and they include the following:

1. Obeying (consulting) persons or deity. Should obey; get consent (should consult, persuade)
2. Blaming (approving). Should be blamed for; disapproved (should be approved)
3. Retributing (exonerating). Should retribute against (should exonerate)
4. Having a right (having no right)
5. Having a duty (having no duty)[20]

Value elements address the final justifications and values that surpass norms and modal elements and establish the moral philosophy of a given individual.[21] They include the following:

Egoistic consequences:

6. Good reputation (bad reputation)
7. Seeking reward (avoiding punishment)

Utilitarian consequences:

8. Good individual consequences (bad individual consequences)
9. Good group consequences (bad group consequences)

Ideal or harmony-serving consequences:

10. Upholding character
11. Upholding self-respect
12. Serving social ideals or harmony
13. Serving human dignity and autonomy

Fairness:

14. Balancing perspectives or role-taking
15. Reciprocity or positive desert
16. Maintaining equity
17. Maintaining social contract or freely agreeing[22]

Kohlberg's technique for assessing stages of moral reasoning was based on structured interviews. It was during these interviews that subjects were presented with moral dilemmas, such as the infamous Heinz dilemma. The presentation of this dilemma was then followed by a series of questions to determine the subjects' justifications and explanations for their decision. This process emphasizes focus on the structure of the subjects' response, which reflects their level of moral thinking.[23]

Kohlberg presented three levels of moral reasoning, with two stages at each level. Every person goes through the stages and levels in the same order but the speed and endpoint of development may differ by individual and by culture. The Preconventional Level is when societal expectations are maintained external to one's "self."[24] Following rules for nothing other than to avoid trouble, satisfy one's needs, and maximize self-interest is prevalent at this level. In Stage 1, an action's physical consequences are not separable from psychological consequences.[25] One's social interactions can only be taken from one point of view at a time. The individual is not yet capable of considering multiple viewpoints simultaneously. In Stage 2, the individual becomes capable of realizing that different people have their own points of view, needs, interests, and intentions.[26] People are viewed as interacting on a superficial "give and take" basis.

At the Conventional Level, conventions, rules, obligations, and expectations are now experienced as being part of "the self."[27] This "self" learns to identify and heed to personal as well as societal obligations and expectations. In Stage 3, the individual sees him/herself as intertwined in a wide variety of interpersonal relationships.[28] They develop moral roles, which are based on their specific interpersonal relationships, emphasizing the general characteristics of what they consider a "good person."[29] Stage 4 allows the individual to take on the viewpoint of an institutional or social system to which they are able to connect their moral actions and expectations while simultaneously finding meaning and justification for them.[30]

At the Postconventional Level, the individual now has developed abstract principles of freedom, equality, and solidarity stemming from specific societal and interpersonal expectations, laws, and norms.[31] Seeing oneself as separate from external expectations, the individual also finds him/herself capable of heeding to principles, which are required for all members of society and humanity. At Stage 5, one's moral reasoning now reflects a prior-to-society perspective of the rational individual, meaning we as individuals are bound to society by an imagined social contract reinforced and concretized by our legal system.[32] This contract is comprised of principles of trust, individual liberty, and equal treatment for all. This should essentially be the basis for all societal and interpersonal arrangements and relationships. Stage 6 is the final leg of moral development in which the individual takes on a "moral point of view." They are now able to express an impartial respect for people as ends in themselves.[33] By taking on roles in their interpersonal relationships, they are now capable of equal consideration of the points of view of all persons involved in the moral dilemma at hand. Kohlberg considers this mature moral reasoning, or moral autonomy, as the endpoint of moral development.[34]

All of the theorists who impacted Kohlberg's personal, educational, and theoretical development emphasized that the development of moral judgment proceeds from moral heteronomy to autonomy. Kohlberg himself presented three hypotheses addressing the issue of heteronomy versus autonomy. He believed that

1. Moral growth throughout the stages of moral reasoning should be accompanied by a gradual shift toward moral autonomy.
2. Moral autonomy develops most consistently in institutions and societies emphasizing democracy, cooperation, and mutual relationships.
3. Moral autonomy leads to moral behavior because moral autonomy is based upon an interest and respect for moral principles and a sense of inner obligation.[35]

Moral education arose as an area of interest in the 1960s. Lawrence Kohlberg facilitated Socratic discussions of moral dilemmas with his students. They generated three controversial philosophic issues: the cultural relativity of moral development, the assumption that a later stage is a morally more adequate or better stage, and the role of authority and indoctrination in moral education.[36] Regarding moral education in schools, Kohlberg believed that one could not develop a theory addressing something such as this by strictly applying research. In order to develop a theory on building bridges, one must do so by in fact building bridges.[37] The construction of a theory of education requires the collaboration of teachers, students, and educational theorists.

Kohlberg saw a "just community" environment in schools and education as one governed by participatory democracy where there is one vote for every person.[38] He sought to put theories of human development into practice by facilitating the formation of democratic or "just communities" in schools and prisons.[39] Based on his views regarding participatory democracy, it would make sense that moral education would prosper in an environment where everyone had decision-making power. The Connecticut Women's Prison was the first to employ such a community structure, followed in 1974 by Cambridge High School, an alternative school dedicated to democratic decision making, and in 1978 by the Scarsdale Alternative School.[40]

While it is important to understand the fundamentals of the work of any classical theorist, it is just as important to understand what brought him/her to these conclusions about life and humanity. It is essential for a complete understanding of Kohlberg's concern with a universal justice and moral development, as well as those of the individual, to address the potential connections between his biographical history and the development of his theoretical perspectives.

Kohlberg never viewed himself as a highly moral person; his interest in moral development and the idea of a universal justice began upon his completion of high school in 1945. This lack of morality was also apparent in Kohlberg's personal friends at this time of his life. They seemed to have little to no regard for rules in which they had no input. Even in high school, Kohlberg considered the rules that he frequently disregarded to have virtually nothing to do with maintaining justice or protecting the welfare of those who were expected to follow them. At this stage, however, he acted more on an adolescent mentality, questioning the basic functionality of rules, which seemed a general inconvenience to him.

As established in the biographical background, one of Kohlberg's high school teachers suggested that he read Dostoevsky's *Brothers Karamazov*. The moral issues faced by Ivan in this work intellectually awakened Kohlberg. Ivan points out the unending series of cruelties and injustices to the innocent, especially children, and concludes that if there is a God who governs the world where such injustices take place he would want to hand God back his ticket.[41] In an attempt to find explanations for these moral issues that had been brought to light, Kohlberg realized that his intellectual education was not enough to fully understand them. Empirical experience was required to completely comprehend the everyday unjust occurrences in society. There is very little in this world, especially regarding the workings of modern society, that can be understood by basic book-knowledge.

This empirical experience was not far behind. Kohlberg, in his participation in smuggling refugees past the British blockade, did not seem to have any pervasive moral struggle with taking part in defending individuals who had suffered such a significant injustice as the Holocaust and were left with nowhere to call home. While at this time he lacked the understanding as to why he felt that this was the "right thing to do," he was able to act without questioning the right and wrong of the scenario.

Kohlberg's experience at the Israeli kibbutz also seemed to have a significant influence on his personal as well as theoretical development. It presented him with a plethora of issues regarding morality and justice. Questions formed as to whether there was morality or justice in utilizing violence as a means to a just and moral end. It called into question whether one could establish an adequate perspective to participating in war if the final intentions were moral and just. While the Israeli kibbutz represented ideals of social justice he could not help but admire, he questioned whether he was actually required to follow them or potentially live by the more familiar and easier demands of his American ideals.[42] He became intrigued as to whether a universal morality was present or could be established. On the contrary, it was possible that moral decisions were virtually all relative, dependent on one's culture, experience, upbringing, etc. Even still, while it would seem drastically simple and superficial, moral decisions could potentially be based solely on one's own personal and emotional motivations.

These empirical experiences also provided Kohlberg with the motivation he previously lacked to further his education based on these newfound interests. While attending college was something that was naturally expected of his middle-class status, he never had possessed the desire to do so until he wholeheartedly absorbed himself in this drive to understand moral development and justice.

Notes

1. Lisa Kuhmerker, Uwe Gielen, and Richard Hayes, *The Kohlberg Legacy for the Helping Professions* (Birmingham, AL: R.E.P. Books, 1991), 11.

2. Ibid., 12.

3. Ibid.

4. Ibid.

5. Ibid., 13.

6. Ibid.

7. Ibid.

8. Catherine Walsh, "Reconstructing Larry: Assessing the Legacy of Lawrence Kohlberg," *HGSE News, Harvard Graduate School of Education & Ed. Magazine,* 2000.

9. Kuhmerker, Gielen, and Hayes, *The Kohlberg Legacy for the Helping Professions,* 15.

10. Ibid., 16.

11. Ibid., 24.

12. Lawrence Kohlberg and Dawn Schrader, *The Legacy of Lawrence Kohlberg* (San Francisco: Jossey-Bass, 1990), 12.

13. Ibid., 53.

14. Ibid., 52.

15. Ibid., 53.

16. Ibid., 53.

17. Kuhmerker, Gielen, and Hayes, *The Kohlberg Legacy for the Helping Professions,* 25.

18. Anne Colby and Lawrence Kohlberg, *The Measurement of Moral Judgment* (Cambridge: Cambridge University Press, 1987), 167.

19. Ibid., 49.

20. Ibid., 167.

21. Kuhmerker, Gielen, and Hayes, *The Kohlberg Legacy for the Helping Professions,* 26.

22. Colby and Kohlberg, *The Measurement of Moral Judgment,* 167.

23. Kuhmerker, Gielen, and Hayes, *The Kohlberg Legacy for the Helping Professions,* 23.

24. William Boyce and Larry Jensen, *Moral Reasoning: A Psychological-Philosophical Integration* (Lincoln: University of Nebraska Press, 1978), 100, 104.

25. Ibid.

26. Ibid.

27. Ibid.

28. Ibid.

29. Ibid., 100, 105.

30. Ibid.

31. Ibid., 100–101.

32. Ibid., 101, 106.

33. Ibid.

34. Ibid.

35. Colby and Kohlberg, *The Measurement of Moral Judgment.*

36. Kuhmerker, Gielen, and Hayes, *The Kohlberg Legacy for the Helping Professions,* 16, 17.

37. Ibid., 17.

38. Ibid.

39. Walsh, "Reconstructing Larry: Assessing the Legacy of Lawrence Kohlberg."

40. Kuhmerker, Gielen, and Hayes, *The Kohlberg Legacy for the Helping Professions,* 17.

41. Ibid., 12.

42. Ibid., 13.

Bibliography

Boyce, William, and Larry Jensen. *Moral Reasoning: A Psychological-Philosophical Integration*. Lincoln: University of Nebraska Press, 1978.

Colby, Anne, and Lawrence Kohlberg. *The Measurement of Moral Judgment*. Cambridge: Cambridge University Press, 1987.

Kohlberg, Lawrence and Dawn Schrader. *The Legacy of Lawrence Kohlberg*. San Francisco: Jossey-Bass. 1990.

Kuhmerker, Lisa, Uwe Gielen, and Richard Hayes. *The Kohlberg Legacy for the Helping Professions*. Birmingham, AL: R.E.P. Books, 1991.

Walsh, Catherine. "Reconstructing Larry: Assessing the Legacy of Lawrence Kohlberg." *HGSE News, Harvard Graduate School of Education & Ed. Magazine* (2000), http://www.gse.harvard.edu/news/features/larry10012000_page1.html.

15

Robert D. Hare

Christina Molinari

It is impossible to detach the concept of deviance from psychopathy. The behavioral manifestations used as diagnostic criteria for this personality disorder, in one way or another, relate to conduct that deviates from social norms. Whether or not it constitutes as criminal, psychopathic behavior assaults our social conscience. From Ponzi schemes to murder, many people become the unfortunate victims of these shameless deeds. Accordingly, many efforts have been made to better understand the psychopathic personality.

A significant portion of the current scholarly knowledge and resources on this topic come from the work of Robert D. Hare. Before this, he, as well as most clinicians, relied heavily on the seminal work of Hervey Cleckley.[1] Hare points out that Cleckley "wrote dramatically about his patients and provided the general public with the first detailed view of psychopathy."[2] This suggests that, historically, accounts of psychopathic individuals were subjective. Addressing a need for more objective methods, Hare and his colleagues established a scientific tool used to measure and diagnose this disorder.[3]

From psychologists to parole officers, professionals in many different fields utilize the breadth of Hare's experience, research, and diagnostic tools in an effort to aptly navigate through the dark and convoluted minds of psychopaths. While these unconscionable individuals once held the upper hand by means of public ignorance, academic and mental health professions now identify them more easily and more consistently.

Robert D. Hare

By all accounts, Robert D. Hare had a typical childhood. In 1934, he was born in Calgary, Alberta. His mother was a French Canadian and his father spent much of his time hitching rides on trains, looking for work as a roofing contractor during the Depression era. In high school, Hare found his classes easy, was able to maintain decent grades, and played several sports, including football.[4]

When Hare enrolled at the University of Alberta for his undergraduate degree, ancient history and archaeology interested him; however, a psychology class left quite an impression. Hare took more psychology-related classes and, ultimately, graduated with his bachelor's degree before attending the University of Alberta for his master's degree.[5]

Subsequently, Hare took a job at the British Columbia Penitentiary as the only psychologist on staff.[6] He left the prison after less than a year and went on to study experimental psychology, receiving his PhD from the University of Western Ontario.[7] There, he wrote his doctoral dissertation on the topic of punishment and its effects on human performance and learning; it was through the research Hare conducted for his dissertation that he was first exposed to writings on psychopathy.[8]

After receiving his PhD, Hare went on to work and continue his research at the University of British Columbia for several decades, where he currently holds an Emeritus Professor position.[9] Hare's work led to his development of the Psychopathy Checklist and Psychopathy Checklist–Revised. Several byproducts of these checklists have since been developed, which Hare has coauthored. Additionally, he has written a number of books, most notably *Snakes in Suits: When Psychopaths Go to Work*, written with Paul Babiak, and *Without Conscience: The Disturbing World of the Psychopaths Among Us*, which Hare authored alone. In addition to books, Hare has also published a multitude of scholarly journal articles related to psychopathy.[10]

Hare has extensive experience consulting with law enforcement agencies, including the Federal Bureau of Investigation (FBI), and has been recognized for his contributions to the field by receiving numerous awards.[11] He also currently served as president of the research and forensic consulting firm, Darkstone Research Group Ltd., where additional methods for the valuation of psychopathy are developed. Training courses on the professional implementation of these assessment tools are also offered.[12]

Theoretical Perspectives: Psychopathy Inception

In the 1960s, while working at the University of British Columbia, Hare began his initial research studying psychopaths at the British Columbia Penitentiary.[13] According to Hare, he had to overcome many hurdles in order to do his research. Psychiatrists and psychologists could not agree on the distinguishing characteristics of this psychological phenomenon.[14] An additional challenge stemmed from difficulties in accurately diagnosing this personality disorder. Traditionally, testing relied heavily on self-reporting measures; however, Hare found that it was not always advantageous to rely on information gathered directly from psychopaths. This is especially true in prison settings, since psychopaths are skilled at presenting themselves in ways that benefit their immediate needs.[15]

The deceptive and manipulative nature of many inmates resulted in inaccurate, conflicting, and often self-serving diagnoses.[16] Hare addressed this problem by avoiding his reliance on self-reports.[17] Instead, he developed a new approach, as he explains,

> The result was a highly reliable diagnostic tool that any clinician or researcher could use and that yielded a richly detailed profile of the personality disorder called psychopathy. We named this instrument the *Psychopathy Checklist*. For the first time, a generally accepted, scientifically sound means of measuring and diagnosing psychopathy became available. The *Psychopathy Checklist* is now used worldwide to help clinicians and researchers distinguish with reasonable certainty true psychopaths from those who merely break the rules.[18]

With a team of qualified clinicians by his side, they identified psychopaths by utilizing lengthy interviews along with a careful examination of their prison files.[19] Over the next 10 years, Hare and his team continued to refine their methods.[20]

The Psychopathy Checklist[21] is a 20-item assessment scale, intended to be completed in a semi-structured interview with the subject. Additionally, data from the subject's clinical chart is used to corroborate information and details obtained in the interview. Each of the items on Hare's checklist has values ranging from zero to 2. Traits that are not present are given a score of zero and traits that are absolutely present receive scores of 2. With 40 being the highest possible score, the cutoff to be a diagnosed psychopath is 30.[22]

Understanding how this diagnostic tool works is important; however, the symptoms explain Hare's theoretical perspectives on psychopathy, defined as ". . . a cluster of both personality traits and socially deviant behaviors."[23] He also insists that "[p]sychopaths are not disoriented or out of touch with reality, nor do they experience the delusions, hallucinations, or intense subjective distress that characterizes most other mental disorders. . . . Their behavior is the result of *choice*, freely exercised."[24] They make conscious, rational decisions to exist hedonistically, regardless whom it affects.

The following sections describe the diagnosing criteria utilized in the Psychopathy Checklist. According to Hare, they fall into two separate categories: emotional and interpersonal aspects, and traits that exemplify a psychopath's lifestyle of socially deviant behavior.[25]

Emotional/Interpersonal Aspects

According to Hare, psychopaths are known to be "glib" and "superficial." Hare states that the charismatic nature of many psychopaths is an asset they often exploit by disarming those around them with laughter, compliments, and clever jokes.[26] They are often likable but, to some, may come off as insincere or "slick." It is also common for psychopaths to assert an expert knowledge in areas such as law, literature, medicine, and psychology.[27] Doing so boosts their fabricated self-image as respectable, trustworthy professionals. Few people would automatically question a new acquaintance who claims to be a doctor. Psychopaths rely on individuals who are unaware of their own credulity.

In addition to a psychopath's superficial charm, they are often "manipulative" and "deceptive." According to Hare, psychopaths are demarcated by their proneness to distorting the truth. In prison, they will often enroll in classes or programs to make it appear as if they are sincere in their attempts to reform. They also make no distinctions between friends and enemies when conning, defrauding, or otherwise deceiving.[28] Not only do psychopaths distort the truth but they tend to relish in the idea of tricking and manipulating someone.[29] They rarely worry about getting caught, as Hare explains.

> With their powers of imagination in gear and focused on themselves, psychopaths appear amazingly unfazed by the possibility—or even by the certainty—of being found out. When caught in a lie or challenged with the truth, they are seldom perplexed or embarrassed—they simply change their stories or attempt to rework the facts so that they appear to be consistent with the lie.[30]

Therefore, it is not skill or foresight that always makes the psychopath a successful manipulator but rather their sheer dedication to deception. Their lack of accountability when caught can be one of the more maddening aspects of dealing with a these individuals.

Psychopaths are also "egocentric" and "grandiose." Hare describes psychopaths as entitled narcissists with overinflated egos. They view themselves as omnipotent and therefore feel warranted in living by their own set of rules.[31] "Psychopaths often come across as arrogant, shameless braggarts—self-assured, opinionated, domineering, and cocky. They love to have power and control over others and seem unable to believe that other people have valid opinions different from theirs."[32] These attributes would make life especially challenging for those who are related to or are in an intimate relationship with a psychopath. Their egocentricity would diminish the reciprocity of respect, appreciation, and love.

When it comes to future plans, Hare states psychopaths often express desires to achieve big goals that they usually have little understanding of and no chance of legitimately attaining. Sometimes, their grandiose self-images pay off. With the right victim, opportunity, or luck, a psychopath can end up ahead, but it is usually at someone else's expense.[33]

"Shallow emotions" are another psychopathic characteristic, according to Hare, who describes this symptom as ". . . a kind of emotional poverty that limits the range and depth of their feelings."[34] He further explains that they often vacillate from cold and detached affects to exaggerated and fleeting emotional displays. Psychopaths also struggle with explaining the subtle differences of many emotional states; for example, Hare states they may attribute feelings of love to the physical response of sexual arousal. Additionally, their emotional forgery is often felt as insincere and peculiar to the astute observer.[35] For those they are able to fool, their ability to mimic emotions allows for the continuation of their ruse. The longer psychopaths keep those around them under the guise they are emotionally congruent, the easier it is for them to perpetuate their manipulation and deceit.

Marked by emotional impoverishment, it follows that another key symptom of this personality disorder is "lack of empathy" for others.[36] Hare describes this as ". . . an inability to construct a mental and emotional 'facsimile' of another person."[37] Hare asserts that psychopaths are individuals who refuse to consider the feelings of others. They tend to view other people as objects and family members as possessions.[38] Any exhibition of benevolence or genuine interest in someone it is not an empathetic response; it is a manipulation tactic geared toward the betterment of their personal interests.

Also, instead of experiencing compassion or pity for vulnerable individuals, Hare states that psychopaths mock them and go out of their way to target those they consider weak. This lack of empathy allows some to commit heinous and disturbingly graphic crimes. While not all psychopaths kill, mutilate, or torture their victims, the ones who do lack appreciation or acknowledgement for how others feel.[39]

A psychopath cannot empathize with others or truly appreciate the depth of his or her destructive actions so, as Hare explicates, psychopaths also experience a lack of guilt or remorse.[40] In many cases, psychopaths will overtly express the fact that they feel no culpability for actions that have hurt others. Other times, psychopaths state they feel remorse, but then later give themselves away with contradicting words or actions. Additionally, resourceful incarcerated psychopaths will say they feel remorse in an attempt further manipulate the prison system.[41]

According to Hare, rationalization plays a major part in a psychopath's ability to cause extraordinary harm with no restraint.[42] They ". . . shrug off personal responsibility for actions that cause shock and disappointment to family, friends, associates, and others who have played by the rules. Usually they have handy excuses for their behavior, and in some cases they deny that it happened at all."[43] Hare also believes that when a psychopath does admit to some action or crime, it will likely be minimized or framed in such a way that completely denies any repercussions to their victims. In fact, psychopaths may even proclaim it is themselves who are the genuine victims.[44] Lacking empathy for others, the pleasure-seeking psychopath would view any obstacle in his/her way as a form of persecution.

Socially Deviant Behaviors

A lack of consideration for potential consequences is a result of the psychopath's "impulsive" nature. Hare explains that delayed gratification is not a strong suit for these individuals; they need immediate pleasure, relief, and satisfaction. Also, unlike most people who learn this skill at an early age, they are unable to compromise and experience the postponement of pleasure. They have a tendency to avoid planning for the future and are generally unconcerned with their lack of accomplishments in life. Instead, psychopaths frequently change their plans and live life one day at a time.[45] Hare highlights this in the following passage:

> One [psychopath] we interviewed used an analogy to explain why he "lived in the moment." "We're always being told to drive defensively, to mentally plan escape routes in case of an emergency, to look well ahead of the car just in front of us. But hey, it's the car just in front of us that's the real danger, and if we always look too far ahead we'll hit it. If I always think about tomorrow I won't be able to live today."[46]

This quote gives away not only this psychopath's impulsivity but also his skill at manipulating the context of social platitudes to rationalize and excuse this behavior.

In addition, psychopaths also have a "need for excitement." Hare asserts that rule breaking is a common way for them to achieve an adrenaline rush. Drug use and frequent job and environment changes alleviate the feelings of monotony and boredom that psychopaths have little tolerance for.[47] Activities or jobs that entail high levels of concentration and are tedious or dull are unlikely to hold their interest.[48] Working as a cashier, mechanic, landscaper, teacher, or cook are just some examples of jobs psychopaths would likely not find interesting.

The impulsive and thrill-seeking psychopath also demonstrates a "lack of responsibility." Hare explains that these individuals often fail to follow through with promises and obligations. They also tend to have poor credit, fail to pay child support, and will regularly be absent from work or exploit the resources of their job. Additionally, psychopaths are known to be abusive or neglectful toward their children.[49] This happens because "psychopaths see children as an inconvenience . . . Typically, they leave children on their own for extended periods or in the care of unreliable sitters."[50] Self-absorbed, even parenthood does not prevent many of them from pursuing immediate gratification, even if puts their own child at risk of physical or emotional harm. If these individuals do act responsibly, they do so as a façade to better meet their selfish needs.

Psychopaths typically have "poor behavior controls" because they react quickly if they feel slighted or insulted.[51] Hare explains that most people have the ability to exercise control over their aggressive behaviors; however, "in psychopaths, these inhibitory controls are weak, and the slightest provocation is sufficient to overcome them."[52] Their low threshold for criticism, according to Hare, causes them to blow up, often over small things. Physical violence and emotional harm are also common. In addition, the context of their outbursts will often come across as inappropriate and will distinctly lack the high level of emotional excitement exhibited by others. Soon after, psychopaths will return to their calm, baseline demeanor as if nothing happened.[53]

Hare lists "adult antisocial behavior" as an additional qualifying symptom for psychopathic individuals.[54] "They consider the rules and expectations of society inconvenient and unreasonable, impediments to the behavioral expression of their inclinations and wishes."[55] As a result, antisocial behavior often begets criminal convictions for these individuals; even within prison walls, the psychopath stands out among the other criminals.[56] Hare notes that "[m]any others do things that, although not illegal, are unethical, immoral, or harmful to others: philandering, cheating on a spouse, financial or emotional neglect of family members, irresponsible use of company resources or funds, to name but a few."[57]

The final symptom of the psychopathic personality is "early behavioral problems." In Hare's experience, psychopaths are often recounted as liars, cheaters, and thieves even in childhood. Setting fires, skipping school, drug use, cruelty to animals, and promiscuousness are all potential behavioral manifestations of the young psychopath. However, Hare warns that there are many children who may display some of these behaviors who do not grow up to be psychopaths. This is especially true for children who are raised in neighborhoods where violence is prevalent or in abusive or disrupted households.[58] Hare discerns that ". . . the psychopath's history of such behaviors is more extensive and serious than that of most others, even when compared with those of siblings and friends raised in similar settings."[59]

Hare notes that the young psychopath may also exhibit extreme brutality toward other children. This may include classmates, neighbors, or siblings. Even at a young age, psychopaths lack the ability to empathize with others and will have nothing stopping them from acting on their impulses to cause pain. While it is not necessary for psychopaths to demonstrate extreme cruelty in childhood, almost all habitually participated in a wide variety of illegal deviant behavior.[60] For example, many children participate in unlawful deviant behaviors, especially when influenced by their friends, and do not grow up to be psychopaths. However, the child who kills neighborhood cats, cuts his sister's hair while she sleeps, and routinely participates in other criminal behavior in the absence of his friends would exemplify the serious and extensive characteristics Hare differentiates as precursory psychopathic behavior.

Influences on Theoretical Development

It is believed that Hare's early experience with a psychopathic inmate played a pivotal role in his future interest, research, and pithy understanding of psychopathy. Hare's description of this prisoner, whom he calls "Ray," suggests this interaction left a lasting impression. Ray motivated Hare's curiosity of psychopathy and left Hare questioning how Ray, and others like him, could behave in such selfish, methodical, and exasperating ways.[61]

Ray was Hare's first patient at a maximum security prison. During their first meeting, Hare explained, Ray maintained intense eye contact and expressed a need for help with a problem—but it was not really help he was looking for. As Ray calmly pulled out a knife, Hare sat nervously. Ray then explained that it was his intention to stab another inmate for making sexual advances on his "partner." Recognizing that this showcase was a test, Hare explained that he was faced with a dilemma: he could report Ray and earn the reputation of being a stiff prison employee who cannot be trusted or become a pushover who says nothing in the hope of building better rapport. Hare ultimately chose to ignore policy and said nothing about Ray's knife.[62]

Throughout the next eight months, Ray's attempts to manipulate Hare were endless. His lies, exaggerations, and constant demands of Hare proved to be cumbersome.[63] Ray's behavior also highlighted his ability to exploit Hare's obvious inexperience with clever and deceptive prison populations.

At one point, Hare was talked into letting Ray work in the prison's kitchen. It was not long before Ray had built a distillery, which subsequently exploded, right under the warden's table in the cafeteria. After some time in solitary confinement, Ray was able, once again, to convince Hare to approve a transfer back to working at his previous job in the prison's auto shop.[64] Hare was ill prepared to engage in a therapeutic relationship with such a sophisticated criminal; without adequate diagnostic tools and no training, he was set up for failure from the start.

After about eight months of working in the prison, Hare left to pursue his doctoral degree. Before leaving, he denied Ray's final request—to allow Ray to work for Hare's father as a roofing contractor. Ray's response was anything but understanding. As Hare explained, his decision to have some work done to his car in the penitentiary's automotive shop would almost cost him his life.[65]

On his way to Ontario, Hare's radiator boiled over. He brought his car to a mechanic, who explained that the float chamber of his carburetor had been filled with ball bearings. Not thinking much of this, Hare got back on the road with his family only to discover soon after that he had no brakes as he barreled down a hill. While no one was hurt, it was uncovered that Hare's brake lines were cut in such a way that fluid in the lines would slowly leak out. Hare explains that the dangerous car problems he experienced could have been merely coincidental; however, he also wrote that he believes Ray was made aware that the car in the auto shop was his.[66]

In a strange turn of events, Hare later bumped into Ray again at the University of British Columbia. As Hare sat at a table helping students register for classes, he heard a familiar voice. There was Ray, lying to another professor about how he had served as Hare's assistant at the prison. Even when confronted, Ray never skipped a beat as he nonchalantly greeted Hare. Reflecting on this, Hare wrote, "[w]hat, in his psychological makeup, gave Ray the power to override reality . . .? As it turned out, I would spend the next twenty-five years doing empirical research to answer that question."[67]

The resources and tools available to clinicians and professionals in the criminal justice field today have undoubtedly benefited from Hare's quest to satiate his curiosity. Through his ordeal with Ray, Hare's firsthand experience undeniably impacted his frame of reference as he began his dissertation research on psychopathy. His ability to identify psychopathic behaviors likely benefited from his past interactions with Ray as well. Additionally, Hare's motivation to depict a clear and accurate portrayal of this personality disorder may have resulted from a feeling of obligation to protect others in his field.

Although Hare's experience with Ray may have catalyzed his interest in psychopathy, Hare acknowledges that many researchers were impacted by Hervey Cleckley's research and theoretical framework on psychopathy.[68] Cleckley's influence is noticeable throughout Hare's work.

Detecting a general lack of attention to what he viewed as a dangerous and pressing concern, Cleckley described the psychopath as the "forgotten man of psychiatry."[69] Responding to Cleckley's apprehension, Hare's devotion has assured psychopaths are no longer overlooked or ignored. He placed a spotlight on this personality disorder and honored Cleckley by refining and progressing his life's work.

As demonstrated with Ray, psychopaths have a keen ability to manipulate power differentials to their advantage and they do this easily because they are devoid of a moral compass. Nevertheless, Hare's theories create more obstacles for these individuals and provide professionals with scholastic weapons of defense. Many psychopaths still find ways to circumnavigate the system, but

Hare's life work has made alleviating the effects of these alpha predators more efficient than ever before.

Conclusion

Deviance defines almost every aspect of a psychopath's personality. Their versatility and malicious nature makes them effective at virtually any crime, resulting in increased academic interest over the past few decades. In addition to the attention given by scholars, trends in current popular culture indicate a morbid infatuation with this dark disorder. Countless movies, books, and television shows depict psychopathic antagonists raping, murdering and otherwise exploiting the trust of others. Viewers are simultaneously enthralled and horrified as they watch each and every one of the attributes Hare has elucidated manifest on the screen.

For professionals who rely on behavioral analysis to understand deviant behavior, Hare's checklist has created a significant advantage. Knowledge of what typifies these individuals increases their predictability and decreases their opportunities to harm. This awareness, in both research and contemporary entertainment mediums, has forced "the forgotten man of psychiatry" out of hiding and under the microscope.

Notes

1. Robert D. Hare, *Without Conscience: The Disturbing World of the Psychopaths Among Us* (New York: Guilford Press, 1999), 28.

2. Hare, *Without Conscience*, 27.

3. Ibid., 32.

4. "Biography – Dr. Robert Hare," http://www.psych.ualberta.ca/GCPWS/Hare/Biography/Hare_bio1.html (accessed November 9, 2013).

5. Ibid.

6. Hare, *Without Conscience*, 9.

7. "Biography – Dr. Robert Hare."

8. Hare, *Without Conscience*, 13–14.

9. "Hare Bio," last modified March 13, 2014, http://www.hare.org/welcome/bio.html.

10. Ibid.

11. Ibid.

12. Ibid.

13. Hare, *Without Conscience*, 28.

14. Ibid., 29.

15. Ibid., 30.

16. Ibid.

17. Ibid., 31.

18. Ibid., 32.

19. Ibid., 31. Hare also explains that the clinicians helping him were extremely familiar with the work of Hervey Cleckley. Hare makes reference to Cleckley several times throughout his book, but specifically states that Cleckley's list of psychopathic traits were provided to Hare's assistants as a guideline while interviewing inmates and reviewing their files.

20. Ibid., 32.

21. Throughout his book, *Without Conscience*, Hare refers to this tool as the "Psychopathy Checklist" and will therefore be referenced as such in this chapter. However, the full name for the updated version that is currently in use is the "Psychopathy Checklist–Revised."

22. "Hare, Robert D.," http://www.encyclopedia.com/doc/1G2-3448300280.html (accessed November 20, 2013).

23. Hare, *Without Conscience*, 25.

24. Ibid., 22.

25. Ibid., 34. The accurate diagnosis of psychopathy using Hare's checklist requires extensive training and a specific scoring manual. Hare emphatically warns readers to not use the symptoms noted in his book to diagnose themselves or anyone else. This warning is also extended to the readers of this chapter.

26. Ibid., 34–35.

27. Ibid., 35.

28. Ibid., 46–50.

29. Ibid., 47. Hare gave an example of a psychopathic woman who bragged about being an amazing liar. She boasted that her skill came from certain tricks she used, such as admitting to something negative about herself as a way to fool the listener into believing the rest of what she said was truthful.

30. Ibid., 46.

31. Ibid., 38.

32. Ibid. To emphasize his point, Hare wrote about one particular psychopath who once described his only weakness as caring about others too much.

33. Ibid., 39.

34. Ibid., 52.

35. Ibid.

36. Ibid., 44.

37. Ibid.

38. Ibid., 45.

39. Ibid.

40. Ibid., 40.

41. Ibid., 40–41.

42. Ibid., 42.

43. Ibid.

44. Ibid., 43.

45. Ibid., 58–59.

46. Ibid.

47. Ibid., 61. Hare exemplified his point by giving an example of a female psychopathic subject who would get a rush from bringing drugs into airports.

48. Ibid., 62.

49. Ibid., 62–63.

50. Ibid., 63. Hare used Diane Downs as a specific example of a psychopathic mother.

51. Ibid., 59.

52. Ibid.

53. Ibid., 59–60.

54. Ibid., 67.

55. Ibid.

56. Ibid., 68.

57. Ibid.

58. Ibid., 66–67.

59. Ibid., 66.

60. Ibid., 67.

61. Ibid., 14.

62. Ibid., 11. According to Hare, Ray never ended up stabbing the other inmate.

63. Ibid., 11–12.

64. Ibid.

65. Ibid., 13.

66. Ibid.

67. Ibid., 14.

68. Ibid., 27.

69. Hervey Cleckley, *The Mask of Sanity,* Rev. ed. (New York: New American Library, 1982), 12.

Bibliography

"Biography – Dr. Robert Hare." University of Alberta. http://www.psych.ualberta.ca/GCPWS/Hare/Biography/Hare_bio1.html (accessed November 9, 2013).

Cleckley, Hervey. *The Mask of Sanity.* Rev. ed. New York: New American Library, 1982.

"Hare Bio" Last modified March 13, 2014. http://www.hare.org/welcome/bio.html.

Hare, Robert D. *Without Conscience: The Disturbing World of the Psychopaths Among Us.* New York: Guilford Press, 1999.

"Hare, Robert D." World of Forensic Science. http://www.encyclopedia.com/doc/1G2-3448300280.html (accessed November 20, 2013).

16

Travis Hirschi

Jessica Vena

It is difficult to understand what motivates an individual to enter a school and unleash a spray of bullets upon innocent victims. School shootings are extremely traumatic in nature, because not only is the possibility for the loss of human life increased but it shatters the idea that schools are a safe haven for children, where violence of this magnitude cannot reach them. Parents send their children to elementary, middle, and high schools expecting them to receive an education, not to be injured or killed.

In reality, school shootings are not a regularly occurring event.[1] However, when one does occur, there is a significant amount of media attention surrounding the incident. Due to the infrequency and the fact that a considerable number of shooters do not survive the event, there is little post-incident evidence as to what drove these individuals to commit such deplorable acts of violence.[2] Each person has a particular personality and demeanor as well as temperament and limits. There are certain life experiences that mold and shape a person into who they are and how they act; but on the other side of that, there are personality characteristics within that affect how a person develops and matures.

It is possible that people have a breaking point, a point at which they can no longer deal with the feelings they have or the situations they are in. It seems that for school shooters, maladaptive coping skills were utilized to ease the tensions they felt, either psychological tensions or interpersonal ones. By looking at classical theories from Travis Hirschi and Howard Becker, understanding the characteristics of school shootings, the shooters involved, and the motivations driving their violence becomes a less daunting and more manageable task.

Even though school shootings are rare, they began to rise beginning in the 1990s, which overlapped with the increased crime rate of the 1960s through the 1990s.[3] This type of school violence differed from other types of violence because instead of being gang related or involving individual disputes, there were attacks on multiple victims, with no specific target; these type of shootings were sometimes deemed "rampage" shootings, and the shooters were not interested in exacting revenge on specific targets but rather on making a declaration with violence and propelling that violence onto their targets.[4] Through these violent acts, it seems that the shooters have a significant amount of built-up hostility and aggression that needs an outlet, and the only way to release that is to engage in a final attention-getting act, such as a school shooting.[5]

Violence of this magnitude does not simply go unnoticed, especially when the shootings end in tragedy. The media plays a significant role in how the slaying of innocent victims is portrayed and how the perpetrators are depicted. Even though the media has a duty to report on incidents like these, Michael Rocque explains that the media can sometimes overreact to school shootings, which leads to the public panicking and miscalculating the risk of violence in their children's schools.[6] The immense amount of media coverage following a school shooting tends to open the door to an intense amount of scrutiny and the creation of a school shooter profile that can lead to an over-identification.[7] Following the Columbine High School shooting, the media profiled the perpetrators by honing in on external facts about Eric Harris and Dylan Klebold, like their interest in violent video games and gothic culture. This might not be a completely rational explanation, but it is an explanation nonetheless. Because of the amplified emotions of people in the aftermath of a school shooting, it seems people find it much easier to place the blame on an external factor that seems just as appalling as the act itself.

However, the media neglected to focus on the internal factors at play, like the depression that was plaguing the young men. Instead, they decided to deem the incident a social problem.[8] It is much easier to place the blame on a social issue rather than on the individual, because school shooters are typically adolescents and it is hard to believe that a person so young can suffer from so much pain; and when a tragedy like this happens, people become terrified and desperately want a way to identify this type of evil so that future events can be stopped or prevented. In order to make sense of a school shooting, the focus needs to be on the psychology of the individual so that future violence can be predicted.[9] In fact, as with most school shootings, the violence came from the perpetrators' own diary entries and poems and not from violent video games or song lyrics.[10]

Moreover, due to the increased number of school shootings, the Federal Bureau of Investigation (FBI) produced a threat assessment specifically for school shooters. This assessment lists characteristics of potential shooters and describes warning signs.[11] However, The FBI does warn against the over-identification of characteristics, stating the following:

No one or two traits or characteristics should be considered in isolation or given more weight than the others. Any of these traits, or several, can be seen in students who are not contemplating a school shooting or other act of violence. The key to identifying a potentially dangerous threat under this four-pronged assessment model is that there is evidence of problems on a majority of the items in each of the four areas. However, there is no "magical" number of traits or constellation of traits which will determine what students may present a problem. Hopefully, subsequent empirical research in this area will determine which are the significant traits and how they should be weighted. However, a practical and common sense application of this model indicates that the more problems which are identified in each of the four prongs, the greater the level of concern for the assessor.[12]

There is no set formula when deciding who is going to become a school shooter and who is not, but instead individual personality characteristics as well as psychological characteristics need to be consulted before making that determination.

The research surrounding the shooters themselves is sometimes limiting because often they commit suicide, but by examining their behavior and personality prior to the incident, a clear pattern emerges. R. M. Holmes and S. T. Holmes (2010) describe a school shooter to be typically a white male who is usually around the age of the victims, a current or past student, resident of a suburban or rural community, middle class, and suffering from feelings of disenfranchisement. Peter Langman, who was also interested in the typology of school shooters, examined 10 school shootings and was able to group the shooters into three categories: traumatized, psychotic, and psychopathic.[13] Langman explains the difference between the three types when he states,

> The traumatized shooters all came from broken homes. They suffered physical and/or sexual abuse. Each had at least one parent with substance abuse problems, and each had at least one parent with a criminal history. Unlike the traumatized shooters, the psychotic shooters all came from intact families with no histories of abuse, parental substance abuse, or parental incarceration. The psychotic shooters exhibited symptoms of either schizophrenia or schizotypal personality disorder, including paranoid delusions, delusions of grandeur, and auditory hallucinations. The psychopathic shooters also came from intact families with no histories of abuse or significant family dysfunction. They demonstrated narcissism, a lack of empathy, a lack of conscience, and sadistic behavior.[14]

It is again important to note that not every individual who suffers from similar personality typology will become a school shooter; instead, there needs to be the perfect combination of factors to result in a person committing such a violent act.

Alongside psychological issues, interpersonal issues of the school shooter need to be addressed. A majority of the potential school shooters suffer from not only depression[15] but also from suicidal thoughts and ideations.[16] Another common theme with school shooters is the psychological suffering over supposed rejection, as well as rejection from groups of peers or society.[17] This rejection is seen in the diaries left behind by the shooters, which express feelings of alienation and vengefulness.[18] In fact, 71 percent of the school shooters studied felt mistreated, bullied, and wronged by others.[19]

This type of social rejection that perpetrators of school shootings identify is not only connected to aggression but comes in three forms: teasing, ostracism, and romantic rejection.[20] Mark Leary, Robin Kowalski, Laura Smith, and Stephen Phillips explain how teasing can have a powerful impact on individuals when they state the following:

> People who are the victims of bullying and teasing receive a clear message that the perpetrators do not like, value or accept them. Furthermore, bullying and teasing typically occur in the presence of other people, thereby providing an element of public humiliation as well. Public attacks may connote even greater interpersonal rejection than private ones because the perpetrator communicates not only that he or she dislikes the victim but is willing to publicly let the rejection be known. In the case of the Columbine shootings, media reports widely acknowledged that the shooters had been taunted and humiliated by other students, raising the question of whether bullying is a common feature of school shootings.[21]

With ostracism, individuals who are unique or different from the normal social characteristics around them stand the chance of being ignored because either others do not give them a second glance or they are ignoring them on purpose.[22] This type of rejection can be clearly seen in the cases of the Columbine shooting, the Dunblane Primary School shooting, and the Virginia Tech shooting. These individuals were ostracized by their peers either on purpose or because they did not give them "the time of day."

The third type of rejection, romantic rejection, occurs when an individual is rejected romantically, which can ultimately ignite feelings of anger and aggression.[23] These types of interpersonal rejection are examined in most school shooting cases,[24] which can lead to a level of paranoia that is lethal. Donald Dutton, Katherine White, and Dan Fogarty explain how deadly paranoia can be when they state,

The paranoid individual is obsessed with revenge and justifies the revenge as "payback" (for a perceived injustice) and is thin-skinned or hypersensitive to perceived slights. It is worth noting that even in non-paranoid populations, vengeance is a powerful motive and capable of altering compassion for the target.[25]

Although individually these factors do not predict that a person will commit a school shooting, a culmination of factors provide an increased risk, which could lead them to engage in various acts of violence and terror, including a school shooting.

It is extremely difficult to understand which motivating factors contribute to such gruesome acts of violence, but by looking at the theoretical perspectives of Hirschi and Becker, a slight understanding can be achieved. Travis Hirschi describes delinquent behavior occurring when an individual's connection to society is weakened or shattered.[26] Hirschi explained further that a lack of attachment to another individual or individuals is not just an indicator of psychopathy but is actual psychopathy, and the resulting violation of societal norms is just a consequence.[27]

By looking at the profiles of school shooters, it seems that a majority of them were loners and outcasts who exhibited behavior that operated on the outskirts of normal society. This detachment that an individual engages in is not simply black and white; as Hirschi explains, it is part of a process that is not just the isolation from others but involves a working interpersonal conflict.[28] The interpersonal conflict that an individual is suffering from can lead to a pool of pent-up hostility and derives from society,[29] and allowing that much hostility and anger to sit and fester does nothing good for the individual and can result in horrific consequences. When researching school shooters, Dutton et al. explain how similar feelings of rejection and resentment were present in their writings and how it could have led to violence:

> A central theme that runs through these diaries is one of feeling rejected, dismissed, disrespected, and devalued by an "in-group" invariably depicted as "jocks and preppies" of wanting vengeance for this mistreatment. The "in-group" is despised for being "superficial" and for getting unwarranted status.[30]

It can be assumed that if an individual detaches from society and society's norms, he will not be responsive to others' opinions, which allows him to be able to deviate how he pleases.[31] This brings emphasis to the idea that attachment plays a major role in the positive social bonding of an individual to society and others, which could possibly prevent deviant behavior from developing.

Howard Becker also explored the idea of individuals as outsiders and their path to deviant behavior. Becker explained that social groups create rules and guidelines for specific people, whom they then label as outsiders, which in turn prompts those newly labeled outsiders to become deviant.[32] That deviance is only a result if the label of outsider has been effectively applied.[33] So if a child in school does not fit in, or is different and unique from most other students, the group that fits the norm collectively decides that the individual should be outcast, therefore leading to that child's deviant behavior. Being labeled an outsider can have a dramatic effect on that individual, both mentally and emotionally. If people label another person as an outsider enough times, an individual might not only believe it but also resent it, which could cause him/her to retaliate by engaging in delinquent behavior. Would Eric Harris and Dylan Klebold have committed such a horrific crime if they had not been cast out by their peers? Did the label of an outsider push them over the edge? The power of a label is so extreme that it can alter how a person sees himself and how others see him to the point that he loses himself.

Becker also explains that the deviance exhibited by the outsider is a direct response to the other individuals' behavior and that the rules that are in place in society can be selectively applied.[34] This only perpetuates the idea that individuals deemed as outsiders can be singled out because they do not follow the norms of society. Allowing the label of outsider to seep its way inside a person can only lead to devastating results, whether they internalize their pain or externalize it.

The human mind is an incredible thing; it can be our greatest asset or our biggest downfall. Every person has their own set of demons they face everyday and perpetrators of school shootings are no different. However, school shooters face their demons in a way that results in the deaths or injuries of innocent victims. Through the research, it is clear that individuals who commit school shootings, like Eric Harris, Dylan Klebold, and Seung-Hui Cho, are plagued with a mental disorder that they could not escape and decided to deal with their issues in a tragic way.

Schools are supposed to be a safe haven where children go to learn and grow, so even though school shootings are rare,[35] their effects are so painful that they completely shatter any trust people have in the idea that schools are a violence-free zone. In order for people to feel safer, they want a way to identify the type of person who can commit such a crime, but unfortunately there is no such profile.[36] However, in most cases of school shootings, another person is aware of their intentions,[37] so the closest possible solution to avoiding such an extreme act of violence is getting the individual the help they need by providing active and early prevention.

Notes

1. Christopher J. Ferguson, Mark Coulson, and Jane Barnett, "Psychological Profiles of School Shooters: Positive Directions and One Big Wrong Turn," *Journal of Police Crisis Negotiations* 11, no. 2 (2011): 141–58, doi:10.1080/15332586.2011.581523, 141.

2. Ibid.

3. Ibid., 142.

4. Michael Rocque, "Exploring School Rampage Shootings: Research, Theory, and Policy," *Social Science Journal* 49, no. 3 (2012): 304–13, doi:10.1016/j.soscij.2011.11.001, 306.

5. Ibid., 308.

6. Ibid., 310.

7. Ferguson, Coulson, and Barnett, "Psychological Profiles," 144.

8. Ibid., 145.

9. Ibid., 152.

10. Ibid., 151.

11. Federal Bureau of Investigation (FBI), "The School Shooter: A Threat Assessment Perspective," FBI.gov. http://www.fbi.gov/stats-services/publications/school-shooter (accessed October 13, 2013), 2.

12. Ibid., 15.

13. Peter Langman, "Rampage School Shooters: A Typology," *Aggression and Violent Behavior* 14, no. 1 (2009): 79–86, doi:10.1016/j.avb.2008.10.003, 81.

14. Ibid.

15. Ferguson, Coulson, and Barnett, "Psychological Profiles," 151.

16. Rocque, "Exploring School Rampage Shootings," 308.

17. Mark R. Leary, Robin M. Kowalski, Laura Smith, and Stephen Phillips, "Teasing, Rejection, and Violence: Case Studies of the School Shootings," *Aggressive Behavior* 29, no. 3 (2003): 202–14, doi: 10.1002/ab.10061, 202.

18. Ibid., 203.

19. Ferguson, Coulson, and Barnett, "Psychological Profiles," 151.

20. Leary, Kowalski, Smith, and Phillips, "Teasing, Rejection, and Violence," 203.

21. Ibid., 203–04.

22. Ibid., 203.

23. Ibid., 204.

24. Ibid., 210.

25. Donald Dutton, Katherine White, and Dan Fogarty, "Paranoid Thinking in Mass Shooters," *Aggression and Violent Behavior* 18, no. 5 (2013): 548–53, http://dx.doi.org/10.1016/j.avb.2013.07.012, 551.

26. Travis Hirschi, "A Control Theory of Delinquency," in *Classics of Criminology*, ed. Joseph E. Jacoby et al., 4th ed. (Long Grove, IL: Waveland Press, 2012), 321–28.

27. Ibid., 322.

28. Ibid.

29. Ibid..

30. Dutton, White, and Fogarty, "Paranoid Thinking in Mass Shooters," 550.

31. Hirschi, "A Control Theory of Delinquency," 322.

32. Howard S. Becker, "Outsiders," in *Classics of Criminology*, ed. Joseph E. Jacoby et al., 4th ed. (Long Grove, IL: Waveland Press, 2012), 354–61.

33. Ibid., 354.

34. Ibid., 355.

35. Ferguson, Coulson, and Barnett, "Psychological Profiles," 141.

36. FBI, "Threat Assessment," 2.

37. Ferguson, Coulson, and Barnett, "Psychological Profiles," 153.

Bibliography

Becker, Howard S. "Outsiders." In *Classics of Criminology*, ed. Joseph E. Jacoby, Theresa A. Severance, and Alan S. Bruce. 4th ed. Long Grove, IL: Waveland Press, 2012, 354–361.

Dutton, Donald, Katherine White, and Dan Fogarty. "Paranoid Thinking in Mass Shooters." *Aggression and Violent Behavior* 18, no. 5 (2013): 548–53. http://dx.doi.org/10.1016/j.avb.2013.07.012 (accessed October 16, 2013).

Federal Bureau of Investigation. "The School Shooter: A Threat Assessment Perspective." FBI.gov. http://www.fbi.gov/stats-services/publications/school-shooter (accessed October 13, 2013).

Ferguson, Christopher J., Mark Coulson, and Jane Barnett. "Psychological Profiles of School Shooters: Positive Directions and One Big Wrong Turn." *Journal of Police Crisis Negotiations* 11, no. 2 (2011): 141–58.

Hirschi, Travis. "A Control Theory of Delinquency." In *Classics of Criminology*, ed. Joseph E. Jacoby, Theresa A. Severance, and Alan S. Bruce. 4th ed. Long Grove, IL: Waveland Press, 2012, 321–28 .

Holmes, R. M., and S. T. Holmes. *Fatal Violence: Case Studies and Analysis of Emerging Forms*. Boca Raton, FL: CRC Press, 2001.

Jacoby, Joseph E. *Classics of Criminology*. 4th ed. Long Grove, IL: Waveland Press, 2012.

Langman, Peter. "Rampage School Shooters: A Typology." *Aggression and Violent Behavior* 14, no. 1 (2009): 79–86.

Leary, Mark R., Robin M. Kowalski, Laura Smith, and Stephen Phillips. "Teasing, Rejection, and Violence: Case Studies of the School Shootings." *Aggressive Behavior* 29, no. 3 (2003): 202–14.

Rocque, Michael. "Exploring School Rampage Shootings: Research, Theory, and Policy." *Social Science Journal* 49, no. 3 (2012): 304–13.

17

Social Disorganization

AnnaMaria Tejeda

In the United States, it is estimated that between 14 percent and 30 percent of all urban youth are involved in a gang at some point in their lives.[1] The average age for a youth gang member is between 12 and 24 years.[2] It has been reported that youth gang members commit approximately 373,000 violent crimes each year, which account for 6 percent of all violent crimes.[3] In 2011, it was estimated that there were 29,900 gangs and 782,500 gang members throughout the United States.[4] It was also reported that gang activity was concentrated in mostly urban areas.[5] The issue raised in this chapter is what leads to the formation of gangs in mostly urban areas. Specifically, if minors join gangs due to lack of structure and monitoring within their community, does the gang offer them the protection they seek and does gang membership protect the minor from violent victimization?

This chapter offers a look into this area from a key perspective, one of prominent research studies. While each of the chapters in this text has established its own approach, this chapter shows the importance of peer-reviewed contemporary research. The chapter compiles research in an explanatory fashion, allowing for the development of theory understanding regarding gang membership and violence, a key component of deviant and criminal behavior in American society.

Clifford Shaw and Henry McKay researched the patterns of crime in the urban areas of Chicago.[6] They found communities were socially disadvantaged due to their poverty level, ethnic and racial mix, and declining population due to migration.[7] The result of the social disadvantage in the community was an increased rate in crime within the urban areas. In addition to the social disadvantage there is a lack of social controls, which results in the inability of the community, parents, and neighborhood to monitor the minors.[8] Delinquency among the minors flourishes within neighborhoods that are socially disorganized and when the community is unable to control crime.[9] Further studies have been conducted to expound upon Shaw and McKay's work. Several studies have identified predictive factors of social disorganization that lead minors to gang involvement.[10] Minors become involved in gangs due to the social disadvantage they experience within their community, the lack of supervision by parents, and lack of social outlets within their community.

By joining a gang, minors feel a sense of bond with others who are in the same socially disadvantaged situation. They feel the bond they have with other minors will protect them from the social problems of their community. The reality is that they are at greater risk for being victimized by fellow gang members and rival gang members. They are oftentimes victimized through an initiation ceremony of being "jumped in" to the gang.[11] Once in the gang, they are exposed to more criminal activity due to their mere involvement in gang life. They are often in possession of weapons and drugs.[12] In addition, they are more likely to be involved in drug sales, which expose them to potential victimization.[13] Minors who are involved in a gang are actually at greater risk of violent victimization and are not protected as they perceived prior to joining the gang.[14]

Shaw and McKay specifically focused their research on an urban environment.[15] They found that crime rates were higher in urban areas due to the social disadvantage of the community.[16] Specifically, the lower economic social class of the residents, the constant migration of an immigrant population, and the mix of ethnic and racial persons in the community contributed to the crime rate.[17] They found key factors explained the social disorganization of a community that had a relationship with the impact of crime within the community. The social disorganization of a community contributes to a weakening of the social controls, which results in an increase in crime and delinquency.

Robert Sampson discussed several causal factors within a community that lead to an increase in crime.[18] A major factor leading to an increase in crime and youth delinquency is unstable families or single-parent families.[19] Some families may not participate in community organizations, which can weaken the effects of formal community social controls. Some families may not properly supervise their children, or they may not become involved in informal social control activities such as neighborhood watch or merely watching over the youth playing outside. All the stated factors lead to social disorganization within a community and an increase in crime. Sampson and W. Byron Groves went on to define both formal and informal controls to support a community and decrease social disorganization. They defined informal controls as ties to neighbors, and formal controls as participating in organized activities within the community. The lack of social controls, poverty, increased mobility of residents, and ethnic heterogeneity lead to social disorganization within a community.[20]

Poverty within a community decreases the ability of the community members to provide controlled youth activities and, thus, the ability to monitor the youth.[21] The migration of various ethnic and racial persons within a community may also reduce the chances for the people of the community to develop strong ties with one another. The constant mobility within a community may also reduce the chances for people to develop bonds with their neighbors and strong ties within the community. All the stated factors lead to further social disorganization within a community and an increase in crime and delinquency.

Due to the level of social disorganization within a community, there is a decrease in the social controls over minors, which increases the potential for crime and delinquency. Due to the lack of social controls and increased social disorganization within a community, minors turn to gangs to replace the social outlet that are missing from their lives. Sampson and Groves discussed that social disorganization explained the inability of a community to supervise and control minors who become involved in delinquent activity and gangs.[22] Siu Wong discussed two main causal reasons for an increase in youth crime and violence. He found that poverty and mobility were associated with violent crimes such as homicide and robbery, which are both related to social disorganization.[23]

David Eitle et al. examined family dynamics that are associated with youth delinquency. They include having a criminal parent or other family member, lack of a bond between the parent and child, inconsistent or overly strict discipline in the home, lack of supervision of the minors, and families with conflict.[24]

Sampson and Groves conducted research to test social disorganization theory as defined by Shaw and McKay. They surveyed 10,905 households from 238 areas in England and Wales in 1982.[25] In 1984, a total of 11,030 households were surveyed again. They found that communities with lower rates of organization, which reported fewer ties to their neighbors and were unable to supervise the minors, had higher levels of crime and delinquency.[26]

Other research examined the level of fear and mistrust within a community based upon the level of social disorganization.[27] It surveyed 2,482 people in Illinois by telephone. The study participants ranged in age from 18 to 92 years. Over half the study sample was female, and 84 percent were white. The study determined that those who reported living in communities where they observed a high level of social disorder (such as graffiti, vandalism, abandoned buildings, etc.) reported higher levels of fear and mistrust of their neighbors.[28] It also found that those who participated in informal social controls (such as improvement association, neighborhood watch, or street beautification) developed more ties with their neighbors and reported lower levels of fear and mistrust.[29] The researchers concluded that it is the community and the level of neighbor participation that determine the level of a person's fear and mistrust of their neighbors.[30]

Wong researched the effect of social disorganization and family disruption as it related to youth crime.[31] He studied the youth crime rates and census data from 483 Canadian municipalities between 1996 and 2001.[32] He found higher levels of social disorganization and family disruption in urban municipalities.[33] Families with a single parent, families with a lower income, and families that lived in ethnically heterogeneous areas were found to have higher rates of youth crime for both males and females.[34] His findings confirm Shaw and McKay's prior work in social disorganization. It was noted that the rates of youth crime were higher in smaller municipalities, which were more susceptible to the problems of social disorganization.[35]

Gang Membership and Associated Victimization

Social disorganization explains that the increased level of social disorganization leads to a lack of social controls and the inability of parents and the community to monitor and supervise the minors. The result is an increase in crime and delinquency. With a lack of structured activities, an area for recreation, or proper supervision, the youth congregate on the street. Without the guidance from schools, churches, parents, adult mentors, or community leaders, the youth turn to gangs to provide the social support they are lacking in their life.

Additional research reported one of the main reasons why youth become involved in gangs is the lack of proper supervision by parents.[36] Paul Bellair and Thomas McNulty determined that gang members who sell drugs in disadvantaged neighborhoods engage in more violent acts of crime.[37] Katrina Rufino et al. reported gang members are actually at greater risk for being victimized by fellow gang members (through involvement in drug use, drug sales, and other criminal activity) and rival members (by assault and drive-by shootings).[38] In addition, girls tend to join gangs to escape other types of abuse (such as physical, sexual, verbal, and emotional) they are suffering in their home.[39] Rufino et al. reported participation in gang activity increases the likelihood of being victimized and reduces the gang members' ties to formal social mechanisms to stop the victimization.[40]

To join the gang, many may be victimized through a "jumping in" ritual in which they are beaten by members of the gang they are attempting to join.[41] In addition, they may also be subject to discipline from their own gang for violations of the rules.[42] Through involvement in gang activities, they are involved in criminal acts such as possession of weapons, drug possession and use, and other violent crimes that expose them to potential victimization.[43] Dana Peterson et al. (2004) report gang members are more likely than non-gang members to be involved in drug sales. This exposes the gang member to an increase in potential victimization.[44] If the gang member is in possession of drugs for sale and is victimized by a rival gang member, he is less likely to report the incident to law enforcement. In addition, law enforcement may be less inclined to follow up on a report of a gang member being victimized by another gang member.[45]

Terrence Taylor et al. discussed several protective factors to prevent violent gang victimization. Specifically, parents monitoring the youth and establishing a bond with their children, the establishment of pro–social peer bonds, a commitment to school, and having structured activities.[46] Within socially disadvantaged communities there is a high possibility that the protective factors are not met, which forces the youth to find alternative social outlets.[47]

Antoinette Farmer and Timothy Hairston discussed various risk factors that predict youth involvement with gangs.[48] They link gang membership with negative personal life events, low self-esteem, lack of family structure, low family socioeconomic status, associating with delinquent peers, lack of engagement in school, and feeling unsafe within their neighborhood.[49] They researched further predictors of gang involvement. They conducted a secondary review of the School Success Profile, which is a survey administered to middle and high school students.[50] The original survey was administered between 2001 and 2005 to 37,354 students from 318 schools across seven states.[51] The secondary data that was reviewed for the study included 19,079 students from 67 schools.[52] The study sample included minors who were between 9 and 23 years old.[53] The average age of the study sample was 13 years old. They concluded that there are specific risk factors that contribute to gang membership. Specifically, being African American, being male, having low self-esteem, being rejected by peers, and perceiving one's neighborhood to be unsafe.[54] It is noted that they did not find any causal link between the minors living in a single-parent household and gang membership.[55]

Eitle et al. researched factors that predict gang membership. The study sample included 1,286 students attending public school in the 1990s.[56] The study was conducted at four intervals. They found that those who reported joining a gang reported being involved in delinquent activities prior to joining the gang.[57] They also found that those who came from "broken and impoverished homes while growing up were more likely to have joined a gang."[58] In addition, growing up with family financial hardship was a predicting factor for youth gang membership.[59]

David Pyrooz, Andrew Fox, and Scott Decker reported that not all socially disorganized neighborhoods encounter a problem with minors joining a gang.[60] They report the level of gang membership is higher in neighborhoods where the level of disadvantage is more pervasive.[61] They researched the relation between heterogeneity, economic disadvantage, and gang membership in a community.[62] They used data from the 2000 U.S. census and the 2000 Law Enforcement Management and Administrative Services.[63] They found that increased ethnic heterogeneity and economic disadvantage relate to an increase in gang membership.[64]

A correlation has been established in the association between gang structure and criminal activity as it relates to victimization. The study sample used data from the Arrestee Drug Abuse Monitoring program of juveniles booked into three detention facilities between 1999 and 2003.[65] The majority of the study sample were male, who reported that 87 percent were current gang members and 74 percent were former gang members. The majority of each group reported there was gang activity in their neighborhood; people who lived on their street were also involved in gang activity, and rival gang members lived in their neighborhood.[66] The researchers concluded that there is a positive relationship between the structural organization of a gang and the involvement in drug crime.[67] Further, as the organization of a gang became more defined, there was an increase in gang members' involvement in criminal activity and exposure to victimization.[68]

Abigail Fagan and Emily Wright researched the association between socially disadvantaged neighborhoods and delinquent offending as it relates to gender differences.[69] They report that social activities for girls are often monitored more closely than activities for boys.[70] As such, girls tend to have more parental supervision and are exposed to more social and community controls than their male counterparts.[71] They surveyed 6,228 children, adolescents, and young adults living in 80 different areas of Chicago.[72] They included only responses from minors aged 9, 12, and 15.[73] The survey took place between 1994 and 1995.[74] They found that peer delinquency was stronger for girls than for boys.[75] In addition, lack of social controls increased the likelihood of violence among girls.[76]

Another study reviewed the motivating factors of ethnic and gender differences as they relate to gang membership. They interviewed 48 self-reported gang members in Hawaii in 1992 and 1993.[77] The study sample included 35 males and 13 females.[78] The average age of the males was 16 years, and the average age of the females was 15 years.[79] Over half the males and three-quarters of the females reported being physically abused.[80] In addition, over half the females reported being sexually abused or assaulted.[81] Nearly all the study sample reported having a sibling who belonged to a gang.[82] They concluded that "boredom, lack of resources, and high visibility of crime in their neglected communities" led the minors to bond with one another and join a gang to provide what was missing from their social outlets within their homes and communities.[83]

Terrence Taylor et al. researched the association between gang membership and victimization. The study sample included 5,935 eighth-grade public school students from 42 schools across 11 states.[84] The study sample was nearly equal for males to females, and 62 percent reported living in a two-parent household.[85] The age of the study sample ranged from 13 to 15 years old.[86] They determined that gang members reported more violent victimization than non–gang members.[87] Notably, those living in a single-parent home were found to have a one-fourth greater chance of being violently victimized.[88] Also, males were twice as likely to be violently victimized than their female gang member counterparts.[89] They concluded that gang membership was associated with unsupervised community activities, use of drugs and alcohol, involvement in delinquent acts, and increased exposure to violent victimization.[90]

Another study researched the relationship between gang membership and violent victimization. Researchers wanted to determine the effectiveness of the Gang Resistance Education and Training (GREAT) program, which is a school-based gang prevention program.[91] The study was conducted in two parts. The first study sample included 5,935 eighth-grade public school students from 42 schools across 11 states who completed a self-report questionnaire in 1995.[92] The second phase took place between 1995 and 1999 and included 3,500 sixth- and seventh-grade students from 22 middle schools across six states who completed surveys.[93] They determined that gang members reported higher levels of victimization than non–gang members prior to joining a gang, that the incidents of victimization were highest when a minor was an active member of the gang, and victimization decreased once the minor left the gang.[94] They also researched whether minors who joined the gang for protection were actually protected by the gang through a decrease in victimization.[95] They concluded that minors who joined a gang for protection are not exposed to less victimization.[96] Thus, joining a gang does not offer any protection from victimization as perceived by those who join.[97] Rather, those involved in a gang are exposed to more violent victimization than those not in a gang.[98]

Perceptions of social disorganization as it relates to gang membership and victimization are vital. Surveys were administered to 2,414 inmates in 14 Florida jails.[99] A total of 370 inmates, or 15 percent, reported being members of a gang.[100] The average age of gang members was 28 years, while the average age of a non–gang member was 33 years.[101] They found that gang members most often reported being the perpetrators of both property and personal crime.[102] Gang members were also more likely to report being victims of both property and personal crimes.[103] Social disorder was found to be the main risk predictor for property crime victimization among gang members.[104] The researchers postulated that gang members may perceive less risk in their community regardless of the social disorder, and feel their association with a gang will insulate them from property victimization. However, the study concluded that gang membership did not insulate them from victimization but instead actually placed them at greater risk than their non–gang member counterparts.[105]

A significant variable in gang membership is the perception of safety. Research examined the link between gang activity and the risk of potential victimization. The study sample included data collected between 1999 and 2003 during the Arizona Arrestee Drug Abuse Monitoring program.[106] The program included self-report information from male and female juveniles booked into two detention facilities. The study sample included 909 juveniles.[107] Of the total, one-quarter had been charged with a violent crime, 20 percent had been charged with a property offense, and 12 percent had been changed with a drug offense.[108] The study sample were 81 percent male, and they were on average 15 years old at the time they were booked into the juvenile detention facility.[109] Of the sample, 444 reported they had never been in a gang, 136 reported to be active gang members, 65 reported to be former gang members, and 264 reported to be gang associates.[110] The researchers concluded that of the reported gang members, 98 percent reported being a victim of violent crime.[111] Regarding reports of violent victimization within the last month, 48 percent of gang members, 92 percent of prior gang members, and 80 percent of gang associates reported violent victimization.[112] This indicates that exposure to victimization does not end once the minor leaves the gang. However, as expected, current gang membership greatly increased the likelihood for violent victimization.[113]

Chris Melde et al. researched actual and perceived victimization by gang members. They report that "gang members are at an increased risk of victimization because of their gang membership."[114] The study sample included 1,450 students from 15 schools in four states during the 2004–2005 school year.[115] There were two parts to the study: a questionnaire and annual follow-up surveys for three consecutive years. The study sample included 46 percent males and 54 percent females.[116] They found that minors who reported being part of a gang reported the suffered more instances of victimization.[117] Minors who reported joining a gang between the original questionnaire and the first follow-up interview reported the highest levels of victimization.[118] Those who reported being part of a gang reported more perceived risk of victimization.[119] Those who reported to have left the gang prior to the first follow-up interview reported lower levels of perceived risk of victimization.[120] Those who reported being part of a gang reported lower levels of perceived fear of crime.[121] While gang membership does not provide protective factors from victimization, it appears the gang members are emotionally protected as they fear crime less due to their gang activity.[122] The researchers also explained the decrease in fear of crime as part of the gang culture to be fearless.[123]

J. C. Barnes et al. researched the genetic and environmental predictors of gang membership and victimization. They reviewed data from the National Longitudinal Study of Adolescent Health that included data from 132 middle and high schools.[124] The study took place in four parts, starting in 1996.[125] The first part included a questionnaire that included 90,000 students. In the second part, a sample of the students was selected to be interviewed at home with their parents or caregivers. In total, 20,745 students and 17,700 parents and caregivers participated in the second part of the study.[126] Approximately four years after the second part, the students were interviewed again. By this stage of the study, many of the students had reached age 18.[127] The last part of the study took place 13 years after the first part and included a personal interview with 15,701 of the original study sample.[128] The researchers concluded there were both genetic and environmental links to gang membership. It was found that if a sibling had joined a gang, there was a 250 percent increased chance that the other siblings would become gang members as well.[129] In addition, gang members were found to have a higher rate of victimization over time.[130]

Rufino et al. researched the link between gang membership and victimization of adults. Given that many minors remain involved in their gang and participate in criminal activity, they expose themselves to potential jail sentences that keep them incarcerated into early adulthood. The area researched was victimization by gang members prior to their incarceration. A total of 84 male inmates of a Texas prison were interviewed for the study.[131] They were identified as gang members through either self-report, identification by the jail operators, or through identification of their tattoos.[132] A control group of 133 inmates were also interviewed who were not part of a gang.[133] The gang members were on average 28 years old, while the non–gang members were on average 34 years old.[134] Gang members reported more often than non–gang members being the victim of assault, aggravated assault, and drive-by shootings.[135] Those gang members who reported being victimized were younger when they joined the gang as compared to the non-victimized gang members, to have visible tattoos regarding their gang, to report having a parent or other family member in their gang, and to have held a special rank within the gang.[136]

Jodi Lane and Kathleen Fox (2012) researched the perceived social disorganization as it relates to their level of fear of personal and gang victimization among incarcerated adults.[137] It was explained that many adult gang members grew up in socially disadvantaged communities and have been involved with gang activity since they were minors, which exposed them to the potential for greater victimization.[138] Fear of crime may lead adults to engage in more crime, such as carrying a weapon, in order to protect themselves from becoming a victim.[139] The researchers postulated that those most likely to be victimized would be most afraid of crime regardless of their gang membership status.[140] Even if a gang member fears crime, they will not express fear due to feeling invincible and to believing the gang will protect them.[141] Their study sample included 2,414 inmates confined to 14 Florida jails between 2008 and 2009.[142] Gang members and former gang members were more likely to report they perceived physical and social disorder in their neighborhood. Gang members reported more violent victimization as compared to former gang members and non–gang members.[143] Perceived risk of personal victimization was reported slightly more often by gang members as compared to former gang members and non–gang members.[144] The researchers postulated that gang members and former gang members live in more socially disorganized neighborhoods as compared to non–gang members. In addition, given the perceived risk of victimization, gang members appear to perceive and acknowledge that their gang activity places them at greater risk for victimization.[145]

Discussion

The work of Shaw and McKay (1942) identified that certain communities are socially disadvantaged due to the poverty level, the high racial and ethnic mix, and the increased migration of the community members within the neighborhood.[146] The social disadvantage was observed to be most prevalent in urban communities.[147] Within a socially disadvantaged community, there are certain factors that predict the level of crime and delinquency. The factors include single-parent households, lack of supervision of the minors, and lack of social controls within the neighborhood.[148] The by-product of a socially disadvantaged community is an increase in crime and delinquency. The average age of a youth gang member is between 12 and 24 years.[149] The youth of the community turn toward gangs to replace the social control and outlets they lack at home and within their neighborhood.[150] Once in the gang, the minors are exposed to more criminal activity than their non–gang member counterparts. Further, prior studies have documented that gang members are at greater risk for being violently victimized once in the gang.[151] In 2010, a total of 4,828 minors between the ages of 10 and 24 years were victims of homicide.[152] Of the victims, 86 percent were male and 14 percent were female.[153] Further, 83 percent were killed with a firearm.[154] Thus, a gang does not provide the protection as perceived by minors. Rather, it places them at an even greater disadvantage and potential for harm within their already disadvantaged situation.

Notes

1. James Howell, "Youth Gangs, Fact Sheet," *Office of Juvenile Justice and Delinquency Prevention* (1997), https://www.ncjrs.gov/pdffiles/fs-9772.pdf.

2. Ibid.

3. Erika Harrell, "Violence by Gang Members, 1993–2003," Crime Data Brief, Office of Justice Programs (2005), http://www.bjs.gov/content/pub/pdf/vgm03.pdf.

4. Arlen Egley and James Howell, "Highlights of the 2011 National Youth Gang Survey, Juvenile Justice Fact Sheet," *Office of Juvenile Justice and Delinquency Prevention* (2013). http://www.ojjdp.gov/pubs/242884.pdf.

5. Ibid.

6. Clifford Shaw and Henry McKay, "Juvenile Delinquency and Urban Areas," in *Classics of Criminology Fourth Edition,* ed. Joseph Jacoby, Theresa Severance, and Alan Bruce (Long Grove, IL: Waveland Press, 2012), 19.

7. Clifford Shaw and Henry McKay, "Differential Systems of Values," in *Classics of Criminology Fourth Edition,* ed. Joseph Jacoby, Theresa Severance, and Alan Bruce (Long Grove, IL: Waveland Press, 2012), 272–73.

8. Ibid.

9. Chris Gibson, "An Investigation of Neighborhood Disadvantage, Low Self-Control, and Violent Victimization Amoung Youth," *Youth Violence and Juvenile Justice* 10, no. 1 (2012): 43.

10. Scott Decker, Chris Melde, and David Pyrooz, "What Do We Know About Gangs and Gang Members and Where Do We Go from Here?" *Justice Quarterly* 30, no. 3 (2013): 374; David Eitle, Steven Gunkel, and Karen Van Gundy, "Cumulative Exposure to Stressful Life Events and Male Gang Membership," *Journal of Criminal Justice* 32, no. 2 (2004): 102; Robert Sampson, "Urban Black Violence: The Effect of Male Joblessness and Family Disruption," *American Journal of Sociology* 93, no. 2 (1987): 352; Robert Sampson and W. Byron Groves, "Community Structure and Crime: Testing Social-Disorganization Theory," *American Journal of Sociology* 94, no. 4 (1989): 778.

11. Katrina Rufino, Kathleen Fox, and Glen Kercher, "Gang Membership and Crime Victimization among Prison Inmates," *American Journal of Criminal Justice* 37 (2012): 325; Dana Peterson, Terrance Taylor, and Finn-Aage Esbensen, "Gang Membership and Violent Victimization." *Justice Quarterly* 21, no. 4 (2004): 797–98; Terrance Taylor, Dana Peterson, Finn-Aage Esbensen, and Adrienne Freng, "Gang Membership as a Risk Factor for Adolescent Violent Victimization," *Journal of Research in Crime and Delinquency* 44, no. 4 (2007): 355.

12. Decker et al., "What Do We Know About Gangs," 371.

13. Ibid., 377

14. J. C. Barnes, Brian Boutwell, and Kathleen Fox, "The Effect of Gang Membership on Victimization: A Behavioral Genetic Explanation," *Youth Violence and Juvenile Justice* 10, no. 3 (2012): 237; Scott Decker, Charles Katz, and Vincent Webb, "Understanding the Black Box of Gang Organization," *Crime & Delinquency* 54, no. 1 (2008): 166; Fox et al., "Do Perceptions of Neighborhood Disorganization," 727; Katz et al., "Understanding the Relationship between Violent," 54; Lane and Fox, "Fear of Crime among Gang," 496; Melde et al., "I Got Your Back," 565; Rufino et al., "Gang Membership and Crime Victimization," 334; Peterson et al., "Gang Membership and Violent Victimization," 813; Taylor et al., "Gang Membership as a Risk Factor," 355.

15. Shaw and McKay, "Juvenile Delinquency in Urban Areas," 19.

16. Shaw and McKay, "Differential Systems of Values," 272–73.

17. Ibid.

18. Sampson, "Urban Black Violence," 352.

19. Ibid.

20. Sampson and Groves, "Community Structure and Crime," 779–81.

21. Sampson, "Urban Black Violence," 352–53.

22. Ibid., 779.

23. Siu Wong, "Youth Crime and Family Disruption in Canadian Municipalities: An Adaptation of Shaw and McKay's Social Disorganization Theory," *International Journal of Law, Crime and Justice* 40, no. 2 (2012): 103–04.

24. Eitle et al., "Cumulative Exposure to Stressful Life Events," 96.

25. Sampson and Groves, "Community Structure and Crime," 782.

26. Ibid., 788.

27. Catherine Ross and Sung Jang, "Neighborhood Disorder, Fear, and Mistrust: The Buffering Role of Social Ties with Neighbors," *American Journal of Community Psychology* 28, no. 4 (2000): 401.

28. Ibid.

29. Ibid., 403.

30. Ibid., 409.

31. Wong, "Youth Crime and Family Disruption," 100.

32. Ibid., 104.

33. Ibid., 105.

34. Ibid., 106.

35. Ibid., 110.

36. Decker et al., "What Do We Know About Gangs," 374.

37. Paul Bellair and Thomas McNulty, "Gang Membership, Drug Selling, and Violence in Neighborhood Context," *Justice Quarterly* 26, no. 4 (2009): 661.

38. Rufino et al., "Gang Membership and Crime Victimization," 326–27.

39. Terrance Taylor, "The Boulevard Ain't Safe for Your Kids . . . Youth Gang Membership and Violent Victimization," *Journal of Contemporary Criminal Justice* 24, no. 2 (2008): 127.

40. Rufino et al., "Gang Membership and Crime Victimization," 324.

41. Taylor et al., "Gang Membership as a Risk Factor," 355.

42. Peterson et al., "Gang Membership and Violent Victimization," 798.

43. Decker et al., "What Do We Know About Gangs," 371.

44. Peterson et al., "Gang Membership and Violent Victimization," 798.

45. Ibid.

46. Taylor et al., "Gang Membership as a Risk Factor," 354.

47. Ibid., 371.

48. Antionette Farmer and Timothy Hairston, "Predictors of Gang Membership: Variations Across Grade Levels," *Journal of Social Service Research* 39, no. 4 (2013): 530.

49. Ibid., 531–32.

50. Ibid., 533.

51. Ibid.

52. Ibid., 534.

53. Ibid.

54. Ibid., 540.

55. Ibid.

56. Eitle et al., "Cumulative Exposure to Stressful Life Events," 98.

57. Ibid., 102.

58. Ibid.

59. Ibid., 103.

60. David Pyrooz, Andrew Fox, and Scott Decker, "Racial and Ethnic Heterogeneity, Economic Disadvantage, and Gangs: A Macro-Level Study of Gang Membership in Urban America," *Justice Quarterly* 27, no. 6 (2010): 870.

61. Ibid.

62. Ibid., 873.

63. Ibid., 874.

64. Ibid., 879.

65. Decker et al., "Understanding the Black Box," 160.

66. Ibid., 161.

67. Ibid., 166.

68. Ibid., 166–67.

69. Abigail Fagan and Emily Wright, "The Effects of Neighborhood Context on Youth Violence and Delinquency: Does Gender Matter?" *Youth Violence and Juvenile Justice* 10, no. 1 (2012): 64–65.

70. Ibid., 66.

71. Ibid.

72. Ibid., 68.

73. Ibid.

74. Ibid.

75. Ibid., 73.

76. Ibid.

77. Karen Joe and Meda Chesney-Lind, "'Just Every Mother's Angel': An Analysis of Gender and Ethnic Variations in Youth Gang Membership," *Gender & Society* 9, no. 4 (1995): 416.

78. Ibid.

79. Ibid.

80. Ibid.

81. Ibid.

82. Ibid., 417.

83. Ibid., 418.

84. Taylor et al., "Gang Membership as a Risk Factor," 356.

85. Ibid., 357.

86. Ibid.

87. Ibid., 362.

88. Ibid., 370.

89. Ibid., 369.

90. Ibid., 372.

91. Peterson et al., "Gang Membership and Violent Victimization," 800.

92. Ibid.

93. Ibid.

94. Ibid., 812.

95. Ibid.

96. Ibid.

97. Ibid.

98. Ibid., 813.

99. Fox et al., "Do Perceptions of Neighborhood Disorganization," 723.

100. Ibid.

101. Ibid.

102. Ibid., 726.

103. Ibid., 727.

104. Ibid.

105. Ibid.

106. Katz et al., "Understanding the Relationship between Violent Victimization," 51.

107. Ibid.

108. Ibid.
109. Ibid., 52.
110. Ibid., 53.
111. Ibid., 54.
112. Ibid.
113. Ibid.
114. Melde et al., "I Got Your Back," 567.
115. Ibid., 574–75.
116. Ibid., 576.
117. Ibid., 580.
118. Ibid.
119. Ibid
120. Ibid., 581.
121. Ibid.
122. Ibid., 585.
123. Ibid., 586.
124. Barnes et al., "The Effect of Gang Membership," 231.
125. Ibid., 232.
126. Ibid., 231.
127. Ibid., 232.
128. Ibid.
129. Ibid., 235.
130. Ibid., 237.
131. Rufino et al., "Gang Membership and Crime Victimization," 325–26.
132. Ibid., 326.
133. Ibid.
134. Ibid., 327.
135. Ibid.
136. Ibid., 330.
137. Lane and Fox, "Fear of Crime among Gang and Non-Gang Offenders," 491.
138. Ibid., 492.
139. Ibid., 493.
140. Ibid., 496.
141. Ibid.
142. Ibid., 498–99.
143. Ibid., 502.
144. Ibid.
145. Ibid., 512.
146. Shaw and McKay, "Differential Systems of Values," 272–73.
147. Shaw and McKay, "Juvenile Delinquency in Urban Areas," 19–20.
148. Eitle, "Cumulative Exposure to Stressful Life Events," 96; Sampson, "Urban Black Violence," 352–53; Sampson and Groves, "Community Structure and Crime," 789.
149. Howell, "Youth Gangs, Fact Sheet."
150. Eitle et al., "Cumulative Exposure to Stressful Life Events," 102; Farmer and Hairston, "Predictors of Gang Membership," 531–32; Pyrooz et al., "Racial and Ethnic Heterogeneity," 867–68; Rufino et al., "Gang Membership and Crime Victimization," 334; Sampson

and Groves, "Community Structure and Crime," 778–80; Wong, "Youth Crime and Family Disruption," 110.

151. Barnes et al., "The Effect of Gang Membership," 237; Decker et al., "Understanding the Black Box," 166; Fox et al., "Do Perceptions of Neighborhood Disorganization," 727; Katz et al., "Understanding the Relationship between Violent Victimization," 54; Lane et al., "Fear of Crime among Gang and Non-Gang Offenders," 492; Melde et al., "I Got Your Back," 565; Peterson et al., "Gang Membership and Violent Victimization," 813; Rufino et al., "Gang Membership and Crime Victimization," 330; Taylor et al., "Gang Membership as a Risk Factor," 351.

152. Centers for Disease Control and Prevention, "Youth Violence: Facts at a Glance" (2012), http://www.cdc.gov/violenceprevention/pdf/yv-datasheet-a.pdf.

153. Ibid.

154. Ibid.

Bibliography

Barnes, J. C., Brian Boutwell, and Kathleen Fox. "The Effect of Gang Membership on Victimization: A Behavioral Genetic Explanation." *Youth Violence and Juvenile Justice* 10, no. 3 (2012): 227–44.

Bellair, Paul, and Thomas McNulty. "Gang Membership, Drug Selling, and Violence in Neighborhood Context." *Justice Quarterly* 26, no. 4 (2009): 644–69.

Centers for Disease Control and Prevention. "Youth Violence: Facts at a Glance" (2012). http://www.cdc.gov/violenceprevention/pdf/yv-datasheet-a.pdf.

Decker, Scott, Charles Katz, and Vincent Webb. "Understanding the Black Box of Gang Organization." *Crime & Delinquency* 54, no. 1 (2008): 153–72.

Decker, Scott, Chris Melde, and David Pyrooz. "What Do We Know About Gangs and Gang Members and Where Do We Go from Here?" *Justice Quarterly* 30, no. 3 (2013): 369–402.

Egley, Arlen, and James Howell. "Highlights of the 2011 National Youth Gang Survey, Juvenile Justice Fact Sheet." Office of Juvenile Justice and Delinquency Prevention (2013). http://www.ojjdp.gov/pubs/242884.pdf.

Eitle, David, Steven Gunkel, and Karen Van Gundy. "Cumulative Exposure to Stressful Life Events and Male Gang Membership." *Journal of Criminal Justice* 32, no. 2 (2004): 95–111.

Fagan, Abigail, and Emily Wright. "The Effects of Neighborhood Context on Youth Violence and Delinquency: Does Gender Matter?" *Youth Violence and Juvenile Justice* 10, no. 1 (2012): 64–82.

Farmer, Antoinette, and Timothy Hairston. "Predictors of Gang Membership: Variations Across Grade Levels." *Journal of Social Service Research* 39, no. 4 (2013): 530–44.

Fox, Kathleen, Jodi Lane, and Ronald Akers. "Do Perceptions of Neighborhood Disorganization Predict Crime or Victimization: An Examination of Gang Member versus Non–Gang Member Jail Inmates." *Journal of Criminal Justice* 38, no. 4 (2010): 720–29.

Gibson, Chris. "An Investigation of Neighborhood Disadvantage, Low Self-Control, and Violent Victimization Among Youth." *Youth Violence and Juvenile Justice* 10, no. 1 (2012): 41–63.

Harrell, Erika. "Violence by Gang Members, 1993–2003." Crime Data Brief, Office of Justice Programs (2005). http://www.bjs.gov/content/pub/pdf/vgm03.pdf.

Howell, James. "Youth Gangs, Fact Sheet." Office of Juvenile Justice and Delinquency Prevention (1997). https://www.ncjrs.gov/pdffiles/fs-9772.pdf.

Joe, Karen, and Meda Chesney-Lind. "'Just Every Mother's Angel': An Analysis of Gender and Ethnic Variations in Youth Gang Membership." *Gender & Society* 9, no. 4 (1995): 408–31.

Katz, Charles, Vincent Webb, Kathleen Fox, and Jennifer Shaffer. "Understanding the Relationship between Violent Victimization and Gang Membership." *Journal of Criminal Justice* 39, no. 1 (2011): 48–59.

Lane, Jodi, and Kathleen Fox. "Fear of Crime among Gang and Non-Gang Offenders: Comparing the Effects of Perpetration, Victimization, and Neighborhood Factors." *Justice Quarterly* 29, no. 4 (2012): 491–523.

Melde, Chris, Terrance Taylor, and Finn-Aage Esbensen. "'I Got Your Back': An Examination of the Protective Function of Gang Membership in Adolescence." *Criminology* 47, no. 2 (2009): 565–94.

Peterson, Dana, Terrance Taylor, and Finn-Aage Esbensen. "Gang Membership and Violent Victimization." *Justice Quarterly* 21, no. 4 (2004): 793–815.

Pyrooz, David, Andrew Fox, and Scott Decker. "Racial and Ethnic Heterogeneity, Economic Disadvantage, and Gangs: A Macro-Level Study of Gang Membership in Urban America." *Justice Quarterly* 27, no. 6 (2010): 867–92.

Ross, Catherine, and Sung Jang. "Neighborhood Disorder, Fear, and Mistrust: The Buffering Role of Social Ties with Neighbors." *American Journal of Community Psychology* 28, no. 4 (2000): 401–20.

Rufino, Katrina, Kathleen Fox, and Glen Kercher. "Gang Membership and Crime Victimization among Prison Inmates." *American Journal of Criminal Justice* 37 (2012): 321–37.

Sampson, Robert. "Urban Black Violence: The Effect of Male Joblessness and Family Disruption." *American Journal of Sociology* 93, no. 2 (1987): 348–83.

Sampson, Robert, and W. Byron Groves. "Community Structure and Crime: Testing Social Disorganization Theory." *American Journal of Sociology* 94, no. 4 (1989): 774–802.

Shaw, Clifford, and Henry McKay. "Differential Systems of Values." In *Classics of Criminology Fourth Edition,* ed. Joseph Jacoby, Theresa Severance, and Alan Bruce. Long Grove, IL: Waveland Press, 2012, 267–74.

Shaw, Clifford. "Juvenile Delinquency and Urban Areas." In *Classics of Criminology Fourth Edition,* ed. Joseph Jacoby, Theresa Severance, and Alan Bruce. Long Grove, IL: Waveland Press, 2012, 19–25.

Taylor, Terrance. "The Boulevard Ain't Safe for Your Kids . . . Youth Gang Membership and Violent Victimization." *Journal of Contemporary Criminal Justice* 24, no. 2 (2008): 125–36.

Taylor, Terrance, Dana Peterson, Finn-Aage Esbensen, and Adrienne Freng. "Gang Membership as a Risk Factor for Adolescent Violent Victimization." *Journal of Research in Crime and Delinquency* 44, no. 4 (2007): 351–80.

Wong, Siu. "Youth Crime and Family Disruption in Canadian Municipalities: An Adaptation of Shaw and McKay's Social Disorganization Theory." *International Journal of Law, Crime and Justice* 40, no. 2 (2012): 100–14.

18

Pedophilia

Sarah A. Strickland

When people hear the word pedophilia, the first thing that comes to mind are the hundreds of pedophile cases involving priests within the Catholic Church. The discovery of this evidence in the church is shocking because such a prestigious, godly institution should not ignore sin cloaked under the guise of priests' robes. While the media may be overexaggerating pedophiles within the church, the fact remains that pedophilia is estimated to be prevalent in 4 percent of the U.S. population. The sad part is that a majority of child sexual assault cases involve someone the child knows, not the suspected registered sex offender who lives a few miles down the road. The best way to combat a disorder such as pedophilia, properly called pedophilic disorder, is to become educated on the definition, symptoms, statistics, and potential causes so that you may properly identify a pedophile and prevent a child under your care from becoming a victim. There is no specific causation of pedophilic disorder, only speculations made by researchers using minute amounts of collected data. Speculations point to physiological and psychological causes. For psychological causes, the work of classical theorists—behaviorists Albert Bandura and B. F. Skinner—can be applied to explain the behaviors shown by those with pedophilic disorder. Although they have not found the ideal answer, scientists and researchers will continue to look for the etiology in hope of creating effective treatment methods for individuals afflicted with the disorder.

The *Diagnostic and Statistical Manual of Mental Disorders* (DSM), written and published by the American Psychiatric Association, is a resource manual used in the United States by mental health professionals, clinicians, researchers, social workers, psychologists, and countless others. It is a standard classification of mental disorders that includes a complete list of diagnostic criteria for every psychiatric disorder recognized in the U.S. health care system. It is used in both clinical settings and community populations. In May 2013, the American Psychiatric Association released the fifth edition of the *Diagnostic and Statistical Manual of Mental Disorders* (DSM-5). This revision included a change in paraphilic disorders' diagnostic criteria, which was improved based on the latest updates in science and effective clinical practices.

Within the DSM-5 are paraphilic disorders, previously called paraphilias. These disorders are characterized by unusual sexual behavior. Not all individuals who have an atypical sexual interest are considered to have a mental disorder. According to the American Psychological Association's Paraphilic Disorders fact sheet (2013), for someone to be diagnosed with a paraphilic disorder requires that people with these interests "feel personal distress about their interest, not merely distress resulting from society's disapproval" or "have a sexual desire or behavior that involves another person's psychological distress, injury, or death, or a desire for sexual behaviors involving unwilling persons or persons unable to give legal consent." The pedophilic disorder, which will be discussed in depth below, has the "persons unable to give legal consent" component. Other paraphilic disorders include exhibitionistic disorder, fetishistic disorder, frotteuristic disorder, sexual masochism disorder, sexual sadism disorder, transvestic disorder, and voyeuristic disorder.[1]

Pedophilia is derived from the Greek words for "child" and "love." What was once called "pedophilia" in the DSM-IV-TR is now called "pedophilic disorder" in the revised DSM-5.[2] The name change was the only significant change to pedophilia in the DSM; the criteria remain the same. Pedophilia is estimated to be the most common paraphilic disorder. Pedophilia has both a medical meaning and a legal meaning. The DSM-IV defines the medical meaning of pedophilia as "recurrent, intense, sexually arousing fantasies, sexual urges, or behaviors involving activity with a prepubescent child or children generally 13 years or younger."[3] The individual must have recurrent pedophilic fantasies or arousals that persist for at least six months and cause significant distress or impairment in daily functioning. Individuals suspected of pedophilia must be at least 16 years of age and must be at least five years older than the prepubescent child. Pedophilia predominantly affects males; females are rarely diagnosed. Unlike the other seven paraphilic disorders, those with pedophilic disorder do not feel true guilt with their "socially unacceptable fantasies, urges, and behaviors."[4] This is not to be confused with the guilt caused by society's unaccepting view of the pedophile. Pedophiles do not feel true guilt for their actions or feelings because they genuinely believe their interest and behaviors with children are appropriate and natural to them. Often, they delude themselves into thinking the child reciprocates the same love for them or that they are actually contributing to the child's development by showing them sexuality. They reach out to children because they do not feel anxiety when with them; they feel anxiety when trying to have an age-appropriate relationship. Pedophiles are not unknown to have adult relationships. This may occur for a number of reasons. For example, adult relationships could be used to hide their pedophilia or they may find the company of a spouse pleasurable, even though it will not ultimately satiate their urges toward children.

L. J. Cohen and I. Galynker (2009) state in their *Psychiatric Times* article on "Psychopathology and Personality Traits of Pedophiles" that it is important to note that "not everyone who sexually molests a child is actually a pedophile" because the person may not have "a persistent attraction to prepubescent children."[5] Studies have shown that about half of child molesters are not sexually attracted to their victims. The individual could just be violent or have a personality disorder. Also, pedophilia can be diagnosed in the absence of any pedophiliac behavior; this would only occur if a person self-reports, which usually only occurs in cases where the individual feels guilty for having these socially unacceptable feelings and urges.[6] The person may not act on their urges; however, they will never go away unless psychological treatment is sought to dampen the urge to manifest their desires. Society often rejects discovered pedophiles so treatments are few for those who come out of the perceived dark and seek them. People with this disorder are usually forced, through court orders, to participate in counseling and treatment.

The act of pedophilia has been deemed illegal by society in order to protect youth. We are protective of our children who, when in the age range from birth to adolescence, are at a crucial stage of development, unable to make decisions on their own. Decisions are made by the legal parent or guardian of the child. Of course, not all guardians have the child's best interests in mind, so safeguards are put in place to guard children from physical and sexual abuse if discovered. The legal meaning of a pedophile is a person who acts on their urges with a prepubescent child or a minor, who is below the legal age of consent, and is caught by law enforcement. It is a forcible act because a minor cannot give consent. Those found guilty are labeled pedophile and/or sex offender for the rest of their life. What differentiates the pedophile and the sex offender is the age of the minor and the state in which the crime occurred. Pedophilia is appropriate when the individual is 13 years of age or younger. Someone can be considered a sex offender but not a pedophile if they engage in sexual interactions with a child between the ages of 14 and 16 years. It depends on what age the state considers a minor; oftentimes it is 16 years of age. And, it could depend on the age of the offender as well. Duane Dobbert, author of *Halting the Sexual Predators Among Us,* gives the act of "sexual activity with pubescent and post-pubescent children, those in middle school and high school"[7] the name "hebephilia," which is not differentiated in the DSM-IV-TR (2004).

The U.S. Department of Justice, Office of Sexual Offender Sentencing, Monitoring, Apprehending, Registering, and Tracking (SMART), created a Web site to raise awareness about sexual abuse. A multitude of facts about sexual abuse are available on the Facts, Myths, and Statistics page. According to the Web site, which gathers information from sources like the National

Crime Victimization Survey and Bureau of Statistics, of the reported child sexual abuse cases, the child knows the person who committed the abuse. In the United States "over 63,000 cases of child sexual abuse were reported in 2010." It has been estimated that as many as "1 in 3 girls and 1 in 7 boys will be sexually abused at some point in their childhood."[8]

Pedophilia has been around for a long time. The only difference now is it is more known due to increased media coverage and technological advances. The Internet alone is making it easier for sexual predators such as pedophiles to act out. It is a venue for like-minded individuals to chat and validate their actions and feelings. It gives them a method to retrieve child pornography and other stimuli, find additional information on a potential victim and their family, or directly contact the victim under the guise of a more appealing alias. Technology, such as social networking, e-mailing, text messaging, videos, and instant messaging are making the pedophile a more effective and successful predator. It has been found in a national survey on Internet-Initiated Sex Crimes Against Minors that the majority of victims meet with their predator willingly. Sixty-seven percent of victims were children between the ages of 12 and 15.[9] Statistics will only climb as our youth continue to mature sooner, use technology at an earlier age, and have technology more readily available.

The world is now a sexual predator's stalking ground thanks to the Internet. Police agencies and their counterparts have adapted to the game and are using similar tactics on pedophiles. Police departments have entire units assigned to monitor the Internet, posing as young children, in hope of entrapping any predators out there stalking social media. While police continue to do their part, researchers, too, are searching for answers as to why sexual predators such as pedophiles exist in hope of preventing future pedophiles if it can be helped. The etiology or origin of pedophilia has been a long-debated topic, one that has not produced a solid answer. Currently, there is no proven answer as to the cause of the pedophilic disorder, since there is not enough empirical data that can point to one specific cause. In the meantime, researchers continue to speculate on multiple reasons, all of which may be true to some extent. In psychology there is rarely only one answer.

The most common theory is that pedophilia stems from psychological influences on a child during the early stage of life, such as being sexually molested himself at a young age. Researchers now believe it may be physiological. Alan Zarembo wrote an article for the *Los Angeles Times* that reveals the new understanding, which was discovered by experts at the Center for Mental Health and Addiction in Toronto. Researchers have used phallometry to measure the attraction and identify men whose "peak attraction is to children."[10] In the study, a man will sit alone in a room where he will see and listen to descriptions of sexual acts that vary with adults and children, male and female. A device is worn on the penis to monitor the flow of blood, indicating arousal.

Pedophiles were found to be attracted most strongly to one gender over the other. Scientists also found that "30% of pedophiles are left-handed or ambidextrous." Since hand dominance is found to be a combination of genetics and womb environment, it is plausible to infer that something is different about pedophiles' birth. Additional discoveries that can be connected to development are that pedophiles were found to be typically an inch shorter in height on average, compared to nonpedophiles examined in the Toronto study, and that they are behind by 10 IQ points on average, in comparison to the nonpedophiles in the same Toronto research. Magnetic resonance imaging (MRI) brain scans have shown that known pedophiles, when compared with criminals who have no sex offenses, show less white matter in the brain. The white matter is involved with connective circuits. Lack of it could imply cross-wiring that would lead to a sexual response toward a child whereas usually it would be a response elicited by an attractive adult. Some men with brain tumors and other brain diseases have been found to suddenly exhibit sexual deviance. All of the above could point to pedophilia as being as intrinsic as heterosexuality. Researchers have been examining not only physiological causes but also psychological causes. Two classical psychologists have proposed cognitive and behavioral theories that can be applied to explain the popular belief that pedophiles were sexually abused in childhood.[11]

The popular belief is that pedophiles experienced childhood sexual abuse. This belief, which could be supported by one of many studies in the past, has been slowly dissolving as the most prominent cause of pedophilia. In 1988, Kathleen Faller wrote a book on child sexual abuse that was an interdisciplinary manual for diagnosis, case management, and treatment. The study in her book showed that all the perpetrators in her sample had "sexual encounters as children, and there was evidence of a relationship between this childhood experience and sexual abuse of children as an adult."[12] Furthermore, the victims were usually the same age and sex of the perpetrator when he was victimized. Perpetrators also tended to use seduction rather than force to ensure cooperation. In the past few decades, however, viewpoints have changed because more studies have been conducted. Not all pedophiles were sexually abuse in their childhood, discounting that childhood sexual abuse is the sole cause of pedophilia. But it cannot entirely be discounted because it does appear in studies frequently and could be of some merit, especially if the work of classical theorist Albert Bandura is applied in the reasoning.

Albert Bandura produced a plethora of theories around the 1960s that had a tremendous impact on cognitive psychology, psychotherapy, and personality development. He is best known for his theory on social learning, the most influential theory of learning and development. Here is his theory summed up in his words: "Fortunately, most human behavior is learned observationally through modeling: from observing others, one forms an idea of how new behaviors are performed, and on later occasions this coded information serves as a guide for action."[13] Basically, through the process of observation learning, or modeling, a child can learn behaviors from those around him. From his theory, Bandura came up with three core concepts: (1) people can learn through observation, (2) internal mental states are essential in the process, and (3) just because something is learned does not mean there will be a change in behavior. His first core concept was shown in his famous 1961 Bobo doll experiment. In this study he showed children a video or live visual display of a man hitting, slapping, kicking, and being verbally abusive to a Bobo doll, a clown-faced model with a rounded bottom that moves back and forth when pushed. Immediately after, children were placed in a room with toys that they were told not to play with. This resulted in an emotional response from the children. They were then moved to a different room where they could play with toys—replicas of the toys in the video or visual display. Eighty-eight percent of the children imitated the aggressive behavior toward the Bobo doll by hitting, punching, slapping, and saying unkind words to it. When brought back eight months later, 40 percent of the children produced the same behavior.[14] This showed that children can learn through modeling others' behavior in the absence of reward or punishment, and the behavior could be retrieved for future use if coded properly. Bandura also discovered three models to facilitate learning: live model, verbal instruction model, and symbolic model.

After the child was done beating up the Bobo doll, he did not receive any type of environmental reinforcement, such as a reward or punishment for his actions. That is because he received intrinsic satisfaction by being able to let out his aggression toward the toy. This sums up the second core concept that internal mental states are important in the observational learning process. This intrinsic satisfaction, or intrinsic reinforcement, will possibly lead to continued observational learning. It is possible that there could be no change at all in behavior.

This third core concept shows that just because something is learned does not necessarily mean that change will occur. The modeling process has four components that must be met if it is to be effective. First, the individual must pay full attention to what is being taught or shown. Second, the individual must retain the information by storing it in their memory subconsciously. Next, the individual must be able to retrieve that information from its stored location and reproduce the behavior. Then, finally, motivation must be present in the form of reward, punishment, or intrinsic motivation if the individual is to imitate the behavior.

A child, in the crucial stages of development who has been sexual abused or fondled by an adult may learn that as a normal behavior because he does not know any differently. Plus, when done gently, especially by a close relative, the child may associate it with love and affection. This is common because the majority of pedophiles and child molesters, statistically, know the child or are closely associated with him or her. So, when the child goes and plays with other children, he may try to show his affections in a similar manner. Sometimes it will go unnoticed if not obvious. This is where parental observation is crucial. Stopping inappropriate behaviors at a young age could prevent future deviant adult behaviors and possibly indicate to the parent that something is wrong. The difficultly lies in differentiating between natural kid tendencies and inappropriate behavior that potentially stems from a more malevolent source. That is when it is important to have that talk with them to see if anyone has been inappropriately touching or abusing them. Pedophiles look just like everyone else. They have been found to take jobs that put them closer to children, like in the priest example.

Not all children who experience childhood sexual abuse necessarily become child predators. Bandura's social learning theory states that there must be those four stages of the modeling process present for change in behavior to occur.[15] Depending on the age, children may not retain the experience because it was too traumatic. The children who associate the abuse with love and affection are most inclined to have pedophilic tendencies in the future because they received intrinsic reinforcement through pleasure and satisfaction brought on by affection shown toward them. Eventually, the child grows into a testosterone-infused adolescent and then that adolescent becomes a testosterone-fueled adult who, if never corrected or caught, will have uncontrollable tendencies that have continued to be reinforced through other means.

For an individual to be diagnosed with pedophilic disorder, he must have a recurrent, intense sexual arousal toward individuals under the age of 13 and experience significant distress or impairment in daily, important functioning.[16] One typically causes the other. The person will have such a recurrent, intense sexual arousal causing anxiety if not satiated. This anxiety or distress seeps into and causes impairment in the person's social, occupational, and possibly familial parts of life unless release is found in the form of pornography, masturbation, alcohol, drugs, or other comorbid paraphilias. This anxiety is different from the other paraphilias because it is anxiety produced from not being able to attain a relationship with a child, instead of anxiety created from shame, guilt, or the anticipation of the act. There is also another type of anxiety that occurs when the individual tries to participate in an age-appropriate relationship. They fall back on relationships with children because these are not anxiety producing and easier to attain. This is tied to what behaviorist B. F. Skinner calls operant conditioning.

B. F. Skinner, the father of operant conditioning, made his discovery about behavior when he conducted experiments that involved rats in "Skinner boxes." In these boxes were levers, an electrical floor, indicator lights, and a food dispenser door. The hungry rats were placed individually in the box where they eventually accidentally knocked against the lever, causing a food pellet to be released. The rats were quick to realize that food was released upon hitting the lever, so they would go to it whenever they were hungry. This positive reinforcement would only occur if the rat felt the need of hunger. Skinner also subjected the rats to discomforting electrical current, which was discovered to stop when bumping into the lever. When this negative reinforcement was administered, the rats quickly learned to go press the lever. He even added a warning light that flicked on before the current was administered. The rats eventually figured out that hitting the lever when the light clicked on would stop the electrical current from turning on. If the behavior was not reinforced, then it would weaken. Oppositely, if the behavior was reinforced, it would strengthen over time.[17]

This can be related to anxiety experienced by pedophiles. Anxiety is a negative reinforcement that the pedophile wishes to stop, thus he participates in the known behaviors that reduce or get rid of the anxiety. For example, he will not try to engage in an age-appropriate relationship because it causes anxiety. For the anxiety produced by his disorder, he will seek things to alleviate it by engaging in his pedophilic urges. This can involve direct contact with a child or an indirect manner such as masturbation, pornography, drinking alcohol, or stalking his ideal love child from afar. It is a vicious cycle because the pedophile's anxiety always comes back unless treatment and counseling is sought. Even then it is not guaranteed.

Psychologist use cognitive behavioral therapy, which stemmed from research conducted by Bandura and B. F. Skinner in sex offender treatments. The purpose of the treatment is to teach pedophiles how to normally interact with adults and to get to the bottom of the underlying pattern of sexual arousal geared toward children. To accomplish this goal, psychologists use conditioning-based approaches to change behavior, social ineptness, empathy, and assertiveness. Linda Grossman, who studies the treatment of sex offenders at the University of Illinois, combines aversion therapy with cognitive behavioral programs. For example, psychologists have the offender visualize a deviant fantasy that elicits a reaction, then the psychologists has them image the consequences of getting caught, arrested, placed in prison, and sexually assaulted in prison.[18] What this is doing is showing the negative consequences or punishments that could occur if caught. For few, this is a deterrent; for many, it will take a greater variety of treatment methods. Some of these treatments include the use of medications that target the physiological causes or reactions of pedophilia.

Pedophilic disorder, previously called pedophilia, is a disorder that is prevalent in approximately 4 percent of the population. The specific cause of pedophilia is yet to be determined, but at this time it has been speculated that causes are both physiological and psychological in nature. The theories of classical theorists Albert Bandura and B. F. Skinner can be applied in explaining potential causes of pedophilia. Pedophilia should not be taken lightly and ignored. Our culture has labeled it as abnormal, but to pedophiles it is normal. Children need to be safeguarded by their parents. The best way to do so is not to ignore but instead to be aware of the signs in your child and the people surrounding your child, especially since children are more commonly sexually assaulted by someone close to them. Researchers and psychologists continue to bring this disorder to light so that advancements in treatment methods can be sought and we can effectively halt the sexual predators among us.

Notes

1. American Psychiatric Association, *Diagnostic and Statistical Manual of Mental Disorders*, 5th ed. (Arlington, VA: American Psychiatric Publishing, 2013).

2. Ibid.

3. Ibid.

4. Ibid.

5. L. J. Cohen and I. Galynker, "Psychopathology and Personality Traits of Pedophiles: Issues for Diagnosis and Treatment." *Psychiatric Times*, 26, no. 6 (June 2009), 25. http://go.galegroup.com/ps/i.do?id=GALE%7CA201495087&v=2.1&u=gale15690&it=r&PPPC&sw=w&asid=34950acaa23a671f963d45e6cfd93ce.

6. Ibid.

7. D. Dobbert, *Halting the Sexual Predators Among Us* (Westport. CT: Praeger, 2004).

8. U.S. Department of Justice, SMART, "Raising Awareness about Sexual Abuse: Facts, Myths, and Statistics" (2013), http://www.nsopr.gov/en/Education/FactsMythsStatistics?AspxAutoDetectCookieSupport=1.

9. U.S. Department of Defense, *Internet-Initiated Sex Crimes Against Minors* (Washington, DC: U.S. Printing Office, 2013).

10. A. Zarembo, "Many Researchers Take a Different View of Pedophilia," *Los Angeles Times* (January 14, 2013), http://articles.latimes.com/2013/jan/14/local/lame-pedophiles-20130115.

11. Ibid.

12. K. C. Faller, *Child Sexual Abuse: An Interdisciplinary Manual for Diagnosis, Case Management, and Treatment* (New York: Columbia University Press, 1988).

13. A. Bandura, *Social Learning Theory* (Englewood Cliffs, NJ: Prentice Hall, 1977).

14. M. D. Isom, "The Social Learning Theory," *FSU Criminology* (November 30, 1998), http://www.criminology.fsu.edu/crimtheory/bandura.htm

15. Bandura, *Social Learning Theory*.

16. American Psychiatric Association, *Diagnostic and Statistical Manual of Mental Disorders*.

17. B. F. Skinner, *The Behavior of Organisms: An Experimental Analysis* (New York: Appleton-Century, 1938).

18. University of Wisconsin, *Treating Pedophiles* (2002), http://whyfiles.org/154pedophile/2.html.

Bibliography

American Psychiatric Association. *Diagnostic and Statistical Manual of Mental Disorders*. 5th ed. Arlington, VA: American Psychiatric Publishing, 2013.

American Psychiatric Association. *Paraphilic Disorders*. American Psychiatric Publishing, 2013. http://www.dsm5.org/Documents/Paraphilic Disorders Fact Sheet.pdf.

Bandura, A. *Social Learning through Imitation*. Lincoln: University of Nebraska Press: Lincoln, 1962.

Bandura, A. *Social Learning Theory*. Englewood Cliffs, NJ: Prentice Hall, 1977.

Cohen, L. J., and I. Galynker. "Psychopathology and Personality Traits of Pedophiles: Issues for Diagnosis and Treatment." *Psychiatric Times* 26, no. 6 (June 2009), 25. http://go.galegroup.com/ps/i.do?id=GALE%7CA201495087&v=2.1&u=gale15690&it=r&p=PPPC&sw=w&asid=34950acaa23a671f963d45e6cfd93cee.

Dobbert, D. *Halting the Sexual Predators Among Us*. Westport, CT: Praeger, 2004.

Faller, K. C. *Child Sexual Abuse: An Interdisciplinary Manual for Diagnosis, Case Management, and Treatment*. New York: Columbia University Press, 1988.

Isom, M. D. "The Social Learning Theory." *FSU Criminology* (November 30, 1998). Retrieved from http://www.criminology.fsu.edu/crimtheory/bandura.htm.

Skinner, B. F. *The Behavior of Organisms: An Experimental Analysis*. New York: Appleton-Century, 1938.

Skinner, B. F. *The Behavior of Organisms: An Experimental Analysis*. New York: Appleton-Century, 1938.

University of Wisconsin. "Treating Pedophiles" (2002). *The Why Files* Retrieved from http://whyfiles.org/154pedophile/2.html.

U.S. Department of Defense. *Internet-Initiated Sex Crimes Against Minors*. Washington, DC: U.S. Government Priniting Office, 2013.

U.S. Department of Justice, SMART. "Raising Awareness about Sexual Abuse: Facts, Myths, and Statistics" (2013). http://www.nsopr.gov/en/Education/FactsMythsStatistics?AspxAutoDetectCookieSupport=1.

Zarembo, A. "Many Researchers Take a Different View of Pedophilia." *Los Angeles Times* (January 14, 2013). http://articles.latimes.com/2013/jan/14/local/la-me-pedophiles-20130115.

19

Competency and Culpability

Joseph McCluskey

There are three distinct concepts that are used by lawyers and mental health professionals working in the criminal justice system. The concepts are capability, capacity, and competence. This chapter defines these terms and identifies their applications within the state and federal criminal justice arenas. Capability refers to various definitions given to minimum ages before which a child or juvenile is deemed not able, or presumed to be unable, to commit crimes generally or to commit specific classes of crimes. Capacity, which for terms of this chapter is defined as the "ability to form a certain state of mind or motive, understand or evaluate one's actions, or control them," is discussed in terms of children/juveniles, the mentally retarded/intellectually disabled, and the insane.[1] In addition to discussing the constitutional parameters and legal significance of capacity, the chapter also discusses the mental health and neuroscience fields' roles in helping to identify those who have or lack the requisite legal capacity. Competence deals primarily with constitutional rights, as they are defined by U.S. Supreme Court decisions, pertaining to matters related to a defendant's ability to meaningfully participate in matters surrounding a trial and to receive a fair trial. There is also a discussion of the efforts the mental health and neuroscience professions are making to identify competence using scientific methods.

In the legal system, there are a host of defenses defense attorneys can raise to excuse client conduct that would otherwise constitute a criminal act. There are also defenses that can be raised that, while not excusing criminal acts, may mitigate the punishment. This chapter discusses three topics—capability, capacity, and competence—as they relate to the criminal behavior of those lacking mental maturity, those with mental retardation, or those with severe mental illnesses meeting the legal definition(s) of insanity.

The headline of the June 10, 2011, online ABC News publication read "5-Year-Old Could Face Murder Charge in Drowning Death of Crying

Toddler."[2] The news report explained that "Kansas City police are trying to determine whether to charge a 5-year-old girl with murder after she admitted that she dragged a crying toddler into a bathtub and held him under water until he stopped crying."[3]

Can a five-year-old really be charged with murder?

Can she be tried as an adult?

Can she be sent to prison?

The answers to these questions appear to be thus: a five-year-old probably could not be charged with murder because a "juvenile" for purposes of the Kansas Juvenile Justice System is defined as someone between the ages of 10 and 18 and there are no provisions for trying five-year-olds for alleged crimes.[4] Ten is the minimum possible age for a child/juvenile to be tried as an adult in Kansas.[5] Even if a five-year-old could be prosecuted as an adult, she could only end up in prison if she were tried as an "extended jurisdiction juvenile" (EJJ).[6] If convicted as an EJJ, she would be transferred from juvenile detention to the prison system upon reaching the age of 23 and only if she violated the terms of her EJJ.[7]

The defense of incapability of children to commit crimes goes back hundreds of years. In the early 14th century, judges and writers began to describe an infancy defense based on a child's incapacity to discern good from evil and to form a wicked intent.[8] A 1313 case reports that a child less than seven years old cannot be held liable for his crimes "because he knoweth not of good or evil."[9]

Ultimately, at common law, children under seven years of age (hereinafter years of age will be referred to simply in terms of years, e.g., seven) were incapable of committing crimes.[10] For children from seven to under 14, to be convicted of a crime at common law, the evidence of malice "ought to be strong and clear beyond all doubt and contradiction."[11] Children over 14 were presumed capable of committing crimes.

Today, approximately 22 states have not defined a minimum age of capability. These states could individually either rely on the common law rule or create their own definition by statute or create a state common law rule or decide the issue case by case, weighing relevant considerations. The federal government and some states have established age minimums for when a child (hereinafter "child" and "juvenile" are used interchangeably) is capable of committing crimes generally and/or for committing specific crimes. The ages of incapacity and the presumptions for certain ages vary widely from state to state.

In North Dakota, children under seven are incapable of committing any crime.[12] In Washington State, "Children under the age of eight are deemed incapable of committing crime . . . [c]hildren between eight and under twelve . . . are presumed incapable . . . but this presumption may be removed by proof that they have sufficient capacity to understand the act or neglect, and to know that it was wrong."[13] The Nevada law is similar to Washington's. A child younger than eight is incapable of committing a crime. However, children between eight and 14, as opposed to Washington's age 12, are presumed to be incapable of committing a crime, absent "clear proof" that at the time of the commission of the crime, "they knew its wrongfulness."[14]

In South Dakota, children under 10 are incapable of committing crimes. Children aged 10 to under 14 are incapable of committing crimes "in the absence of proof that at the time of committing the act or neglect charged, the child knew its wrongfulness."[15]

In Minnesota, "[c]hildren under the age of 14 are incapable of committing crime."[16] In California, children under 14 are incapable of committing crimes "in the absence of clear proof that at the time of committing the act charged against them, they knew its wrongfulness."[17] Although the California statute would appear to be essentially as favorable to children as the Minnesota statute, it is not. In Minnesota, children under 14 cannot be prosecuted for any crime. In contrast, children in California, at any age, are capable of committing crimes if there is clear evidence they knew the wrongfulness of their acts.

New York's law is complex. It provides that children less than 16 are not criminally responsible for crimes, except

1. Children 13, 14, and 15 are capable of committing second-degree murder (requiring intent, depraved indifference, or while committing sexually motivated felonies); and
2. Children 14 and 15 are capable of committing crimes such as rape, kidnapping, arson, assault, manslaughter, burglary, etc.[18]

At common law, males under 14 were presumed to be incapable of committing rape.[19] Florida and South Carolina, for example, have expressly overruled the common law.[20]

At the present time, the determination of capability is based on chronological age, although mental age can be used as a mitigating factor when determining the appropriate sentence. Some thought ought to be given to determining capability using the lower of the chronological or mental age of the subject.

The discussion of capacity that follows includes the capacity of (1) children, who are capable of committing crimes, to be held to the same standard as adults; (2) the mentally retarded; and (3) the insane and/or mentally ill. Also, for purposes of this chapter, "capacity" has the same definition as that applied by the U.S. Supreme Court in *Clark v. Arizona*: the "ability to form a certain state of mind or motive, understand or evaluate one's actions, or control them."[21]

All 50 states have juvenile justice laws and practices. A juvenile law may, for example, give the juvenile justice system jurisdiction to deal with crimes alleged to have been committed by children aged 10 to less than 18. Many states also have exceptions that allow children to be tried as adults. Some laws require that juveniles of specified minimum ages who are accused of certain crimes be tried as adults.[22] As with capability to commit crimes, state laws vary concerning the minimum age at which children can be tried and/ or treated as adults. During the 1990s, numerous states passed laws expanding the crimes for which juveniles could be tried as adults.[23] In fact, between 1992 and 1999, 48 of the 50 states "revised or rewrote their transfer laws to broaden the scope of transfer—lowering age/offense thresholds, moving away from individual and toward categorical handling, and shifting authority from judges to prosecutors."[24]

During this period, 35 states expanded the crimes for which juveniles could be tried as adults, 27 states either lowered the minimum ages for which juveniles could be tried as adults or at least broadened the eligibility of juveniles for adult prosecution, 13 states created presumptions to try juveniles as adults for certain or all crimes, and 11 states expanded the role prosecutors play in determining whether to exercise adult jurisdiction over juveniles.[25]

These changes were part of the overall "get tough" on crime agenda that took place during this time frame.[26] The purported justification for bringing more juveniles into adult court was to stem the number of homicides and other violent crimes committed by juvenile offenders.[27]

There are myriad examples of state laws that allow children to be tried as adults. According to the Office of Juvenile Justice and delinquency Prevention (OJJDP), a 10-year-old in Kansas can be tried as an adult for "[a]ny criminal offense," and in Indiana a child of 10 can be tried as an adult for murder.[28] A 10-year-old in Vermont can be tried for murder and certain crimes against persons or property, and the same is true for 12-year-olds in Colorado.[29] In Illinois, Mississippi, and Wyoming 13-year-old juveniles can be tried as adults for any crime.[30] In Georgia and New Hampshire, 13-year-old juveniles can be tried for murder and/or capital crimes.[31] Fourteen-year-olds can be tried as an adult for any crime in Alabama, Florida, Idaho, Iowa, Nevada, and New Jersey; 14-year-olds can be tried for murder or capital crimes in Arkansas, Kentucky, Louisiana, New Jersey, and Wisconsin.[32] Three and five states, respectively, allow 15- and 16-year-olds to be tried as adults for any crime.[33] There are also state statutes that allow juveniles at various ages, ranging from 13 to 17, to be tried as adults for violence against persons and/or property, and/or drug and weapons offenses.[34]

The concept of trying children/juveniles as adults has not met with universal acceptance. For example, a 2011 article explained that recent research in neuroscience and psychology does not support the proposition that sub-18-year-olds have the decision-making maturity or capabilities of adults and suggests that they should not be held to the adult criminal standard.[35] Primary influences on decision making include a "person's 'maturity of judgment' which can be broken down into two facets: cognitive capacity and psychosocial factors."[36] "'Maturity of judgment' . . . refers to the way that the process of decision-making changes with development."[37]

The brain, like the rest of the body, matures. The lateral prefrontal cortex includes the cognitive control system that rules "higher executive functioning activities such as impulse control, future orientation and deliberation"[38] It also controls "planning, weighing risks and rewards, and the simultaneous consideration of multiple sources of information"[39] The maturation process in this area does not rise to the level of adult competence until age 16.[40]

Psychosocial factors include impulsivity, ability to consider all consequences, ability to see different perspectives, responsibility, and antisocial decision making (degree to which individual makes "socially sanctioned" choices).[41] A study by Elizabeth Cauffman and Laurence Steinberg found that psychosocial maturity increases at a high rate between the ages of 16 and 19 and seems to be fully mature by age 21.[42] This lack of psychosocial maturity, in the below 19 age group (as well as the below 21 group), leads to risk taking and getting into trouble.[43] Thus, research suggests that decision-making capabilities, at least with regard to risk taking and antisocial decision making, do not rise to the adult level until sometime after age 18. If one accepts this research, it follows that those under 19, at a minimum, should not be held to the same legal standard as adults.

The youngest person ever executed in the United States was George Stinney Jr. in 1944. He was an African American male who was convicted in the beating deaths of two white girls, ages 7 and 11. He was convicted on the basis of a confession some believe was coerced. He had neither the benefit of legal nor parental counsel at the time of his confession. He was convicted and then executed 87 days later. At the time of his execution, Stinney was just 14 and one-half years old, stood 5 feet 1 inch, and weighed approximately 90 pounds. The electric chair used to execute Stinney was not designed for children. The electric chair's straps and headgear were too large for Stinney's small frame and became dislodged during the execution, which in turn prolonged the time it took to complete the execution and the pain inflicted on Stinney.[44] Also in 1944, a 16-year-old was executed for rape and three 17-year-olds were also executed.[45]

In 1988, the U.S. Supreme Court (Supreme Court or Court), in *Thompson v. Oklahoma*, determined that it was unconstitutional to execute a person for a crime committed when he was 15.[46] The *Thompson* Court based its decision on Eighth Amendment to the U.S. Constitution considerations, which makes it unconstitutional to inflict "cruel and unusual punishment."[47] (The decision was extended to the states via the due process clause of the Fourteenth Amendment.)[48] The decision was based on three primary factors. First, the

Court reasoned that children held a special status under the law.[49] The Court noted that children had limited or no rights as they pertained to making contracts, committing torts, voting, serving on juries, marrying without parental consent, the purchase of cigarettes, the purchase and consumption of alcohol, etc.[50] The Court also noted that children held a special status under criminal law.[51] Next, the Court found that the execution of a person who was 15 at the time of the crime "would offend civilized standards of decency."[52] The Court explained that this view "has been expressed by respected professional organizations, by other nations that share our Anglo-American heritage, and by the leading members of the Western European community."[53]

The second factor found by the *Thompson* Court was that there was a national consensus against executing individuals for crimes committed when they were younger than 16. The Court noted that there appeared to have been only 18 or 20 people executed in the United States since 1900 for crimes committed when they were younger than 16 and that no such execution had occurred for more than 40 years.[54] The Court also found statistical support for a national consensus against executing this class of criminals. The Court explained that only five of the 1,393 individuals in the United States who received a death sentence between 1982 and 1986 where younger than 16 when they committed the crime for which they received the ultimate sentence.[55] The Court reasoned, "Statistics of this kind of this kind can, of course, be interpreted in different ways, but they do suggest that these five young offenders have received sentences that are "cruel and unusual in the same way that being struck by lightening is cruel and unusual."[56]

The third issue the *Thompson* Court considered was whether a lowered juvenile culpability for crime rendered cruel and unusual an execution in the case before the Court.[57] The Court explained that the two key purposes served by the death penalty are retribution and deterrence. The Court found that the reasons, for a lower culpability for adolescents vis-à-vis adults, was "too obvious to require extended explanation,"[58] stating "Inexperience, less education, and less intelligence make the teenager less able to evaluate the consequences of his or her conduct while at the same time he or she is much more apt to be motivated by mere emotion or peer pressure than an adult.[59]

Thus, the Court found the same act committed by a juvenile to be less "morally reprehensible" than if it had been committed by adult.[60] The Court also determined that because the death penalty is imposed so infrequently for those who committed a crime before they were 16, the death penalty would not serve as a deterrent.[61] The Court declined, however, the invitation to create a bright line rule barring the execution of anyone who committed their crime before the age of 18 because that issue was not before the Court.[62]

One year after the *Thompson* decision, a plurality of the Court, in *Stanford v. Kentucky*, found that the execution of those who committed their crimes when they were 16 or 17 was not prohibited.[63] According to the Death Penalty Information Center, nineteen 17-year-olds were executed in the United States between 1989, the year the of the *Stanford* decision, and 2005, the year of the *Roper v. Simmons* decision, which, as discussed below, banned all executions of individuals who were under 18 when they committed the crime for which they could otherwise receive the death penalty.[64] The *Roper* decision essentially follows the same reasoning as *Thompson*.[65] There are some points of note, however, in *Roper*. The *Roper* Court recognized that mental health professionals are not able to diagnose people under 18 as psychopaths or sociopaths.[66] The Court reasoned that jurors therefore should not be charged with making decisions, similar to those that professionals cannot make, when deciding the fate of juvenile criminals. The Court also stated, "Our determination that the death penalty is disproportionate punishment for offenders under 18 finds confirmation in the stark reality that the United States is the only country in the world that continues to give official sanction to the juvenile death penalty."[67]

In *Graham v. Florida*, the defendant, a 16-year-old when he committed the crime, was sentenced to life in prison.[68] Because Florida had abolished the parole system, the defendant was effectively sentenced to life in prison without the possibility of parole (LWOP).[69] When the *Graham* case wound its way to the U.S. Supreme Court, the Court considered whether LWOP for a person who was under 18 at the time of the crime constituted cruel and unusual punishment in violation of the Eighth Amendment. (This holding is in stark contrast to *Thompson v. Oklahoma*, discussed above, where the Court declined to extend a case, involving a 16-year-old, to all persons under 18.[70]) The Court explained that consideration of the "cruel and unusual" issue involved not only the punishment itself but also a moral component that changes as societal mores change.[71] When considering the cruel and unusual issue, the Court explained, "the Court's precedents consider the punishment challenged not as inherently barbaric, but as disproportionate to the crime. The concept of proportionality is central to the Eighth Amendment."[72] The Court explained that it has taken, depending on the circumstances, two different approaches to determine the proportionality issue. The Court either has considered the issue from a "term-of-years" perspective or by making "categorical distinctions" (such as no death penalty for person who committed murder when under the age of 18), the latter of which had been previously considered only in death penalty cases.[73] (The Court reasoned that the categorical distinction was appropriate for the case before it.[74])

The Court's decision followed the pattern of the *Thompson* and *Roper* death penalty cases. Although recognizing that a majority of states permitted imposing LWOP for juvenile offenders, the Court found a national consensus against sentencing juveniles to LWOP based on the fact that only 123 juveniles in the United States were serving such sentences for non-homicide crimes, and of that number, 77 were in Florida and the remainder were spread out among just 10 states; thus, 39 states did not have a single person under 18 serving a LWOP sentence.[75] The Court also noted that it had previously found less culpable, "defendants who do not intend to kill or foresee that life will be taken."[76] Citing *Roper*, the Court also noted that it had previously recognized that juveniles are considered less culpable and, thus, less deserving of the "most severe punishments."[77]

The Court, once again, found support for its position in the mental health sciences. The Court stated that "developments in psychology and brain science continue to show fundamental differences between juvenile and adult minds."[78] The Court also found that LWOP did not advance the goals of deterrence or retribution; because of their youth, juveniles could not be determined to be an incorrigible, forever danger to society; and there is a global consensus against such punishments[79] The Court concluded ultimately, "[t]he Constitution prohibits the imposition of a life sentence without parole on a juvenile offender *who did not commit homicide*."[80] To ensure that a state would not be able to do indirectly what it could not do directly, the Court went on to explain, "[a] State need not guarantee the offender eventual release, but if it imposes a sentence of life it must provide him or her with some realistic opportunity to obtain release before the end of that term."[81] Thus, for example, one would expect that a court could not sentence a juvenile offender, tried as an adult, to five terms of 99 years, to run consecutively. Although the juvenile offender might live long enough to be eligible for parole on the first and possibly second 99-year sentences, he/she almost surely would not survive long enough to be paroled for the fifth 99-year sentence.

In 2012, the Court extended the prohibition against providing LWOP sentences to individuals who were under 18 when they committed a homicide crime.[82] In *Miller v. Alabama*, the underlying circumstances involved two individuals, tried as adults for murders committed when they were 14, who received LWOP sentences.[83] The Court determined that LWOP for juveniles who committed homicide violated the Eighth Amendment.[84] The Court, following the precedents of *Roper* and *Graham*, noted that juveniles were considered less culpable than adults.[85] The Court also explained why LWOP for juveniles served the purposes of neither retribution nor deterrence. The Court citing, inter alia, *Graham* and *Roper* explained that desire for retribution against juveniles is not as strong as it is for adults.[86] It also found, as noted in *Graham*, that LWOP would not serve effectively as a deterrent for juveniles because "their immaturity, recklessness, and impetuosity—make them less likely to consider potential punishment."[87] In sum, juvenile offenders cannot be sentenced, for any offense, either to death or life in prison without the reasonable possibility of parole.

"Mens Rea" means "guilty mind," and it expresses the intent to commit an act.[88] "The existence of a mens rea is the rule of, rather than the exception to, the principles of Anglo-American criminal jurisprudence."[89] As discussed below, the incompetence of a defendant is an absolute bar to waiver of *Miranda* rights, and to trials, plea bargains, guilty pleas, and self-representation.[90] Thus, a person with severe mental retardation will lack the mental capacity to even form the mens rea necessary to commit a crime.[91]

Mental capacity can also be taken into account in determining the appropriate sentence for mentally retarded persons convicted of crimes. For example, the U.S. Sentencing Commission's 2012 USSC Guidelines Manual allows for a downward departure from the sentencing guidelines "if (1) the defendant committed the offense while suffering from a significantly reduced mental capacity; and (2) the significantly reduced mental capacity contributed substantially to the commission of the offense." [92]

In 1989, the U.S. Supreme Court in *Penry v. Lynaugh*, determined that a defendant, in a case where the death penalty may be imposed, must be permitted to present evidence of his mental retardation as mitigation to the death sentence, and the jury must be made aware that it may consider and give effect to this mitigating evidence in considering whether to impose the death penalty.[93] Defendant Penry argued that imposing the death penalty on the mentally retarded constitutes "cruel and unusual punishment" in violation of the Eighth Amendment.[94] Defendant made two arguments to support his position. The first was that the impaired reasoning abilities of the mentally retarded make them less morally culpable than individuals of normal intelligence and, therefore, less deserving of the death penalty.[95] The second argument was that there was a national consensus against executing the mentally retarded.[96] The *Penry* Court rejected these arguments.[97]

The Supreme Court revisited the "cruel and unusual punishment" argument, as applied to the execution of the mentally retarded, in *Atkins v. Virginia*.[98] This time the Court changed course and determined that such executions do amount to cruel and unusual punishment.[99] The Court explained the mentally retarded are less culpable than most defendants because of their disabilities in "reasoning, judgment, and control of impulses."[100] The Court explained that the mentally retarded are more likely to give "false confessions," are less able to "make a persuasive showing of mitigation," are "less able to give meaningful assistance to their counsel," "are typically poor witnesses," and "their demeanor may create an unwarranted impression of lack of remorse for their crimes."[101] The Court also explained that the "execution of mentally retarded criminals will [not] measurably advance the deterrent or the retributive purposes of the death penalty."[102] Finally, the Court concluded that in the 13 years since the *Penry* decision, "the American public, legislators, scholars, and judges have deliberated" the execution of the mentally retarded issue and a national consensus has developed that they should not be executed.[103]

The *Atkins* Court noted that there could be disagreements about what degree of retardation is necessary to fall within lowered culpability standards for escaping the death sentence. In discussing definitions for mental retardations, the Court cited the definitions developed by the American Association on Mental Retardation (AAMR) (since renamed "American Association on Intellectual and Developmental Disabilities" [AAIDD]) and the American Psychiatric Association (APA).[104] The Court subsequently explained that "clinical definitions of mental retardation require not only subaverage intellectual functioning, but also significant limitations in adaptive skills such as communication, self-care, and self-direction that became manifest before age 18."[105] To meet the definition of mental retardation under the AAMR and APA standards, which essentially are the same, the person has to have (1) significant sub-average general intelligence functioning; (2) limitations in two or more of the following adaptive skills areas: "communications, self-care, home living, social skills, community use [use of community resources], self direction, health and safety, functional academics, leisure, and work"; and, the onset must occur before age 18.[106] Apparently, the requirement that the onset of retardation begin before 18 is so that, in cases in which the person was determined to be mentally retarded before he commits the crime, there is no ability for someone 18 or over to feign mental retardation to escape the death penalty. The Court also said that it was up to the individual states to define mental retardation.[107]

The definition of mental retardation, for death penalty purposes, varies among the states. For example, Arkansas law defines "mental retardation" as "(A) Significantly subaverage general intellectual functioning accompanied by a significant deficit or impairment in adaptive functioning manifest in the developmental period, but no later than age eighteen (18) years of age; and, (B) A deficit in adaptive behavior."[108] Arkansas also creates a "rebuttable presumption" of mental retardation if the individual has an intelligence quotient (IQ) of 65 or below.[109] The Nebraska, Tennessee, and Washington State laws, respectively, are similar to Arkansas's law, except they do not create the IQ-specific rebuttable presumption and instead use an IQ of 70 or below.[110] The definition is essentially the same for North Carolina, except it defines "adaptive skills" much like they are defined by the APA and AAMR, discussed above, and sets the IQ bar at 70 or below (mentally retarded defendants; death sentences prohibited).[111]

Kansas has opted to use the term "intellectual disability" in lieu of mentally retarded (sentencing for capital murder and mandatory terms of imprisonment; determination if defendant is a person with intellectual disability)[112] It defines intellectual disability to include requirements that there be evidence of "subaverage general intellectual functioning" and of "deficits in adaptive behavior" "to an extent that substantially impairs one's capacity to appreciate the criminality of one's conduct or to conform one's conduct to the require-ments of law."[113] Kansas does not have a numeric IQ cutoff; instead, it defines "sub-average general intellectual functioning" to mean "performance which is two or more standard deviations from the mean score on a standardized intelligence test."[114] Kansas also requires a showing that the individual did not appreciate the criminality of his actions or was unable to conform to the "requirements of the law."[115] (As discussed below, the last part of the Kansas requirements is very similar to its requirements for finding insanity). In *Atkins*, the Court noted that,

> mentally retarded persons frequently know the difference between right and wrong. . . . Because of their impairments, however, by definition they have diminished capacities to understand and process information, to commu-nicate, to abstract from mistakes and learn from experience, to engage in logical reasoning, to control impulses, and to understand the reactions of others. . . . Their deficiencies do not warrant an exemption from criminal sanctions, but they do diminish personal culpability.[116]

Although the Supreme Court said in *Atkins* that it was up to the individual states to define "mental retardation" for death penalty purposes, one would expect that there is an as-of-yet undefined minimum standard for determin-ing retardation, below which a state could not go and still pass constitutional muster.[117] It will be interesting to see if the "did not understand the criminality of his actions" requirement in the Kansas statute runs afoul of the Supreme Court's willingness to assign less criminal culpability to the mentally retarded in death penalty cases. An argument that could be made would be this: the defendant by most legal and medical definitions is mentally retarded; he is able to appreciate that what he did was a criminal act; he was able to conform his actions to the requirements of the law, but did not do so; nevertheless, because of mental impairments inherent with mental retardation, he is con-sidered less culpable and to execute him would constitute cruel and unusual punishment.

The Louisiana statute does not contain any maximum IQ requirement and simply defines "mental retardation" as "a disability characterized by sig-nificant limitations in both intellectual functioning and adaptive behavior as expressed in conceptual, social, and practical adaptive skills.[118] The onset must occur before the age of eighteen years."[119] Nevada law mirrors the Louisiana definition.[120]

Virginia's and Florida's, definitions, respectively, also include the adaptive behavior and below age 18 onset requirements, and they require an IQ that is two standard deviations below the mean of a normal score.[121]

Using the *Atkins* decision as the basis for a federal mental retardation definition, the definition requires that the onset begin before the age of 18 and that it meet the AAMR and DSM-IV-TR definitions. (AAMR has been renamed and the DSM-IV-TR has been superseded).

An issue that has arisen concerning executions and the mentally retarded concerns the application of the "Flynn effect" to state statutes that have defined IQ ceilings. The Flynn effect is a phenomenon that has been replicated in numerous studies in the United States. It refers to gains "in intelligence-quotient . . . scores over time. . . . Scores are increasing at an average rate of 0.3 points per year."[122] An argument defense counsel can make is that because of the Flynn effect, the maximum IQ score for mental retardation/intellectual disability purposes, should be raised one point every three and one-third years. This issue was dealt with by the U.S. Tenth Circuit Court of Appeals in *Hooks v. Workman* in a habeas corpus proceeding.[123] The defendant, who had been sentenced to death, argued that, among other things, if the Flynn effect had been taken into account, he would have been deemed to be retarded and, thus, could not be sentenced to death.[124] The Tenth Circuit rejected this argument under the standards that are mandated for habeas actions. The Court stated, "failure to account for and apply the Flynn Effect was not 'contrary to' or an 'unreasonable application of' clearly established federal law."[125] The Flynn effect has not been used successfully to raise the highest numerical requirement for a finding of mental retardation.[126]

As discussed above, the mentally retarded/intellectually disabled are assigned a special status, in the criminal law sense; because of their limited mental capacities, they are deemed to be less culpable for committing, at least, capital crimes. (Their intellectual capacity can also be considered as a mitigating factor at sentencing.) Thus, it would be cruel and unusual punishment to execute them for capital crimes, although they can still be incarcerated for those crimes.

Capacity of the Insane

Are the insane, like the mentally retarded, considered less culpable?

How does the mental health profession define insanity?

How does the legal profession define insanity?

Is there a constitutional right to plead not guilty by reason of insanity?

What percentage of those charged with crimes plead not guilty by reason of insanity (NGRI)?

Of those who plead NGRI, how many are actually determined to be not guilty?

Each of these questions will be covered in the following discussion, although not necessarily in the order presented above.

The insanity defense:

> has long tantalized defendants and mystified jurors. . . . [T]he concept that certain people may not be held responsible for their actions by reason of their mental state generates feelings of anger and disparity among some individuals. The insanity defense is viewed by some as a "loophole" for defendants and a scheme that clever attorneys and mental health professionals exploit to acquit their criminal clients and permit dangerous people to roam freely in society.[127]

In the United States, defendants plead NGRI in approximately 1 percent of all criminal cases. Of those who plead NGRI only about 10 percent to 25 percent prevail.[128] The average layperson believes these percentages are much higher and, generally, they have a negative view of the insanity defense.[129]

> The concept of excusing a criminal act based on the presence of an identifiable mental disease or defect and its impact on cognitive and/or volitional capacity has been in existence for centuries. . . . It is designed to protect those who are not considered blameworthy.[130]

The concept of insanity is legal. One who is insane may be relieved from the typical punishment for a crime. Because the mental health profession is designed to diagnose and treat disorders, it has no definition for the generic term "insanity." That is not to say that the mental health profession plays no role in the legal identification of insanity or that it will not play a greater role in the future.

There is much neuroscience research under way that may eventually help identify those who should be found NGRI. As discussed in greater detail below, a typical insanity defense may provide either that the individual lacked the knowledge or capacity to recognize that an act was wrongful and/or because of a mental disorder was unable to conform his conduct to the requirements of the law.[131]

One area where neuroscience may assist in determining insanity is to diagnose whether there is some type of neurobiological disorder that impairs a person's decision-making abilities, for example, by virtue of an impulse or "intermittent explosive disorder," from a dysfunction of the medial orbitofrontal cortex; from the ventromedial/orbital prefrontal cortex; or, from the brain's distribution of serotonin and/or dopamine.[132] Other neurobiological research is being conducted to see what, if any, effect brain lesions might have on criminal responsibility.[133]

Insanity Laws

There appears to be no right under the U.S. Constitution to raise insanity as a defense to a crime. Dicta in *Clark v. Arizona* suggests that there is no constitutional requirement for a state to allow for an insanity defense, although evidence of the mental state at the time of the crime may be used to negate the mens rea element of some crimes.[134]

In 1984, John Hinckley was found not guilty by reason of insanity for, inter alia, shooting and attempting to kill President Ronald Reagan and others. The public outrage created by the Hinckley verdict led the federal government and several states to modify their insanity defense laws.[135] The Federal Insanity Defense Reform Act of 1984 significantly modified the standard to prove insanity, moved the burden of proof of insanity from the prosecution to the defendant, limited the scope of expert witness testimony, and, for the first time, included a provision that would automatically trigger a commitment proceeding if the verdict was NGRI.[136]

Idaho, Kansas, Montana, and Utah have abolished the NGRI insanity defense. In its place, Utah allows a jury to find a defendant "guilty but mentally ill," and Montana allows a "guilty but insane" verdict. Twelve states allow a verdict of guilty but mentally ill.

There are four general definitions of insanity used by the states. Some states "variously combine [these definitions] to yield a diversity of American standards."[137] Many of the state definitions vary the language sufficiently to make them difficult to categorize with 100 percent degree of assurance that the categorization is accurate. (The term "approximately" is used to indicate this uncertainty.) The original test used in the United States is based on the 1843 English M'Naughten case.[138] The M'Naughten test says a person is NGRI if at the time of the act, because of a mental disease or defect, he did "not know the nature and quality of the act he was doing, or if he did know it that he did not know he was doing wrong."[139] The part of the test dealing with "not knowing the nature or quality of the act" is what the Supreme Court refers to as the "cognitive capacity" element and the "not know what he was doing is wrong" is referred to as the "moral capacity" element.[140] Currently, approximately 17 states and the federal government use the M'Naughten test. Approximately four states modify the M'Naughten test to include a provision to the effect that the defendant is NGRI if, because of a mental disease or defect, the defendant is "unable to control his actions"; at least one of these states, Arizona, dropped the cognitive incapacity element.[141] Alaska is the only state to define insanity to include only the cognitive incapacity element.[142]

American Law Institute's (ALI) The Model Penal Code defines insanity as:

A person is not responsible for criminal conduct if at the time of such conduct as a result of mental disease or defect he lacks substantial capacity either to appreciate the criminality [wrongfulness] of his conduct or to conform his conduct to the requirements of law.[143]

Approximately 14 states follow the Model Penal Code definition.[144]

Approximately 10 states use the irresistible impulse standard that "asks whether a person was so lacking in volition due to a mental defect or illness that he could not have controlled his actions."[145]

Only New Hampshire follows the Durham test that originated from the case of *Durham v. United States*.[146] The *Durham* test provides that a person is NGRI if the "unlawful act was the product of a mental disease or defect"[147]

"Competence" for criminal law purposes is like insanity in that it is a legal standard.[148] In *Dusky v. United States*, the U.S. Supreme Court, quoting language from the U.S. Solicitor General, declared that for a defendant to stand trial he must be mentally competent and the test for this is whether the defendant "has sufficient present ability to consult with his lawyer with a reasonable degree of rational understanding—and whether he has a rational as well as factual understanding of the proceedings against him."[149] If a legally incompetent defendant is tried, his constitutionally protected due process rights are violated.[150] This competence standard applies not only to the beginning of trial, but also throughout the course of trial.[151] In *Godinez v. Moran*, the Supreme Court held that this same competence standard applied to pleading guilty and waiving a right to trial.[152] The same competence standard also applies to a waiver of right to counsel.[153]

In *Indiana v. Edwards*, the Supreme Court was asked to determine if a person who is competent to stand trial is also necessarily competent to waive his right to counsel and to conduct his own defense.[154] The Supreme Court seemed to struggle with the issue of applying two different competence standards; it did so, nonetheless. The Court reasoned that: "[m]ental illness itself is not a unitary concept. It varies in degree. It can vary over time. It interferes with an individual's functioning at different times in different ways."[155] The Court went on to explain "a right of self-representation at trial will not 'affirm the dignity' of a defendant who lacks the mental capacity to conduct his defense without the assistance of counsel."[156] Ultimately, the Court concluded a state could conclude that while defendants are competent to stand trial, they "still suffer from severe mental illness to the point where they are not competent to conduct trial proceedings by themselves."[157]

In *Sell v. United States*, the Supreme Court determined that a court could order that a defendant who is facing serious criminal charges and who poses a danger to himself or others be forcibly administered antipsychotic drugs if there is no less intrusive alternative to the drugs and rendering the defendant competent furthered an important governmental trial-related interest.[158]

The Supreme Court also has held that a requirement that a defendant prove by clear and convincing evidence that he is incompetent to stand trial is unconstitutional because the requirement violates the defendant's due process rights.[159] In *Ford v. Wainwright*, the Court was asked to determine if a person has to be sane at the time of execution so as to render the execution not cruel or unusual.[160] The *Ford v. Wainwright* Court stated that the minimum standard of sanity/competence was whether the defendant was capable of "comprehending the reasons for the penalty or its implications."[161] The standard of comprehension the Supreme Court announced, however, sounds more like the second prong of the competency standard announced in *Dusky v. United States*.[162]

As with insanity, courts look to the neuroscience and mental health professionals to make a legal competency determination. Neuropsychological tests are being developed with an aim of determining whether individuals with certain brain injuries meet the competency definition.[163] For example, neuroscientists examine the frontal lobe of the brain to determine if there may be a change in executive functioning abilities because of some type of injury. Making this determination may be aided by neuroimaging using such techniques as Magnetic Resonance Imaging, Fluid-Attenuated Inversion Recovery, Positron Emission Tomography, or Single Photon Emission Computed Tomography.[164] There are also a host of neuropsychological tests used in an effort to establish competence, or the lack thereof, including, for example, the Wisconsin Card Sorting Test, the Stroop Colour Word Test, the Oral Word Fluency Test, and the Halstead Category Test.[165] The Competence Assessment to Stand Trial For Defendants With Mental Retardation (CAST*MR) is an assessment tool, as its name suggest, used specifically to determine if a mentally retarded/intellectually disabled person is competent to stand trial.

The concepts of capacity, capability, and competence play important roles in the criminal justice system. These three concepts are difficult to apply and this difficulty is magnified by the differing definitions in the various states and the federal government. With respect to capacity, the current approach is to apply traditional definitions of age in determining capacity. It may be time, however, to apply some type of "mental age" standard. The difficulty in applying capability and competence are exacerbated by the evolving Eighth Amendment requirements applied to them.

The mental health and neuropsychology disciplines are conducting research and creating tests that, hopefully, in the future may make the determination of mental age capacity, capability, and competence more precise and more accurate.

Notes

1. *Clark v. Arizona*, 548 U.S. 735, 749 n. 7 (2006) (WestlawNext).

2. Katie Kindelan, "5-Year-Old Could Face Murder Charge in Drowning Death of Crying Toddler," ABC News (June 10, 2011), http://abcnews.go.com/US/murder-charge-considered-girl-drowned-crying-toddler/story?id=13811620.

3. Ibid., 1.

4. Kan. Stat. Ann. §38.2302(i)(1) (WestlawNext 2013).

5. *Id.* at § 38-2347(a)(1).

6. *Id.* at §38-2347(a)(4).

7. *Id.* at §38-2376 (a).

8. Anthony Platt and Bernard L. Diamond, "The Origins of the 'Right and Wrong' Test of Criminal Responsibility and Its Subsequent Development in the United States: An Historical Survey," *California Law Review* 53 (August 1966): 1233, http://scholarship.law.berkeley.edu/cgi/viewcontent.cgi?article=2914&context=californialawreview.

9. Andrew M. Carter, "Age Matters: The Case for a Constitutionalized Infancy Defense," *Kansas Law Review* 54 (April 2006): 687 (quoting Y.B., 6 & 7 Edw. 2, in 24 Selden Society 109 (1909)), https://1.next.westlaw.com.

10. *Angelo v. People of Ill.*, 96 Ill. 209, 211 (1880).

11. *Id.* (quoting Blackstone, vol. 4, 23).

12. N.D.C.C. §12.1-04-01 (WestlawNext 2013).

13. Wash. Rev. Code Ann. §9A.04.050 (WestlawNext 2013).

14. Nev. Rev. Stat. §194.010.1-2 (WestlawNext 2013).

15. S.D. Stat. Laws §22-3-1 (WestlawNext 2013).

16. Minn. Stat. Ann. 609.055, subd.1 (WestlawNext 2014).

17. Cal. Ann. Penal Code §26, One (WestlawNext 2014).

18. McKinney's N.Y. Penal Law Art 40 (WestlawNext 2014).

19. Fla. Stat. Ann. §794.02 (WestlawNext 2013).

20. *Id.*; S.C. Code Ann. §16-3-659 (WestlawNext 2013).

21. *Clark v. Arizona*, 548 U.S. 735, 749 n. 7 (2006) (WestlawNext).

22. Franklin E. Zimiring, "The Power Politics of Juvenile Court Transfer: A Mildly Revisionist History of the 1990s," *Louisiana Law Review* 71 (Fall 2010): 6, https://1-next-westlaw-com.ezproxy.fgcu.edu/Document/I02922dcef83a11df9b8c850332338889.

23. Ibid., 5–6.

24. U.S. Department of Justice, Office of Justice Programs (OJP), "States That Changed Their Transfer Laws, 1992–1999, Juveniles Tried as Adults," *Statistical Briefing Book* (1999), http://ojjdp.gov/ojstatbb/structure_process/qa04107.asp?qaDate=1999.

25. Ibid.

26. Zimiring, "The Power Politics," 8.

27. Ibid., 4.

28. U.S. Department of Justice, Office of Justice Programs (OJP), *Trying Juveniles as Adults* (2009), 4, https://www.ncjrs.gov/pdffiles1/ojjdp/232434.pdf.

29. Ibid.

30. Ibid.

31. Ibid.

32. Ibid.

33. Ibid.

34. Ibid.

35. Samantha Schad, "Adolescent Decision Making: Reduced Culpability in the Criminal Justice System and Recognition of Capability in Other Legal Contexts," *Journal of Health Care Law and Policy*, 14 (September 1, 2011): 282–83, http://web.b.ebscohost.com. ezproxy.fgcu.edu/ehost/resultsadvanced?sid=36b72d69-cd46-4e70-92f4-61eabb1e57a4%4 0sessionmgr111&vid.

36. Ibid., 377.

37. Elizabeth Cauffman and Laurence Steinberg, "(Im)maturity of Judgment in Adolescence: Why Adolescents May Be Less Culpable than Adults," *Behavioral Sciences & the Law* 18 (February 5, 2001): 743, doi:10.1002/bsl.416.

38. Ibid.

39. Schad, "Adolescent Decision Making," 377 (quoting Laurence Steinberg, "Adolescent Development and Juvenile Justice," *Annual Review of Clinical Psychology* 5 (April 2009): 459–85).

40. Schad, "Adolescent Decision Making," 381.

41. Cauffman and Steinberg, "(Im)maturity of Judgment," 750.

42. Ibid., 756.

43. Ibid.

44. Juan I. Blanco, "George Stinney," *Murderpedia, the Encyclopedia of Murderers*: 1, http://murderpedia.org/male.S/s/stinney-george.htm.

45. Ibid., 2.

46. *Thompson v. Oklahoma*, 487 U.S. 815, 835 (1988) (WestlawNext).

47. *Id*. at 833-38.

48. *Id*. at 838.

49. *Id*. at 834.

50. *Id*. at 823.

51. *Id*. at 832.

52. *Id*. at 830.

53. *Id*.

54. *Id*. at 832.

55. *Id*. at 832-33.

56. *Id*. at 832 (quoting *Furman v. Georgia*, 408 U.S. 238, 309 (1972)).

57. *Thompson v. Oklahoma* at 835-35.

58. *Id*. at 835.

59. *Id*.

60. *Id*. at 836.

61. *Id*. at 837.

62. *Id*. at 838.

63. *Stanford v. Kentucky*, 492 U.S. 361, 380 (1989) (WestlawNext).

64. "Execution of Juveniles in the U.S. and Other Countries," Death Penalty Information Center, February 23, 2011, http://www.deathpenaltyinfo.org/execution-juveniles-us -and-other-countries.

65. *Roper v. Simmons*, 543 U.S. 551, 569–76 (2005) (WestlawNext).

66. *Id.* at 573.

67. *Id.* at 575.

68. *Graham v. Florida*, 560 U.S. 48, 57 (2010) (WestlawNext).

69. *Id.*

70. *See above* text at endnote 62.

71. *Graham v. Florida,* 560 U.S. at 59.

72. *Id.*

73. *Id.*

74. *Id.* at 61-62.

75. *Id.* at 67.

76. *Id.* at 69.

77. *Id.* at 67.

78. *Id.* at 68.

79. *Id.* at 72, 78, 80.

80. *Id.* at 82 (emphasis added).

81. *Id.* at 82.

82. *Miller v. Alabama*, 132 S. Ct. 2455, 2469 (2012) (WestlawNext).

83. *Id.* at 2469.

84. *Id.*

85. *Id.*

86. *Id.* at 2470-75.

87. *Id.* at 2465.

88. *Clark v. Arizona*, 548 U.S. 735, 742 (2006) (WestlawNext).

89. *Dennis v. United States*, 341 U.S. 494, 500 (1951) (WestlawNext).

90. Stephen Morse, "Mental Disorder and Criminal Law," *Journal of Criminal Law and Criminology,* 101, no. 3 (2011): 885–968, 910–16. http://search.proquest.com.ezproxy.fgcu.edu/docview/926417344/A4FF00B5ABCD4912PQ/6?accountid=10919.

91. J. Gregory Olley, "Definition of Intellectual Disability in Criminal Court Cases," *Intellectual and Developmental Disabilities* 51 (April 2013): 117–21, 117–18. doi:10.1352/1934-9556-51.2.117.

92. U.S. Sentencing Commission, *United States Sentencing Commission Guidelines Manual §5K2.13, 462* (November 1, 2013), http://www.ussc.gov/Guidelines/2012_Guidelines/Manual (accessed March 29, 2014).

93. *Penry v. Lynaugh*, 492 U.S. 340 (1989) (WestlawNext).

94. *Id.* at 313.

95. *Id.* at 328-29.

96. *Id.* at 329.

97. *Id.* at 340.

98. *Atkins v. Virginia*, 536 U.S. 304, 306 (2002) (WestlawNext).

99. *Id.* at 321.

100. *Id.* at 306.

101. *Id.* at 320-21.

102. *Id.* at 321.

103. *Id.* at 317.

104. *Id.* at 307, n. 3.

105. *Id.* at 318.

106. *Id.* at 344 (quoting respectively the APA and AAMR "mental retardation" definitions).

107. *Id.* at 317.

108. Ark. Code Ann., §5-4-618(a)(1) (WestlawNext).

109. *Id.* at §5-4-618(a)(2).

110. Neb. Rev. Stat. §28-105.01(3) (WestlawNext); Tenn. Code Ann. §39-13-203 (a) (using "intellectual disability" instead of mental retardation) (WestlawNext); Wash. Rev. Code Ann. §10.95.030(2)(a)&(c) (also uses intellectual disability).

111. N.C. Gen. Stat. Ann. §15A-2005 (a)(1) (WestlawNext).

112. Kan. Stat. Ann. §21-6622(a).

113. *Id.* at §76-12b01(i).

114. *Id.* at §76-12b01(d).

115. *Id.* at §21-6622(h).

116. *Atkins v. Virginia*, 536 U.S. 304, 318 (2002) (WestlawNext).

117. *Id.* at 317.

118. La. Rev. Stat. Ann. §905.5.1 (H)(1) (WestlawNext).

119. *Id.*

120. Nev. Rev. Stat 174.098(7).

121. Va. Code Ann. §19.2-264.3:1.1(A)(i); Fla. Stat. Ann. §921.137(1).

122. Geraldine W. Young, "A More Intelligent and Just Atkins: Adjusting for the Flynn Effect in Capital Determinations of Mental Retardation or Intellectual Disability," *Vanderbilt Law Review*, 65 (March 20, 2012): 615–75, 617, http://web.b.ebscohost.com.ezproxy.fgcu.edu/ehost/detail?vid=5&sid=cdf29c2e-2c6b-4536-8694-576497c6deee%40sessionmgr112&hid=118&bdata=JnNpdGU9ZWhvc3QtbGl2ZQ%3d%3d#db=a9h&AN=78553493.

123. 689 F.3d 1148, 1159 (10th Cir. 2012) (WestlawNext).

124. *Id.* at 1169.

125. *Id.* at 1170 (quoting 28 U.S.C. §2254(d)(1)).

126. *Walker v. True*, 399 F.3d 315, 322-23 (4th Cir. 2005), remanded on other grounds, 546 U.S. 1086 (2006).

127. *Atkins v. Virginia*, 536 U.S. 304, 306 (2002) (WestlawNext).

128. Ibid., 254.

129. Jennifer Eno Louden and Jennifer L. Skeem, "Constructing Insanity: Jurors' Prototypes, Attitudes, and Legal Decision-making," *Behavioral Sciences & the Law* 25 (May 15, 2007): 449–70, 450. doi:10.1002/bsl.760.

130. Zachary D. Torry and Kenneth J. Weiss, "Medication Noncompliance and Criminal Responsibility: Is the Insanity Defense Legitimate?" *Journal of Psychiatry & Law*, 40 (2012): 219–42, 221, https://login.ezproxy.fgcu.edu/login?url=http://web.b.ebscohost.com/ehost/pdfviewer/pdfviewer?vid=5&sid=cc5cc4a3-6ce2-45a8-8923-1dd715dd5ce2%40sessionmgr110&hid=112.

131. *M'Naughten Case*, 10 Cl. & Fin 200, 8 Eng. Rep. 718 (H.I. 1843), http://www.bailii.org/uk/cases/UKHL/1843/J16.html.

132. Gerben Meynen, "A Neurolaw Perspective on Psychiatric Assessments of Criminal Responsibility: Decision-making, Mental Disorder, and the Brain," *International Journal of Law and Psychiatry* (March/April 2013): 93–99, 95–96. doi:10.1016/j.ijlp.2013.01.001.

133. Shelley Batts, "Brain Lesions and Their Implications in Criminal Responsibility," *Behavioral Sciences & the Law* 27, no. 2 (2009): 261–72, 265. doi:10.1002/bsl.857.

134. *Clark v. Arizona*, 548 U.S. 735, 751 (2006) (WestlawNext).

135. Robert Kinscherff, "Proposition: A Personality Disorder May Nullify Responsibility for a Criminal Act," *Journal of Law, Medicine & Ethics* 38 (Winter 2010): 745–59. doi:10.1111/j.1748-720X.2010.00528.x; Randi Ellias, "Should Courts Instruct Juries as to the Consequences to a Defendant of a 'Not Guilty by Reason of Insanity' Verdict?" *Journal of Criminal Law and Criminology* 85 (April 01, 1995): 1062–083, http://www.jstor.org/stable/10.2307/1144093?ref=search-gateway:f5ec02e0283bcd1598b98421df321b9f.

136. U.S. Department of Justice, "Insanity Defense Reform Act of 1984," *USSC Guidelines Manual*, §5K2.13, 462. http://www.justice.gov/usao/eousa/foia_reading_room/usam/title9/crm00634.htm (accessed March 31, 2014).

137. *Clark* at 548 U.S. at 749.

138. *M'Naughten Case,* 10 Cl. & Fin 200, 8 Eng. Rep. 718 (H.I. 1843), http://www.bailii.org/uk/cases/UKHL/1843/J16.html.

139. Henry Campbell Black, Joseph R. Nolan, and Michael J. Connolly, *Black's Law Dictionary: Definitions of the Terms and Phrases of American and English Jurisprudence, Ancient and Modern* (St. Paul: West Publishing, 1979), 905.

140. *Clark* at 548 U.S. at 747.

141. *Id.* at 752.

142. Alaska Stat. Ann. §1247.010 (a) (WestlawNext).

143. *Clark* at 548 U.S. at 751, n. 15 (quoting American Law Institute (1962), Model Penal Code, §4.01(1) (proposed draft), 66).

144. *Clark* at 751.

145. *Id.*

146. Howard P. Rome, M.D., "McNaughten, Durham and Psychiatry," *Federal Rules Decisions* (1964), 93–110, 93.

147. *Durham v. U.S.*, 214 F.2d 862, 875 (D.C. Cir. 1954) (WestlawNext).

148. G. Michelle Reid-Proctor, Karen Galin, and Michael A. Cummings, "Evaluation of Legal Competency in Patients with Frontal Lobe Injury," *Brain Injury* 15 (May 1, 2001): 377–86, 378. doi:10.1080/02699050010005977.

149. *Dusky v United States*, 362 U.S. 402, 402 (1960) (WestlawNext).

150. *Pate v. Robinson*, 383 U.S. 375, 378 (1966) (WestlawNext).

151. *Drope v. Missouri*, 420 U.S. 162, 181 (1974) (WestlawNext).

152. *Godinez v. Moran*, 509 U.S. 389, 401 (1993) (WestlawNext).

153. *Westbrook v. Arizona*, 384 U.S. 150, 150 (1966) (WestlawNext).

154. *Indiana v. Edwards*, 554 U.S. 164, 174 (2008).

155. *Id.* at 175.

156. *Id.* at 176 (internal citations omitted).

157. *Id.* at 178.

158. *Sell v. United States*, 539 U.S. 166, 197 (2003) (WestlawNext).

159. *Cooper v. Oklahoma*, 517 U.S. 348, 369 (1996) (WestlawNext).

160. *Ford v. Wainwright*, 477 U.S., 399, 417-18 (1986) (WestlawNext).

161. *Id.* at 417.

162. *Dusky v United States*, 362 U.S. 402, 402 (1960) (WestlawNext).

163. Reid-Proctor, "Evaluation of Legal," 380–84.

164. Ibid., 380–85.

165. Ibid., 382.

Bibliography

Associated Press. "George Stinney, Black Teen Executed in 1944, Gets New Trial" (November 10, 2013). http://www.huffingtonpost.com/2013/11/10/george-stinney-black-teen-executed-new-trial_n_4250315.html (accessed March 29, 2014).

Batts, Shelley. "Brain Lesions and Their Implications in Criminal Responsibility." *Behavioral Sciences & the Law* 27, no. 2 (2009): 261–72. doi:10.1002/bsl.857.

Black, Henry Campbell, Joseph R. Nolan, and Michael J. Connolly. *Black's Law Dictionary: Definitions of the Terms and Phrases of American and English Jurisprudence, Ancient and Modern.* St. Paul, MN: West Publishing, 1979.

Blanco, Juan I. "George Stinney." *Murderpedia, the Encyclopedia of Murderers.* http://murderpedia.org/male.S/s/stinney-george.htm (accessed March 26, 2014).

Carter, Andrew M. "Age Matters: The Case for a Constitutionalized Infancy Defense." *Kansas Law Review* 54 (April 2006): 1227–260. https://1-next-westlaw-com.ezproxy.fgcu.edu/Document/I79d759a14b1e11db99a18fc28eb0d9ae.

Cauffman, Elizabeth, and Laurence Steinberg. "(Im)maturity of Judgment in Adolescence: Why Adolescents May Be Less Culpable than Adults." *Behavioral Sciences & the Law* 18, no. 6 (February 5, 2001): 741–60. doi:10.1002/bsl.416.

Ellias, Randi. "Should Courts Instruct Juries as to the Consequences to a Defendant of a 'Not Guilty by Reason of Insanity' Verdict?" *Journal of Criminal Law and Criminology* 85, no. 4 (April 1, 1995): 1062–083. http://www.jstor.org/stable/10.2307/1144093?ref=search-gateway:f5ec02e0283bcd1598b98421df321b9f (accessed March 29, 2014).

"Execution of Juveniles in the U.S. and Other Countries." Death Penalty Information Center (February 23, 2011). http://www.deathpenaltyinfo.org/execution-juveniles-us-and-other-countries (accessed March 29, 2014).

Griffin, Patrick, Sean Addie, Benjamin Adams, and Kathy Firestone. "Trying Juveniles as Adults: An Analysis of State Transfer Laws and Reporting." *U.S. Department of Justice, Office of Juvenile Justice and Deliquency Juvenile Offenders and Victims: National Report Series Bulletin* (September 2011): 1–27. https://www.ncjrs.gov/pdffiles1/ojjdp/232434.pdf (accessed March 29, 2014).

Kindelan, Katie. "5-Year-Old Could Face Murder Charge in Drowning Death of Crying Toddler." ABC News (June 10, 2011). http://abcnews.go.com/US/murder-charge-considered-girl-drowned-crying-toddler/story?id=13811620 (accessed March 29, 2014).

Kinscherff, Robert. "Proposition: A Personality Disorder May Nullify Responsibility for a Criminal Act." *Journal of Law, Medicine & Ethics* 38, no. 4 (Winter 2010): 745–59. doi:10.1111/j.1748-720X.2010.00528.x.

Louden, Jennifer Eno, and Jennifer L Skeem. "Constructing Insanity: Jurors' Prototypes, Attitudes, and Legal Decision-making." *Behavioral Sciences & the Law* 25, no. 4 (May 15, 2007): 449–70. doi:10.1002/bsl.760.

Meynen, Gerben. "A Neurolaw Perspective on Psychiatric Assessments of Criminal Responsibility: Decision-making, Mental Disorder, and the Brain." *International Journal of Law and Psychiatry* 36, no. 2 (March/April 2013): 93–99. doi:10.1016/j.ijlp.2013.01.001.

Morse, Stephen. "Mental Disorder and Criminal Law." *Journal of Criminal Law and Criminology (1973-)* 101, no. 3 (2011): 885–968. http://search.proquest.com.ezproxy.fgcu.edu/docview/926417344/A4FF00B5ABCD4912PQ/6?accountid=10919 (accessed March 29, 2014).

Olley, J. Gregory. "Definition of Intellectual Disability in Criminal Court Cases." *Intellectual and Developmental Disabilities* 51, no. 2 (April 2013): 117–21. doi:10.1352/1934-9556-51.2.117.

Platt, Anthony, and Bernard L. Diamond. "The Origins of the 'Right and Wrong' Test of Criminal Responsibility and Its Subsequent Development in the United States: An Historical Survey." *California Law Review* 53, no. 3 (August 1966): 1227–260. http://scholarship.law.berkeley.edu/cgi/viewcontent.cgi?article=2914&context=californialawreview.

Reid-Proctor, G. Michelle, Karen Galin, and Michael A. Cummings. "Evaluation of Legal Competency in Patients with Frontal Lobe Injury." *Brain Injury* 15 (May 1, 2001): 377–86. doi:10.1080/02699050010005977.

Rome, Howard P., M.D. "McNaughten, Durham and Psychiatry." In *Federal Rules Decisions*, Vol. 34. Eagan, MN: West Publishing, 1964, 93–110.

Schad, Samantha. "Adolescent Decision Making: Reduced Culpability in the Criminal Justice System and Recognition of capability in Other Legal Contexts." *Journal of Health Care Law and Policy*, 14 (September 1, 2011): 375–403. http://web.b.ebscohost.com.ezproxy.fgcu.edu/ehost/resultsadvanced?sid=36b72d69-cd46-4e70-92f4-61eabb1e57a4%40sessionmgr111&vid=3&hid=118&bquery=Adolescent+decision+making%3a+Reduced+culpability&bdata=JmRiPWE5aCZ0eXBlPTEmc2l0ZT1laG9zdClsaXZl.

Steinberg, Laurence. "Adolescent Development and Juvenile Justice." *Annual Review of Clinical Psychology* 5, no. 1 (April 2009): 459–85. doi:10.1146/annurev.clinpsy.032408.153603.

Torry, Zachary D., and Stephen B. Billick. "Overlapping Universe: Understanding Legal Insanity and Psychosis." *Psychiatric Quarterly* 81 (April 6, 2010): 253–62. doi:10.1007/s11126-010-9134-2.

Torry, Zachary D., and Kenneth J. Weiss. "Medication Noncompliance and Criminal Responsibility: Is the Insanity Defense Legitimate?" *Journal of Psychiatry & Law*, 40 (2012): 219–42. https://login.ezproxy.fgcu.edu/login?url=http://web.b.ebscohost.com/ehost/pdfviewer/pdfviewer?vid=5&sid=cc5cc4a3-6ce2-45a8-8923-1dd715dd5ce2%40sessionmgr110&hid=112.

U.S. Department of Justice. "Insanity Defense Reform Act of 1984." *US Attorney Criminal Resource Manual*, Title 9, §634. Retrieved from: http://www.justice.gov/usao/eousa/foia_reading_room/usam/title9/crm00634.htm.

U.S. Department of Justice. Office of Justice Programs, Office of Juvenile Justice and Delinquency. "States That Changed Their Transfer Laws, 1992–1999, Juveniles Tried as Adults." *Statistical Briefing Book* (October 31, 2009). http://ojjdp.gov/ojstatbb/structure_process/qa04107.asp?qaDate=1999 (accessed March 29, 2014).

U.S. Department of Justice. U.S. Attorney's Office. *Criminal Resource Manual 637 Insanity-Present Statutory Test-18 U.S.C. Sec. 17(a)*. Washington, DC: Department of Justice, U.S. Attorneys Office. http://www.justice.gov/usao/eousa/foia_reading_room/usam/title9/crm00637 (accessed March 29, 2014).

U.S. Sentencing Commission. *United States Sentencing Commission Guidelines Manual §5K2.13, 462.* Washington, DC: United States Sentencing Commission, November 1, 2013. http://www.ussc.gov/Guidelines/2012_Guidelines/Manual (accessed March 29, 2014).

Young, Geraldine W. "A More Intelligent and Just Atkins: Adjusting for the Flynn Effect in Capital Determinations of Mental Retardation or Intellectual Disability." *Vanderbilt Law Review* 65, no. 2 (March 20, 2012): 615–75. http://web.b.ebscohost.com. ezproxy.fgcu.edu/ehost/detail?vid=5&sid=cdf29c2e-2c6b-4536-8694-576497c6deee% 40sessionmgr112&hid=118&bdata=JnNpdGU9ZWhvc3QtbGl2ZQ%3d%3d#db=a9h &AN=78553493 (accessed March 29, 2014).

Zimiring, Franklin E. "The Power Politics of Juvenile Court Transfer: A Mildly Revisionist History of the 1990s." *Louisiana Law Review* 71 (Fall 2010): 1–15. https://1-next-westlaw-com.ezproxy.fgcu.edu/Document/I02922dcef83a11df9b8c850332338889 (accessed March 29, 2014).

About the Editors and Contributors

EDITORS

Duane L. Dobbert, PhD, is a full professor in Justice Studies and also Forensic Behavioral Analysis at Florida Gulf Coast University, Fort Meyers. A criminal justice practitioner, educator, and consultant for 40 years, Dobbert is also adjunct faculty at Capella University, a Fellow of the American College of Forensic Examiners, a Diplomate with the American Board of Psychological Specialties, a Commissioner with the Commission on Forensic Education, a lifetime Juvenile Court Administrator with the National Council of Juvenile and Family Court Judges, and a certified social worker. His previous books include *Understanding Personality Disorders* (Praeger 2007), which was translated into Korean and published in 2011.

Thomas X. Mackey, PhD, is an adjunct professor in Justice Studies at Florida Gulf Coast University, Estero, teaching courses including homeland security, criminal justice theory and practices, juvenile justice, criminal evidence, and research in violent behavior. Previously a police officer in Brooklyn, New York, and later a detective at the Sag Harbor (New York) police department, he was honored in the latter role as Police Officer of the Year in 1998 and in 2009. Mackey is a certified homicide investigator, fingerprint specialist, narcotics crime investigator, and family crisis counselor; he has been awarded 22 medals for acts of service in police work, as well as three lifesaving service medals. He developed the complete curriculum, including text choice, for the Homeland Security course now offered at Florida Gulf Coast University.

CONTRIBUTORS

Danica Ivancevich earned a bachelor of science in psychology and criminology from Florida Southern College and is pursuing a master of science in

Forensic Studies from Florida Gulf Coast University. She is currently a behavior technician in the applied behavior analysis field, providing therapy services to individuals with behavior problems.

Joseph McCluskey, J.D., graduated with honors from the University of Richmond Law School where he served as editor-in-chief of the *Law Review*. He is now a retired attorney who practiced law in Virginia for about 25 years. He is in the Florida Gulf Coast University master of arts, Forensic Studies program, with a concentration in criminal behavioral analysis.

Christina Molinari holds a bachelor's degree in sociology with emphasis in criminology and is currently pursuing a master's degree in Forensic Studies, with a forensic behavior analysis concentration. She has five years experience working with both male and female juvenile offenders, the last two years spent supervising a residential treatment facility for juvenile sex offenders. She is currently focusing her studies on sexual predators and serial murder.

Sarah Norman is currently enrolled in the Forensic Studies master's program at Florida Gulf Coast University where program leader Professor Duane Dobbert pushes the efficacy of real life practitioner work along with theoretical integration to think outside the box. She completed an undergraduate degree from the University of Louisville in 2006 and went on to complete mortuary school in 2010. She is presently a forensic investigator for the District 21 Medical Examiner's Office in Southwest Florida.

Inna Angelina Olson was born in the former Soviet Union and raised in the Crimea. She immigrated to the United States in 2003 to fulfill her academic thirst and ambition. A summa cum laude graduate of Florida Gulf Coast University, where she studied Criminal Justice, and hereafter completed the law enforcement basic training program at the Southwest Florida Public Service Academy. She currently serves her community as a law enforcement officer with an ultimate goal and desire for investigative work. She strongly believes in improving the lives of others by working hard and working toward her final goal—a doctorate program in Forensic Behavioral Analysis.

Kimberly Ortiz is a U.S. Army veteran. She completed a bachelor's degree in Legal Studies from Strayer University and is currently completing the master's degree in Forensics Studies at Florida Gulf Coast University, with emphasis on Forensic Behavioral Analysis.

Lindsey Page, a graduate student at Florida Gulf Coast University, holds a bachelor's degree in Criminal Justice, with minors in psychology and Spanish, from York College of Pennsylvania. She recently completed her master's degree in Behavioral Forensic Analysis at Florida Gulf Coast University.

Lucy Papp is originally from Miami, Florida. She has received both her undergraduate and graduate degrees from Florida Gulf Coast University. She is currently pursuing a doctoral degree from Nova Southeastern University. She is married and the parent of two children.

Cynthia Penna graduated from Fort Myers High School in 2004, earned an associate's degree from Edison State College in 2009, a bachelor's degree in Criminal Justice and Forensic Studies in 2013, and is now working on a master's degree in Forensic Studies.

Shauna Stoeger, MS, grew up Medina, Wisconsin, where she lived until graduating as valedictorian from New London High School in 2008. Stoeger next attended the University of Wisconsin–Eau Claire, where she graduated in 2012 with honors and two bachelor's degrees, in psychology and Spanish. Stoeger received her master of science in Criminal Forensic Studies with an emphasis in Forensic Behavioral Analysis from Florida Gulf Coast University in May 2014. Stoeger's main interests are crime and deviance as they relate to human rights and the environment.

Sarah A. Strickland is a native Floridian who grew up in Brevard County. She attended Florida Gulf Coast University in Fort Myers and graduated with a dual bachelor's degree in Criminal Justice and Forensic Studies. She is currently completing a master's degree in Homeland Security at Wilmington University.

AnnaMaria Tejeda earned a master's degree in Criminal Justice at Florida Gulf Coast University, and a bachelor's degree in Criminology, Law, and Society from the University of California, Irvine. She has been employed more than 18 years with the U.S. Probation Office. Currently assigned as a Senior U.S. Probation Officer in the Middle District of Florida, she is supervising a high-risk caseload of convicted sex offenders, crime family members, and severe mentally ill offenders.

Ashley Veasy attended the University of Massachusetts, Amherst and graduated with a bachelor's degree in psychology and a minor in history. She currently attends Florida Gulf Coast University, working on her master's in Forensic Studies with a concentration in Forensic Behavioral Analysis.

Jessica Vena graduated from Fort Myers High School in 2008 with International Baccalaureate Diploma, then attended the University of Florida, where she graduated with a bachelor's degree in psychology and a minor in history in 2012. She is currently enrolled in the master's degree program in Forensic Science, with an emphasis on Forensic Behavioral Analysis, at Florida Gulf Coast University.

Nicholas Zarrillo, MS, is originally from Caldwell, New Jersey. He attended Florida Gulf Coast University, where he first received his bachelor of science in Criminal Justice with a minor in political science, and later his master of science in Criminal Justice. Zarrillo is currently a law enforcement officer with a local law enforcement agency in southwest Florida.

Index